Praise for *Powered by*

'The world needs organisations to d
Powered by Purpose is a practical g
that fulfils both of these needs.'

Bill Winters, CEO, Standard Chartered Bank

'*Powered by Purpose* demystifies the black box of being purpose-driven. Sarah combines research, theory and experience into practical and actionable insights for those creating purpose-led teams and organisations.'

Morag Watson, Vice President, BP

'With the world, your customers and your staff expecting more from business than only generating shareholder value, Sarah has written a must-read for any leader wishing to power their organisation or team by purpose. If you read just one book this year – read this one!'

Jan Slaghekke, CEO, Sungevity
International – Powering Lives with Sunshine

'*Powered by Purpose* is a go-to text for leaders of organisations who can't quite remember their reason for being.'

Sarah Maguire, Chief Executive, Choice Support

'Occasionally a book comes along that is of its time – I believe that this book is one of those. Over the last decade conversations about "purpose" have risen up the strategic agenda in many organisations. Since the financial crisis in 2008, more and more people have looked to companies for more than just financial performance. "Why do we exist?" and "what is our role in society?" have become critical questions. This book goes to the heart of this challenge and provides a map for leaders to follow if they are to become what is needed as we move forward in 21st century. It is a pleasure to recommend it.'

Dr Andrew White, Associate Dean for Executive
Education, Saïd Business School, University of Oxford

'*Powered by Purpose* is compulsory reading for any leader searching for purpose and looking to authentically transform their organisation, people and planet for positive impact.'

Esther Foreman, CEO, The Social Change Agency

'Today, successful leadership is not just being good at what you do. You also need to be inspired by what you are doing and embody a sense of purpose greater than power, money and ego alone. You are called to show up with your humanity. Sarah's book beautifully guides you back to your purpose and what truly inspires you.'

Nick Williams, mentor, speaker and best-selling author of 18 books including **The Work We Were Born To Do** *www.iamnickwilliams.com*

'Having a powerful purpose is not about purpose statements; it's about ambition, passion and commitment to make a difference in the world around you. Sarah offers the means of how to do that in a book that's both accessible and enjoyable to read. She offers practical steps that not only make sense, they work!'

Marina Bolton, Director for Leadership and Organisation Development, and Design, UK Civil Service

'*Powered by Purpose* is a different business book to any other I have read. Sarah writes based on her unique combination of experience and skill, drawing on a wide range of sources to share insights that work in the real world.'

Onno Ruhl, General Manager, Aga Khan Agency for Habitat; former World Bank Country Director for India

'The "how" of purpose we all needed. Sarah articulates in a clear and compelling way the leadership journey executives and their teams must embark on to unleash the power of purpose in their organisations.'

Sabine Vinck, UK lead, Leadership Advisory Services, Spencer Stuart; former Associate Dean, London Business School

ACKNOWLEDGEMENTS

There are many people who have contributed to the writing and birthing of this book. I have been deeply touched by the kindness and commitment of many colleagues, family and friends. Without their support, *Powered by Purpose* would never have come into being. A heartfelt thank you to all.

I am hugely grateful to Paul Polman for his contribution of the foreword and his bold, purpose-led leadership during these testing times. Geoff McDonald kindly introduced my writing to Paul and Michael Hann connected Geoff and me. Life really is one conversation followed by another and then another.

Dr Victoria Hurth, who has generously written the Epilogue, kept my thinking sharp and my spirits buoyant with her depth of understanding. Michael Cahill, with his brilliant mind, was fantastically generous with his insights and stretched my thinking into new dimensions. Peter Owen gave amazing feet-to-the-fire encouragement and kept my focus on fluidity and bite. Jan Rakowicz read every page tirelessly and added value (and humour!) at every turn.

Eloise Cook, my editor, with her hands-on help honed the book in ways I could never have imagined; sincere thanks to the whole Pearson Education team. KT Forster, Alison Jones and Stefan Wagstyl supported the writing process from inception to completion. Steph McGonigle and Dave Smith created the original set of graphics.

Ed Rowland, founder of The Whole Partnership (TWP), fanned the flame inside me around purpose. During the four years we worked together, Ed's artistry with constellating systems was truly inspiring to witness. He had the original idea to create the Purpose Diamonds, which we co-evolved with clients. I am grateful to the students and clients of TWP, including co-founder Mark Stanley, for the many fulfilling hours spent diving into systemic work.

It has been a real honour to work with all the leaders – named and unnamed – whose stories are in this book. Countless other coaching and consulting experiences have also informed my writing. I am grateful to all the leaders who have trusted me to work with them and their teams; sitting in the circle has been a life-enriching experience.

Simon Cavicchia has provided 'super vision' to my work for over 12 years, bringing balanced perspective, particularly with my missteps and screw-ups. Sarah-Jane Menato has gifted me an understanding of how to integrate the deep feminine into leadership work. Claus Springborg has shown me how to experience essence in leadership settings. Rob Lake revealed the part that better dialogue has to play in impact investing. I am grateful to Nick Udall, founder of nowhere, Andy Kitt and all the 'nofolk' for the many laughs and insights. Lynn Stoney, supported by Paul Stoney and Michael Cahill, constellated the emerging manuscript with a 'field walk' of the chapters and brought incisive insights to edit the text.

Tricia Grace-Norton, my mentor and friend for over 20 years, has given unstinting support, along with Karen Scholes, Janet Curran, Roger Cross, Elina Koussis, David Adams, Andrew Woodgate, Anita Hughes, Chris Frampton, Chrissie Astell, Peter Danby, Chris Wood, Phil Cartwright, Julia Hollenbery and her daughter, Ruby. Rev. Phil Cansdale and the 10:45 congregation at Trinity Churches, Shrewsbury have provided ongoing spiritual nourishment, connecting me with the 'Heart of my own heart', as we've sung many times.

Conversations with caring colleagues and purpose pioneers shaped the book significantly: Alastair MacGregor, Alison Miles, Brian Davenport, Catherine Knight, Cees Kramer, Charles Wookey, Cliff Penwell, Dik Veenman, Emma Ashru Jones, Jason Jay, John Blakey, Julia Rebholz, Liam Black, Loughlin Hickey, Louise Mossman, Martha Morris Graham, Morag Dwyer, Peter Thompson, Robin Alfred, Robin Shohet, Ruth Dobson, Sam King, Steve Lang, Steve Waygood, Vanessa Hartnoll and others too numerous to name here. Thank you for all your fuel for my fire.

A deep thank you to the teachers of the Ridhwan School, founded by A. H. ('Hameed') Almaas. I have been a member of the school since 2016 and am grateful to Rob Merkx, Tejo Jourdan, Candace Harris and all the 'UK4' teachers for their expertise in the teaching of the 'Diamond Approach' to inner realisation. Inquiry with my fellow students has helped to deepen my presence and felt experience of True Nature.

Most importantly, my thanks to my family who have given me deep roots, wings to take flight and much other delight. Mum and Dad, my siblings and their partners – Anna, Johnty and Lucie, Emily and Tom – and my 'niblings' (to whom the book is dedicated) mean more to me than words can ever say. Finally, a huge thank you to Anna Rakowicz for welcoming me into her home where much of this book was written and to Jan Rakowicz for all his good loving, unending kindness and for giving me all the space that I needed to write.

PUBLISHER'S ACKNOWLEDGEMENTS

Text credit

xxvi **Business Roundtable:** Business Roundtable Redefines the Purpose of a Corporation to Promote 'An Economy That Serves All Americans' Updated Statement (August 19, 2019); xxvi **Chartered Management Institute:** Hurth V, Ebert C and Prabhu J (2018) The What, the Why and the How of Purpose: A Guide for Leaders, Chartered Management Institute; xxvii **FINANCIAL TIMES REPUBLICATION:** Caulkin S (24 January 2016) Companies with a purpose beyond profit tend to make more money, Financial Times © 2019 Financial Times Limited. All rights reserved; xxvii **FINANCIAL TIMES REPUBLICATION:** Andrew Hill, (July 5 2019), Simon Sinek: The next generation must test leaders' finite mindset, Financial Times © 2019 Financial Times Limited. All rights reserved; xxviii **PwC:** CEO Pulse (May 2019) Connecting the dots: how purpose can join up your business, PwC; xxix **Yale University Press:** McGilchrist, Iain (2009). The Master and His Emissary: The Divided Brain and the Making of the Western World. Yale University Press; xxix **FINANCIAL TIMES REPUBLICATION:** Rana Foroohar (14 July 2019) Why management by numbers doesn't add up. Financial Times © 2019 Financial Times Limited. All rights reserved; 3 **Berrett-Koehler Publishers:** Jaworski J, (2011) Synchronicity: The Inner Path of Leadership, Berrett-Koehler; 4 **Penguin Random House:** Whyte D. (2002) Crossing the Unknown Sea: Work as a Pilgrimage of Identity. Riverhead Books; 44051 **Business and Sustainable Development Commission:** Better Business, Better World Report (2016), The Business and Sustainable Development Commission; 11 **Elevate Publishing:** Hurst A, (2013) The Purpose Economy, Elevate; 15 **Chartered Management Institute:** Hurth V, Ebert C and Prabhu J (2018) The What, the Why and the How of Purpose: A Guide for Leaders, Chartered Management Institute; 16 **Patagonia:** Mission statement of Patagonia. "Our Business and Climate Change." Patagonia. Used with permission from Patagonia; 16 **Unilever:** Mission statement of Unilever. "Our Strategy for Sustainable Growth." Unilever Global Company Website, © Unilever 2020. Used with permission from Unilever; 16 **GUARDIAN NEWS AND MEDIA LIMITED:** Pratley N, (2017) Paul Polman: 'I could boost Unilever shares. But cutting costs is not our way', The Guardian, 20 May 2017; **17 JOHN WILEY AND SONS INCORPORATED:** Kouzes, J. M., & Posner, B. Z. (1995). The leadership challenge: How to keep getting extraordinary things done in organizations (2nd ed.). San Francisco, CA, US: Jossey-Bass; **17 Pearson Education:** Yukl, G.A., State University of New York, Albany (2013) Leadership in Organizations, 8th Edition, Pearson Education; **17 Berrett-Koehler Publishers:** Scharmer, O. & Kaufer K. (2013) Leading from the Emergent Future: From Ego-System to Eco-System Economies. Berrett-Koehler; **22 Government Digital Service:** On A Mission in the UK Economy (2016) Advisory panel to mission-led business review: Final report Department for Digital, Culture, Media & Sport, UK Government publication; **25 FINANCIAL TIMES REPUBLICATION:** Hill A. (2019) Beyond the bottom line: should business put purpose before profit? Financial Times (4 January 2019) © 2019 Financial Times Limited. All rights reserved; **27 Patagonia:** Marcario, Rose. "Record-Breaking Black Friday Sales to Benefit the Planet." Patagonia Outdoor Clothing & Gear, 10 Feb. 2020; **27 Simon and Schuster:** Kirkpatrick D, (2010) The Facebook Effect, Simon & Schuster; **29 Harvard Business Publishing:** The Business Case for Purpose (2015) EY Beacon Institute and Harvard Business Review Analytic Services. Copyright © 2015 Harvard Business School Publishing; **30 Deloitte Development LLC:** Core beliefs & culture survey (2014) Culture of Purpose — Building business confidence; driving growth, Deloitte Development LLC; **30-31 The Boston Consulting Group:** BCG Insights (October 2017) Total Societal Impact: A New Lens for Strategy, Boston Consulting Group; **32 FINANCIAL TIMES REPUBLICATION:** Tett G. (21 September 2018), Millennial heirs to change investment landscape, Financial Times © 2019 Financial Times Limited. All rights reserved; **32 FINANCIAL TIMES REPUBLICATION:** Edgecliffe-Johnson A (3 January 2019) Beyond the bottom line: Should business put purpose before profit? Financial Times © 2019 Financial Times Limited. All rights reserved; **33 Lisa Earle McLeod:** Lisa Earle McLeod. "Why Millennials Keep Dumping You: An Open Letter to Management." LinkedIn; **33-34 Authentic Investor/ RD Lake:** Authentic Investor. Millennial Voices: stories from the heart of the investment industry. Authentic Investor Limited, 2019. Used with permission from Authentic Investor; **34 Academy of Management Learning & Education:** Sumantra Ghoshal (2005) Bad management theories are destroying good management practices, Academy of Management Learning & Education, 4(1), 75-91; **36 Penguin Random House:** McLuhan M & Fiore Q. (1967) The Medium is the Massage: An Inventory of Effects, Penguin; **37 Government Digital**

Service: On A Mission in the UK Economy (2016) Advisory panel to mission-led business review: Final report Department for Digital, Culture, Media & Sport, UK Government publication; **47 Harvard Business Publishing:** Rooke D. and Torbert W. R (April 2005). Seven Transformations of Leadership, Harvard Business Review; **49 Nelson Parker:** Laloux F. (2014) Reinventing organizations: A Guide to Creating Organizations Inspired by the Next Stage of Human Consciousness, Nelson Parker; **52 Bloomsbury Publishing:** Winner D (2012). Brilliant Orange: The Neurotic Genius of Dutch Football, A&C Black; **52 Johan Cruyff:** Reported by Leo Messi on Twitter 24 March 2016; **52 Bloomsbury Publishing:** Winner D (2012). Brilliant Orange: The Neurotic Genius of Dutch Football, A&C Black; **53 Penguin Random House:** Mihaly Csikszentmihalyi (30-Mar-2004) "Good Business: Leadership, Flow, and the Making of Meaning", Penguin Random House; **53 FINANCIAL TIMES REPUBLICATION:** Sarah Gordon (8 March 2019) I covered the City for 20 years – and here's what I learnt, Financial Times. © 2019 Financial Times Limited. All rights reserved; **54 Taylor & Francis:** Barrett R., (2013) The Values-Driven Organization: Cultural Health and Employee Well-Being as a Pathway to Sustainable Performance, Routledge; **55-56 Business Insider:** Benjamin Zhang, (23 May 2019) American Airlines CEO reveals the most important lesson he learned from the legendary founder of Southwest Airlines. Business Insider; **56-57 Iceland Foods Ltd:** Walker R., (20 May 2019) "Palm Oil Was All about Doing The Right Thing, Not a Marketing Gimmick." About Iceland, 20 May 2019; **57-58 THE ECONOMIST:** Choosing plan B (9 August 2018) Danone rethinks the idea of the firm, The Economist; **58 Rose Marcario:** Marcario R., (28 November 2018) Our Urgent Gift to the Planet, LinkedIn. Used with permission from Rose Marcario; **59 Penguin Random House:** van der Post L., (1958) The Lost World of the Kalahari, Vintage Publishing (2002 edition); **65 Berrett-Koehler Publishers:** Scharmer O. (2009) Theory U: Learning from the Future as It Emerges. Berrett-Koehler Publishers; **67 HarperCollins:** Collins J., (2001) Good to Great: Why Some Companies Make the Leap... and Others Don't. Harper Business, 2001; **68 DailyGood:** Scharmer O. (9 July 2013) Uncovering The Blind Spot of Leadership, The Daily Good; **68 Berrett-Koehler Publishers:** Scharmer, O. & Kaufer K. (2013) Leading from the Emergent Future: From Ego-System to Eco-System Economies. Berrett-Koehler; **71 Fortune Media IP Limited:** Leaf C., (15 October 2019) Salesforce Founder Marc Benioff: What Business School Never Taught Me, Fortune, Inc; **73 Simon and Schuster:** Benioff M. and Langley M., (2019) Trailblazer: The Power of Business for the Greatest

Platform for Change, Simon and Schuster; **73 The New York Times Company:** Gelles, D. (2018, June 15). Marc Benioff of Salesforce: 'Are We Not All Connected?'; **73 Shambhala Publications:** Almaas, A. H. (2008). The unfolding now: realizing your true nature through the practice of presence. Boston, Mass: Shambhala, p. 136; **74 Henley Business School:** Hawkins P., (2017) Tomorrow's Leadership and the Necessary Revolution in Today's Leadership Development, Henley Business School; **75-76 Claus Springborg:** How to disarm your inner critic. Claus Springborg. Used with permission from Claus Springborg; **76 Shambhala Publications:** Byron Brown (1998) Soul Without Shame: A Guide to Liberating Yourself from the Judge Within. Shambala Publications Inc; **76 HarperCollins:** Chade Meng Tan (2012) Search Inside Yourself: The Unexpected Path to Achieving Success, Happiness (and World Peace). HarperOne; **94 Dik Veenman:** Dik Veenman. The Listening Spectrum. The Right Conversation. Used with permission from Dik Veenman; **95 Otto Scharmer:** Adapted from Scharmer's model of the Four Fields appears in Isaacs W. (1999) Dialogue and the Art of Thinking Together. Bantam Doubleday Dell Publishing Group. Used with permission from Otto Scharmer; **99-100 A Blueprint for Better Business:** Adapted from Blueprint for Better Business (May 2018) How can investors identify purpose-led companies?; **104 Kogan Page Ltd:** Hawkins P., (2017) Leadership Team Coaching: Developing Collective Transformational Leadership, Kogan Page; **107-109 Springer:** Clayton M., (2014) The Influence Agenda: A Systematic Approach to Aligning Stakeholders in Times of Change, Palgrave Macmillan; **111 Google:** Mission statement of Google; **112 Greta Thunberg:** Frazee, G. (2019, September 23). Read climate activist Greta Thunberg's speech to the UN; **116 Nelson Parker:** Laloux F. (2014) Reinventing Organizations: A Guide to Creating Organizations Inspired by the Next Stage in Human Consciousness. Nelson Parker; **118 GUARDIAN NEWS AND MEDIA LIMITED:** Nicholls-Lee, D. (2018, February 28). Fishing for plastic: the Amsterdam canal tour with a difference; **119 Edward Rowland/Sarah Rozenthuler:** Organisational Purpose Diamond by Edward Rowland and Sarah Rozenthuler (www.wholepartnership.com) is licensed under the Creative Commons Attribution-ShareAlike 4.0 International License; **121 Pearson Education:** O'Brien J. and Cave A. (2017) The Power of Purpose. Pearson Education; **122 Patagonia:** Mission statement of Patagonia. "Our Business and Climate Change." Patagonia. Used with permission from Patagonia; **130 NS Media Group:** Dr Whitaker, (2015) "How Labour broke the NHS – and why Labour must fix it", New Statesman, 5 March 2015; **130 Cambridge Judge Business School:** Hurth V., Ebert C. & Prabhu J.

(2018) Organisational Purpose: The construct and its antecedents and consequences. Cambridge Judge Business School, Working Paper No. 02/2018; **136 Kogan Page Ltd:** Whittington J., (2012), Systemic coaching and constellations: An Introduction to the principles, practices and application. Kogan Page; **143 Simon and Schuster:** Heffernan M (2015) Beyond Measure: The Big Impact of Small Changes. Simon & Schuster; **151 Ernst & Young Global Limited:** The Business Case for Purpose (2015) EY Beacon Institute and Harvard Business Review Analytic Services. Copyright © 2015 Harvard Business School Publishing; **153 Business Roundtable:** Business Roundtable Redefines the Purpose of a Corporation to Promote 'An Economy That Serves All Americans' Updated Statement (August 19, 2019); **154 Council of Institutional Investors:** Council of Institutional Investors Responds to Business Round table Statement on Corporate Purpose. (August 19, 2019); **154 FINANCIAL TIMES REPUBLICATION:** Tett G., (September 6, 2019) Does capitalism need saving from itself? Financial Times © 2019 Financial Times Limited. All rights reserved; **157 Jack Ma:** Ma J., (20 September 2017) Building the Economy of the Future, https://www.youtube.com/watch?v=BhCCAbDSsNc, Bloomberg, YouTube LLC; **157 McKinsey & Company:** De Smet A. & Gagnon C. (2017 Number 4) Safe enough to try: An interview with Zappos CEO Tony Hsieh, The Quarterly McKinsey & Company; **161 THE ECONOMIST:** The Economist (22 August 2019) What are companies for?; **162 GUARDIAN NEWS AND MEDIA LIMITED:** Weale, S. (2019, April 15). Fifth of teachers plan to leave profession within two years; **162-163 Penguin Random House:** Based on Sinek S. (2011) Start with Why: How Great Leaders Inspire Everyone To Take Action, Portfolio; **163 Harvard Business Publishing:** James C. Collins and Jerry I. Porras (1996) Building Your Company's Vision Harvard Business Review; **170 Forbes Media LLC:** Gallo C., (9 December 2013) What Starbucks CEO Howard Schultz Taught Me About Communication And Success, Fortune; **171 Harvard Business Publishing:** Katzenbach, John R and Smith, Douglas K, (2009) The Discipline of Teams, Harvard Business Review Classics; **173 Edward Rowland/Sarah Rozenthuler:** Team Purpose Diamond by Edward Rowland and Sarah Rozenthuler (www.wholepartnership.com) is licensed under the Creative Commons Attribution-ShareAlike 4.0 International License; **181 Éditions de la Maison française, Inc:** Antoine de Saint Exupéry (1942) Pilote de Guerre. Editions de la Maison Francaise; **181 Harvard Business Publishing:** Marcus Buckingham, Ashley Goodall (2019) "The Feedback Fallacy" Harvard Business Review; **185 Penguin Random House:** Whyte D. (2002) Crossing the Unknown Sea: Work as a

Pilgrimage of Identity. Riverhead Books; **188 Elsevier Inc:** Michele W. Gazica and Paul E. Spector (2015) Journal of Vocational Behavior. Elsevier; **190 Steve Jobs:** Stanford University (2008) Steve Jobs' 2005 Stanford Commencement Address; **190 Edward Rowland/Sarah Rozenthuler:** Personal Purpose Diamond by Edward Rowland and Sarah Rozenthuler (www.wholepartnership.com) is licensed under the Creative Commons Attribution-ShareAlike 4.0 International License; **191 JOHN WILEY AND SONS INCORPORATED:** Palmer P (1999) Let Your Life Speak: Listening for the Voice of Vocation. Jossey Bass; **193 Penguin Random House:** Hillman J., (1997) The Soul's Code: In Search of Character and Calling, Ballantyne Books; **193 The Big Issue Company Ltd:** Graham J., (14-20 March 2016) Paul Merton: "I wanted my dad to be a hero, but he was very distant" The Big Issue; **194 BBC:** Smale, W. (2019, May 20). 'The bullying got worse and worse and I snapped'; **194 Inner City Books:** Hollis J. (2000) Creating a Life: Finding Your Individual Path, Inner City Books; **197 University of California:** Based on Luft, J.; Ingham, H. (1955). "The Johari window, a graphic model of interpersonal awareness". Proceedings of the western training laboratory in group development (Los Angeles: UCLA); **198 Macmillan Publishers:** Pearce N (2019) The Purpose Path: A Guide to Pursuing Your Authentic Life's Work. St Martin's Essentials; **201 Richard Branson:** Admin. "Look after Your Staff." Virgin, 27 Apr. 2017; **214 Victoria Hurth:** Epilogue: A New Dawn by Dr Victoria Hurth. Used with permission from Victoria Hurth; **205 Westburn Publishers Ltd:** Porter, M. E., & Kramer, M. R. (2011). Shared value: How to reinvent capitalism—and unleash a wave of innovation and growth. Harvard Business Review, 89(1/2), 62-77; **208-209 Beacon Press:** Viktor Emil Frank (1992) "Man's Search for Meaning: An Introduction to Logotherapy" Beacon Press; **209 Politeia:** Freeman, R. E., & Ginena, K. (2015). Rethinking the purpose of the corporation: Challenges from stakeholder theory. Notizie di Politeia, 31(117), 9-18; **211 Oxford university press:** Bolden, R., Hawkins, B., Gosling, J., & Taylor, S. (2011). Exploring leadership: Individual, organizational, and societal perspectives. OUP Oxford; **211 SAGE Publication:** Kempster, S., Jackson, B., & Conroy, M. (2011). Leadership as purpose: Exploring the role of purpose in leadership practice. Leadership, 7(3), 317-334; **213 Pearson Education:** Yukl G (2006) Leadership in Organizations, 6th edn. Upper Saddle River, NJ: Prentice-Hall; **213 JOHN WILEY AND SONS INCORPORATED:** Drath, W. H. (1998). Approaching the future of leadership development. In C. D. McCauley, R. S. Moxley, & E. Van Velsor (Eds.), The Center for Creative Leadership handbook of leadership development (pp. 403–432). San Francisco: Jossey-Bass; **214 Chartered Management Institute:** Hurth V, Ebert C and Prabhu J (2018) The What, the Why and the How of Purpose: A Guide for Leaders, Chartered Management Institute.

Photo credit

26 Patagonia: Don't buy this Jacket. Patagonia Inc. Used with permission;

FOREWORD

By Paul Polman

Business has rarely been under as much pressure as it is today to justify its role in the world. Trust is at an all-time low and corporate leaders face fundamental questions about what they are doing and why. And rightly so. The globe faces huge social, economic and environmental challenges with the onset of climate change, growing inequality, and operating within the planetary boundaries to name just a few.

As I have long argued, business leaders have responsibilities that go far beyond delivering returns to shareholders. They must have a wider purpose. Profit alone cannot be an objective; it should rather be the result of working for the greater good. Moving from profit as sole objective to not even profit *and* purpose but ultimately to profit *through* purpose.

As this book admirably explains, companies that are powered by purpose are ultimately more successful, including in generating profits, than those that are not. Nor can purpose be reduced to hollow exhortation. The chief executive should, as Sarah writes, make sure that purpose is tightly bound into the organisational fabric of the corporation. It ultimately becomes the strategy.

To give meaning to purpose, a leader must walk the walk as well as talk the talk. When I was young, I decided to be a priest and later a doctor. Both are professions with purpose. Serendipity had it that my life took a different turn and I ended up in business. Initially, I did not find it motivating, but the more I got involved and climbed the ranks the more I realised that business too can have great purpose. I always believed that business cannot be a bystander in a system that gives it life in the first place and, for it to be accepted long term, needs to ultimately be a positive contributor to society. After all there is no business case in enduring poverty.

As chief executive of Unilever for a decade, I had a glorious opportunity to see how powerful this is. When the Lever brothers, the company's founders, launched Sunlight, the world's first packaged soap, it was not to report quarterly profits or pay out dividends to shareholders. It was to improve hygiene in nineteenth-century Britain. When I became CEO, we simply reframed it to making sustainable living commonplace. Never has this been so important than now.

Contemporary psychiatrists have warned about the risks of ignoring the RH workings of our brain. Iain McGilchrist has highlighted how the 'unopposed action of a dysfunctional left hemisphere' had led to an increasingly mechanistic world where many people feel separated from one another and a sense of emptiness. In organisations, the narrow, profit-focused, cost-cutting perspective of leaders comes from a LH-dominated thinking mind that drives for certainty through short-term thinking and quarterly reporting.[10]

It is essential for human survival that leaders, whose actions can impact millions, find a way to become more balanced as they make their decisions. As one example among many, Rana Foroohar, author of *Makers and Takers*, highlights how risk-taking in order to maximise profit at Boeing has become problematic.[11] Following the grounding of the Boeing 737 Max aircraft after two separate crashes, Boeing is now at risk of being overtaken by Airbus as the world's biggest plane maker. While there were many factors behind the crash, outsourcing to engineers who were paid just $9 an hour, charging extra for certain safety features and rushing the aircraft to market in order to beat Airbus were key elements in the mix.

'Wise chief executives and board members should think hard before they look to financial engineering to save them.' The mindset of management by numbers, cost cutting and 'shareholder value', which preaches that executives should worry only about the share price of their company, can 'end up being so pricey in the long run'.

Leadership is not only about rational problem solving, goal attainment and pragmatic solutions (the LH territory); it is also about drawing on the intuitive, imaginative and embodied intelligence we have (the RH domain). To manifest the bold vision that all companies become purpose-driven, leaders will need to be courageous and vulnerable, responsible and pioneering, protectors of well-being and agitators of change. As individuals become more balanced, they will be better able to lead a purposeful enterprise, and this calls for leaders developing their capacity to lead in ways that re-humanise the workplace.

THE FOUR CORE CAPACITIES OF PURPOSE-LED LEADERSHIP

Powered by Purpose outlines the core capacities that leaders need to develop in order to go on the journey to deliver purpose. The model, which forms the crux of the book, arises out of recent research, practitioner expertise and close observations of corporate leaders over 20 years. To turn the concepts into experience, I give practical guidance on how to develop these capacities through experiential exercises that will enable you to bring purpose to life in your organisation. The four interrelated core capacities of purpose-led leadership are:

- **Cultivate leadership presence.** To step forward courageously onto new ground, leaders need to deepen their self-awareness. By being in touch with the reality of the present moment and their felt sense of 'rightness' about future direction, leaders act in a way that others are inspired to follow. Through embodied wholehearted awareness, leaders deal with inner obstacles to presence such as reactivity and bring a sense of ease to their interactions. They act on their desire to serve the well-being of others, which in turn increases their own well-being.

- **Make dialogue authentic.** To manage the tensions that inevitably crop up on the path to achieving the dual goals of purpose and profit, leaders need to be skilful at dialogue. They listen actively, surface critical questions and name any 'hard truths' that need to be addressed – rather than languishing in the short-term comfort of avoidance. They remain open to challenge and address issues such as competition for resources, divergent views about how to reach strategic goals and decisions about profit allocation. They discern what wants to flow through their organisation in order to bring something new and 'right' into the world.

- **Engage your stakeholders.** To articulate a compelling organisational purpose that engages and energises team members, leaders need to see the larger system of which they are part. They need to connect with a wide set of stakeholders – both internal and external – rather than serve shareholders alone. By mapping their ecosystem of stakeholders, they see who is critical to include and who is at risk of being excluded. When leaders attune to the energetic field of these stakeholders, this enables them to live out the deeper potential of their organisation and the positive social change it can create in the world.

- **Connect on purpose.** To encourage everyone to pull in the same direction, purpose-led leaders foster a culture of collaboration. They discern where the 'acupressure points' for change are and attend to any invisible dysfunctional dynamics that impede day-to-day interactions. By developing their systemic intelligence, they disable silos and activate a free flow of positive energy throughout the system.

CHAPTER 1

WHY PURPOSE IS KEY TO A BETTER FUTURE

Leadership is discovering the company's destiny and having the courage to follow it ... Companies that endure have a noble purpose.[1]

Joe Jaworski

We are living through intense, uneasy and extraordinary times. Darkness is falling wherever we look, and yet there are pinpricks of light too. Never has the potential for humanity to address urgent and global issues – economic inequality, societal polarisation and environmental dangers – been greater. And never has the risk of systemic failure – whether from cyber-attacks, stand-offs between nations, or the catastrophic consequences of climate change – been higher. We are poised right on the edge of destiny-changing times.

What will it take for our collective and individual lives to cascade down a path of shared prosperity and greater well-being rather than widening inequality? How can we make a successful transition to a truly global society where each person has a sense of belonging and their 'right' place? How can individuals, nations and organisations have a deeper sense of their role in the world without becoming imperialistic or narcissistic?

To address the twenty-first-century challenges we face as a global society, we need to rekindle our imaginations about who we are and what we are capable of. If we slide into despair about how dangerous our leaders are, how intractable our problems have become and how fragmented our global village is, then nothing will change for the better. To find hope, we might have to dig deep but dig we must. We need a fresh perspective more than ever and to pay attention to the new and inspiring ways of leading that are emerging.

Amid all the challenges, there is a tremendous opportunity emerging. The movement towards 'purpose-driven' business, which puts solving social and environmental problems at the heart of organisations, is under-way and gathering strength. High-performing companies that are purpose-ful, profitable and socially aware are catalysing new ways of working. Top teams are tuning into how a potent purpose harnesses the energy of team members to do great work. And pioneering leaders are showing an unwa-vering commitment to creating a vibrant economy, a true humanity and a sustainable planet that will benefit us all.

THE FUTURE OF LEADERSHIP

This chapter explores the need for a fundamentally different approach to leadership given the scale of the challenges facing us. This shift, which can be framed broadly as a move from 'command-and-control' to 'purpose-led leadership', is already taking place both in companies and the not-for-profit sector. We are witnessing old models of leadership breaking down and new forms that are more fit-for-purpose emerging.

While leadership is a huge and hot topic, leadership research has mostly focused on theories of leadership. The question often remains: leading for the sake of what? Purpose answers this question by focusing leadership beyond the burning platform. Leadership can only be sustainable if it's powered by a 'towards' motivation. As Brexit has demonstrated, there's no leadership in knowing what you don't want. Purpose is having real preci-sion and clarity on what you are looking to create as well as the unwavering commitment to do it.

Becoming powered by purpose is the real cutting edge of organisational development today. In our rapidly changing world, there is a huge opportu-nity emerging for organisations and leaders to play a positive role in society by orientating around an inspiring purpose. Purpose is unique in its power to help an organisation to become a 'force for good' in the world rather than simply chase the dollar sign or growth for growth's sake.

The power of purpose is that it touches us, moves us and stirs us into action. Purpose brings feeling to a business in a way that a vision alone often doesn't. We need passion, energy and enthusiasm to generate the will to act. As the poet David Whyte says, 'The antidote to exhaustion is wholeheartedness'.[2] When our heart, head and gut are aligned, we are engaged and energised to do great work.

This chapter covers the following territory:

- Why purpose is key to a better future.
- What it means to be powered by purpose.
- How being powered by purpose looks in practice.

WHY WE NEED A BRIDGE TO A BETTER FUTURE

My sense of optimism comes from the shifting landscape I see around leadership. While it's true that we live in times of deep turmoil, it's also true that leaders are starting to spark a different conversation about what it means to lead in our rapidly changing, digitally connected world. In my consulting work as a business psychologist, I've seen how a disparate group of people, all pulling in different directions, can come together to become a true team in service of something larger than themselves.

For far too long, the dominant narrative in organisational, economic and political life has cast human beings as self-interested, self-maximising and separated. This story is not only incomplete but inaccurate. Recent thinking in psychology, neuroscience and evolutionary biology confirms that our true nature as a human species is to be empathic, altruistic, sensitive to the needs of others and collaborative more than competitive when – and this is a big caveat – the systems we are in are set up supportively (see page 133). Our 'prosocial' tendencies enabled us to survive the African savannahs and outwit predators faster and stronger than ourselves by being supreme co-operators.[3]

In the corporate world, the story that we've been telling ourselves about ourselves in recent decades has tended to be a long way from this reality. The narrative of rampant individualism, extreme competition and scarce resources has thwarted our collective ability to create a thriving global community that treats people and the planet well. The drive for constant economic growth driven by consumer demands is now at loggerheads with the environmental crisis creating pressure to review and renew our story.

The good news is that this narrative, resting on shaky foundations, is losing ground. There is a new guiding story beginning to emerge. Leaders around the world are discovering their power to become a force for good, not just for their immediate stakeholders but for society as a whole. This movement towards 'purpose-led leadership' is exciting because it reflects the reality of the interconnected web in which we live and aligns with our deeper potential as humans. A tangible bridge to the better future we crave is starting to appear.

HEARING THE CALL

Before I set some further context, I'll first share what sparked my passion for leadership that taps into the power of purpose.

When I was 21 years old, I graduated in psychology with flying colours from the University of Nottingham. I'd completed a four-year degree course, with the encouragement of my parents who'd been keen for me to jump a year at school and fast track to a successful career. I was fortunate enough to spend my 'industrial placement' year working for a top consultancy where I loved working directly for clients to improve performance by applying insights from business psychology.

After I finished my degree, instead of doing the sensible thing by accepting the offer of a graduate job from the consultancy, the spirit of adventure got the better of me. I rode off into the sunshine with my boyfriend in an old camper van with the plan to teach English for a year. After driving through the Alps and doing day work on yachts in Antibes, we had enough cash stashed to drive south to Spain. Friends from university who'd set up home in Valencia told us of fiestas, fun and sun. Our happy reunion came to an abrupt end, however, when we discovered that while we'd been out having cervezas our camper van had been broken into. We lost virtually all our possessions – the little money we had, all our clothes and our much-loved stereo too.

With no fixed address and no clothes to wear except old t-shirts and scruffy denim shorts, we didn't get a single interview at a language school. We soon found ourselves without a job nor a Peseta in our pockets (this was over twenty years ago, pre-Euro). Hanging out in plazas, we soon met other 'travellers', or 'Thatcher's refugees', as some liked to call themselves, who were adept at earning a living on the street. To avoid having to borrow money from my parents and returning to the UK with my tail between my legs, I set out learning to busk.

The plan to spend a year teaching English turned into four years living on the road. I learnt how to juggle three balls, three plastic clubs, followed by three fire clubs and finally three knives. A turning point came when a US magician, a seasoned street performer, taught me how to pull a crowd, entertain them and pass the hat.

THE TURNING POINT

After four years of full-on adventure and hard graft, I had my first successful season doing a solo show. As the long days shortened to autumn, my spirits started to sag. Although I'd 'made it' as a busker, having saved up enough money for a winter of not working, I began to feel really down. After several weeks of going to bed crying and waking up crying, I bought a flight back to the UK and went to visit my parents. My mum and I had what turned out to be a life-changing conversation and the turning point on my journey of feeling so lost.

'You're not happy because you're not fulfilled. And you're not fulfilled because you're not using all your talents,' Mum said.

My self-esteem was so low, I couldn't actually figure out what my talents were. I guessed that I probably wasn't using all of them. I knew that while I enjoyed making people smile and children laugh, I sensed that there was more to life than this. There had to be more to work than this. There had to be more to me than this.

After some heart searching, I left my itinerant life and moved back into my parents' home. The funds that would have seen me through a winter hibernating in Spain suddenly seemed very small. I was 25 and life had never felt so challenging. It had been tough on the road, but this inner pain was different from the hunger I'd felt on the streets. The same thoughts went round and round my head:

'Everyone has a life apart from me.'

'I've burnt all my bridges.'

And ... again and again –

'Is this it?'

My 'crash' turned out to be hugely instructive. I had wandered off my path and my internal radar knew it. I gradually came to accept what my mum had seen so clearly. I hadn't been using the abilities I had that were so effortless I hardly even noticed I had them: communicating with diverse people, synthesising different information and asking provocative questions. In their absence, a light had gone out inside.

It took over a year to write my CV, go to some interviews and find a job. I was eventually offered a position in what is now the Department of Work and Pensions at their head office in Sheffield. I travelled around to different job centres – Wigan, Barnsley and Cardiff – testing staff on newly developed recruitment tests to check that they didn't have any adverse impact on women or people from minority backgrounds. Hardly my dream job, but I was grateful to have been given a break. By returning to my passion – helping people and organisations to thrive – the light inside started to shine again.

Since then, I've seen time and time again how individuals who are in touch with their passion have a wellspring of energy. Their eyes are bright, their presence is magnetic and their vision is energising for others. When people believe in what they do, they not only have a purpose, they embody it too.

There is a well-shared story that illustrates the difference that purpose makes. During a visit to the NASA space centre in 1962, President John F.

Kennedy noticed a janitor carrying a broom. He interrupted his tour, walked over to the man and said, 'Hi, I'm Jack Kennedy. What are you doing?'

'Well, Mr President,' the janitor responded, 'I'm helping put a man on the moon.'

To most people, this janitor was simply cleaning the building. But in the larger story, the janitor was aware that he was helping to serve what was widely believed to be a vital step for humanity. When we live purposefully, no matter how large or small our role, we contribute in a meaningful way to the bigger story unfolding through us.

Beyond autonomy, recognition, flexibility or any other factor that organisational psychology tells us is key to job satisfaction, it is being true to our purpose that makes us thrive. It propels us to participate wholeheartedly in our own lives and in the world.

FORGING A DIFFERENT PATH

Living our personal purpose is not, however, enough. To create a truly sustainable planet for us all, whole-scale change is needed. Resolving systemic challenges will require courageous action not just by individuals but by groups of people. There is increasing recognition that in order to solve the most pressing issues of our time – world hunger, environmental degradation and social inequality – governments, companies and not-for-profits will need to work together. We need to find not just an individual path to our own fulfilment, but a collective path that leads to long-term well-being for us all.

'It's time to change the game,' states the Better Business, Better World report presented at Davos in January 2017. The report is a call to action for leaders from all walks of life to build an economy that is just, sustainable and inclusive, and is one of many similar such calls for action from within the business community. The report is the work of the Business and Sustainable Development Commission that includes 35 leaders including CEOs of global organisations such as Aviva plc, Pearson plc, Investec Asset Management, Ericsson, Women's World Banking and Mars.[4]

The report emerged on the back of the socially disruptive events of 2016. The outcome of the Brexit referendum and the US election has left many people feeling deeply unsettled. These socio-political events have revealed the extent to which significant sectors of the population feel angry, frustrated and disenfranchised with what has been called the 'globalisation hangover'.

Despite technological progress, better health standards and an overall reduction in poverty over the last 30 years, the report states that we have also witnessed the rise of climate change, armed conflict and youth unemployment. Globalisation has an 'unacceptable face' and the current model of business is 'deeply flawed'. The report states:

> *Solutions are urgently needed. We see the next 15 years as critical, with change starting now and accelerating over the period. Business as usual is not an option: choosing to 'kick the can down the road' over the next four years will put impossible environmental and social strains on a stuttering global economy. But if enough leaders act now and collectively, we can forge a different path, one that eases the burden on finite resources and includes those currently left behind or excluded from the market, helping to address today's political grievances* [my emphasis]

Fortunately, cross-sector collaboration of business, government and civil society is starting to happen. The 17 Sustainable Development Goals (SDGs) ratified at the 2015 United Nations summit are one glimmer of hope on the horizon.[5] Also known as the 'Global Goals', these are ambitious targets to address the three most pressing needs of our global society: end extreme poverty, address social inequality and tackle climate change. Together with their 169 associated targets, the SDGs offer a powerful framework to bring about fundamental change. Replacing the Millennium Development Goals, which expired at the end of 2015, these are goals for all countries and for all people.

BUSINESS AS THE 'BRIDGE'

The Better Business, Better World report makes a bold claim about how far along the journey to purpose we have come. Acknowledging that the business case for a more sustainable growth model is already strong – purpose-driven companies across the globe are delivering attractive returns to shareholders – the report goes one step further. It maps the economic prize available to business if the 17 SDGs are achieved.

Incorporating the Global Goals into core growth strategies, value chain operations and policy positions would open up US$12 trillion worth of market opportunities in terms of business savings and revenue. It would also help to create 380 million new jobs with a living wage across supply chains and distribution networks by 2030.

A new socially focused business model is therefore about recognising that successful businesses of the future are good global citizens. Shell, for example, has developed 'gravity lights' to replace kerosene lamps in Africa, leveraging the power of their engineering, technology and brand to create positive change in the lives of millions. If their intentions shift from mere profit to profitable good, companies become uniquely placed to scale creative ideas, taking them from the lab to the living room where they have real impact.

The report *On A Mission in the UK Economy* (2016)[6] produced by an advisory panel of top-level leaders at the request of Rob Wilson, Minister for Civil Society, calls the increasing engagement of business with a wider set of stakeholders in order to create benefits for employees and society at large a new 'movement'. The report also underlines the growing evidence base of a link between purpose-driven business and earnings out-performance. They cite the following as key pieces of data:

- 54% of consumers want to buy sustainable products, research by Unilever has found. More recently, Unilever has reported that its Sustainable Living Brands such as Lifebuoy, Ben & Jerry's and Dove grew 50% faster than the rest of the business and delivered more than 60% of Unilever's growth.[7]

- Two-thirds of consumers are willing to pay more for purpose-driven brands, according to the Global Corporate Sustainability Report. 'Purpose' as a purchasing factor has risen 26% globally since 2010.[8]

The next chapter covers more about the evidence for the business benefits of being powered by purpose. This movement will not sustain itself if it's understood as simply a good thing to do or a merely because of a moral push. What's exciting is when business becomes a real 'bridge' for the conversation between entrepreneurs and society, as we've seen in the case of Shell.

With the growing success of companies such as Whole Food Markets, Unilever, Honest Tea and Etsy, 'doing well' and 'doing good' are becoming increasingly understood as intertwined. These companies make a difference and they make a profit, successfully. Whether through more sustainable environmental impact, improving health or the sale of handcrafted goods, these companies are seizing new 'market opportunities'. They are championing goals that hold meaning for their stakeholders, because this is where true value-creation lies. Meaning is being recognised as having more currency than money.

In his book, *The Purpose Economy*, social entrepreneur Aaron Hurst places the movement towards purpose-driven business in an evolutionary context. Starting with the agrarian economy, which lasted 8,000 years, Hurst shows how this gave rise to the industrial evolution, which dominated for 150 years, through new methods of working and organising. Within the last 50 years, the information economy can be seen as emerging out of the industrial economy as the demand for new capacities such as data storage and software development formed new markets. Business opportunities such as sustainable energy, resource sharing and improving well-being are now emerging as new ways to create value.[9]

Purpose-driven organisations are 'moving markets' and setting the course for redefining business. Hurst uses the term 'purpose economy' to capture how society is going through another fundamental restructure as purpose becomes the new business imperative. He sees running an organisation today without a central emphasis on purpose as similar to running an organisation in the early 1990s and failing to implement technology – in other words, fatally myopic. This nascent economy is, as Hurst says, 'the first economy built for humans'. It taps into our innate desire to orientate ourselves towards what's meaningful, as recent developments in brain science demonstrates. Purpose-driven business will, therefore, require a more human-centred leadership, as we shall see.

With purpose as the driver of the new economy, the opportunity to improve the lives of billions of people and create truly successful companies that people want to support is huge. An invigorating social and economic system is emerging where value creation that creates real well-being in the long term. Figuring out what leadership capabilities are required both to bring about and then sustain this new 'purpose economy' is the critical leadership challenge of our time.

PURPOSE AS A FORGOTTEN GEM

While the movement towards purpose-driven business could be seen as the defining pattern of our era, it is also, in some ways, nothing new. Professor Colin Mayer traces the roots to the Roman corporation that combined corporate with social purpose by performing public works, building public infrastructure and generating a financial return.[10]

Andy Last, co-founder of the communications agency Salt, highlights how public-minded nineteenth-century industrialists such as George Cadbury, Joseph Rowntree and Jesse Boot founded their businesses on the premise that their organisations were not just about making money but serving society as well. Leaders from the Quaker tradition clearly understood that the growth of their businesses would be stronger if it was aligned with social progress. Last traces the development of Lifebuoy – now one of Unilever's most successful and profitable brands – back to the vision of William Hesketh Lever. Concerned about cholera and other infectious diseases spreading through the slums of Liverpool, Lever created a bar of soap that would be available to the masses who were at risk of dying – a mission that is still consistent with how the soap is marketed in India today.[11]

Turn the clock forward to the twenty-first century and we are witnessing what many businesses would call their rediscovery of 'social purpose', which was lost in the heady days of the 1980s and 1990s. Thatcher's declaration that 'there is no such thing as society' summarises the dominant mindset in six words. The comical but obnoxious 'Loadsamoney' played by Harry Enfield was a defining character of that era.[12]

Business leaders such as Emmanuel Faber of Danone, Rose Marcario of Patagonia and Adam Elman of Marks & Spencer are leaders of today who also see the growth of business and the progress of society as inextricably linked. From a historical perspective, purpose-driven business is the next iteration of the enlightened approach that Roman and Victorian entrepreneurs took to building enduring enterprises.

Coalescing around a potent organisational purpose is, therefore, a forgotten gem. Leaders are increasingly seeing the need to reclaim an inspiring organisational purpose. The 'enlightened self-interest' of visionary leaders created towns with civic pride and good design such as Bourneville and Letchworth in the late nineteenth and early twentieth centuries. Contrast these with Grenfell and the 'sink estates' of the 1960s and the difference that purposeful leadership makes comes sharply into focus.

THE BIG CONVERSATION

While purpose-driven business is not a new paradigm, the context in which organisations are now operating is distinctly different from what has gone before. Given this changing landscape, there is a big conversation going on about purpose globally.

According to research by EY Beacon Institute and Saïd Business School at Oxford University, the dialogue on purpose-driven business has grown exponentially among CEOs, consultants and 'conscious business' change agents over the last five years.[13] The fact that three of the Big Four accounting firms – EY, PwC and Deloitte – have each carried out research into this area in recent times also points to the incoming tide of purpose.

A unique combination of circumstances is creating pressure to change the current state of leadership, business and capitalism. Chief among these forces for change is the need to rebuild trust in organisations. The 2019 Edelman Trust Barometer found that only one in five feel that the system is working for them, and nearly half of the mass population feel that the system is failing them.[14]

A further factor creating the pressure to change is the widespread and well-documented high level of disengagement among workers. Ongoing research by Harvard Business School has revealed that fewer than 20% of managers have a strong sense of their own personal purpose.[15] In 2018 Gallup reported that the percentage of 'engaged' employees in the USA – those who are involved in, enthusiastic and committed to their work and workplace, is 34%. Around 17% are 'actively disengaged' costing the US economy billions per year through loss of productivity.[16]

Finally, the 'purpose generation' is also creating the pressure for change. Research shows that for six out of ten millennials a 'sense of purpose' is part of the reason they choose to work for their current employer (eight out of ten for the 'super-connected' who are high users of social networking tools).[17]

WHAT IS ORGANISATIONAL PURPOSE?

Despite the mounting interest and growing business case, there is a lack of know-how about how to activate purpose-led leadership. There is acknowledgement that the journey to become purpose-driven takes time and that there are obstacles along the way but the question remains: what exactly is organisational purpose and how does it differ from what has come before?

Despite all the focus on purpose in recent years, however, unanswered questions remain and criticisms abound. Objections include:

- Purpose overlaps with similar concepts such as mission and vision, creating conceptual confusion.
- The lack of an agreed definition, in turn, creates an absence of know-how about how to implement purpose effectively.
- Purpose is just a re-hash of CSR (corporate social responsibility) and adds nothing new.

Lack of clarity about purpose is a key issue. Research by IMD and Burston-Marsteller in 2015 found that one-third of the executives surveyed showed considerable difficulty identifying a single company that they perceived as having an authentic corporate purpose.[18] Not one company stood out as having the most credible or convincing purpose. Of the companies' respondents identified as having a purpose, most received only a single mention. Even the top three companies that respondents identified – Google, Nestlé and Apple – received relatively low levels of multiple mentions and have a mixed history of being purpose-led.

The same research also found that while many companies may 'talk the talk', they do not necessarily 'walk the walk' when it comes to their stated corporate purpose. Even if they do 'walk the walk', they may not be perceived as doing so. The researchers concluded that there is a potential 'dearth of leadership' with regard to purpose-driven business.

In response to the call for organisations to play their part in creating a better future for us all, a wealth of literature has appeared about organisational purpose. Consultancies, universities and charities have all articulated more holistic ways of thinking about how organisations can truly benefit society. Blueprint for Better Business, an independent charity in the UK, Professor George Serafeim at Harvard University in the USA and the global consultancies BCG, EY and Deloitte are all providing cutting-edge thinking in this area.

Looking across their publications, several core themes consistently emerge. An organisational purpose needs to be:

- **Compelling** – It is meaningful and resonant for the organisation's stakeholders, including employees, customers, investors and shareholders. It energises and engages team members, encouraging them to act in line with the purpose.

- **Authentic** – It refers to what the organisation actually does, not what it espouses to do. It is prominent in how an organisation communicates with its customers and other stakeholders. It is specific to the organisation and reflects its uniqueness.

- **Practical** – It is clear enough to enable choices to be made. It is used to guide decision making across the organisation and to review what products and services should be developed, retained or dropped.

- **Beneficial** – It contributes to the flourishing of life by improving the well-being of people and/or protecting the resources of the planet. It identifies who the intended beneficiaries of the purpose are, whether human or non-human.

- **Unifying** – It pulls people together to work for a collective venture. It fosters collaboration and commitment in the ecosystem of diverse stakeholders. It provides a clear context for shared understanding and unified action.

- **Long-term focused** – It acts as a guardian for future generations. It generates trust as the organisation actively aims to reduce negative impact and maximise positive impact in the longer term.

These dimensions are reflected in a recent definition of organisational purpose. Dr Victoria Hurth, Charles Ebert and Professor Jaideep Prabhu at Judge Business School at the University of Cambridge carried out research that led to this definition of organisational purpose:

> *An organization's meaningful and enduring reason to exist that aligns with long-term financial performance, provides a clear context for daily decision making, and unifies and motivates relevant stakeholders.* [19]

They also include what makes organisational purpose different from CSR, sustainability and mission/vision. These distinctions bring further clarity:

- Whereas CSR can be seen as a way that an organisation tries to compensate for societal problems, purpose is the core and enduring reason an organisation exists. Purpose is about pursuing a brighter future rather than turning away from a darker tomorrow. Purpose is more compelling than CSR because it has the power to unify stakeholders. Rather than moving away from something we want to avoid, purpose moves us towards something positive.

- While purpose and sustainability are closely related – both focus on a long-term systems view and both focus on well-being – purpose goes beyond addressing environmental, financial and social concerns by including the natural human motivation to serve others and connect with something 'greater than' oneself. Purpose has the power to release the 'emotional capital' of this untapped resource.

- Whereas vision is *what* an organisation is trying to achieve and mission is *how* an organisation goes about it, purpose is the organisation's 'why'. It is the fundamental reason that an organisation exists. A truly compelling purpose is 'company-transcendent' because it contributes to the long-term well-being of all. It is the *raison d'être* of an organisation that people find meaningful because it connects with universal human values of what is 'good'.

More and more companies are articulating and aligning with a purpose along these lines. Examples include:

■ 'Build the best product, cause no unnecessary harm, use business to inspire and implement solutions to the environmental crisis' – Patagonia.

■ 'Make sustainable living commonplace' – Unilever.

Pioneering leaders around the world are attuning their organisations to the power of purpose. In a global marketplace, they understand how a compelling organisational purpose unlocks people, performance and the planet – a shift that cannot come soon enough.

WHAT DOES IT MEAN TO BE POWERED BY PURPOSE?

We had a glimpse of the leadership needed to be more purpose-led in the thwarted Kraft Heinz £115 billion takeover bid of Unilever in spring 2017. With Kraft Heinz's focus more on value extraction, through cost-cutting, rather than value creation through investing in the brand, the two companies were operating on a very different basis. Paul Polman, CEO of Unilever at that time, rejected the advance of 'fast and ruthless' Kraft Heinz with its short-term approach.

The driving force behind Unilever's growth in recent years has been its purpose-driven brands such as Ben & Jerry's and Lifebuoy. Polman pointed to the returns that shareholders had enjoyed under his leadership for the previous eight years and championed a more inclusive business model. In *The Guardian* (20 May 2017) Polman stated:

> The financial market has changed and you need to be clear on
> what you want. Do you want short-term forces – that work for a
> few people, and make a few more billionaires – to be the
> dominant force? Or do you want the system to work
> for the billions that need to be served? It's a
> fundamental choice.[20]

This question strikes at the heart of the issue. Do we want to work for the billions or the billionaires? The viability of our future – individually and collectively – hangs in the balance.

Navigating ridges such as these calls for a much more expansive approach than leaders have typically taken in the past. Purpose-led leadership calls for whole-heartedness and a sense of the whole system that more go beyond the typical notions of leadership. Conventional definitions of leadership include 'leadership is about mobilising others to want to struggle for shared aspirations'[21] and 'leadership is the process of influencing others to ... accomplish shared tasks'.[22]

The classic notions of leadership are out-of-date. What's missing here is the vital connection between the whole self and the whole system. Leadership is not just about how we influence others; it is about how we manage our own energy as we step into uncertainty and co-create with others. Global thought leader Otto Scharmer highlights how the Indo-European root, '*leith*', from which we derive the word leadership, means 'to go forth'. Alternative translations include 'to cross a threshold', 'to let go' or 'to die'. At the heart of leadership is our capacity to step into the unknown. As we sense the pull of the future calling us forward, we need to let go of our old fears and go courageously towards the unfamiliar.

Successful leaders attend to the new disruptive reality surrounding us by 'sensing and actualising the future that wants to emerge'. They are not caught in the trap of formulating fixed five-year plans. They are not focused on moving into a 'planned future'. Instead, they attune to the 'emergent future' – the future that is moving towards them.[23]

The bravery needed to be purpose-led is very different from the bravado of corporate egos. It comes from an inner sense of conviction about what wants to happen. As we saw in the case of Paul Polman standing strong in the face of the potential Kraft takeover, purpose anchors a leader inside. It gives them a sense of direction even when facing uncertainty. A leader is able to take their organisation on the journey to become purpose-driven when they are purpose-led themselves.

Pulling all this together, my own definition of what it means for an organisation to be powered by purpose is:

> *Having a clear, compelling and authentic purpose that*
> *contributes to long-term well-being, guides day-to-day*
> *decision making, and engages and energises people to*
> *do great work.*

CROSSING THE BRIDGE TO A BETTER FUTURE

These are game-changing times and business has a huge contribution to make. To co-create a sustainable future that serves the well-being of all, leaders need to change themselves and change their organisations. When leaders both expand their understanding of leadership and embody a new set of capacities, they activate the deeper potential of their organisation and the people around them.

Coaching leaders in organisations, I have had many conversations exploring what is at the heart of a purpose-led approach. In these conversations, one key theme has emerged. Purpose-led leadership is a call to express more of our humanity. Through increasing our awareness of our interconnectedness, many are calling for more compassion and consideration in how organisations operate in the world.

Senior executives I've spoken with are quick to point out that being more 'human' is not about being 'soft'. It is about being truthful, transparent and courageous. Rather than avoid the difficult conversations – purpose disrupts business-as-usual – effective leaders lean into them. Purpose-led leadership, with its wider agenda of having a positive impact on the world, and the accompanying cynicism, demands robust discussion. Having a different kind of dialogue is often a bridge to 'better'.

In recent research published by Saïd Business School, many CEOs spoke about the increasing expectation for them to be 'human' stewards for stakeholders rather than 'heroic' agents of shareholders. In 'The CEO Report: Embracing the Paradoxes of Leadership and the Power of Doubt', many talked about the growing importance of being perceived as approachable, engaged and caring. The need to build trust across multiple groups is changing how CEOs communicate, listen and make decisions. Collaboration, listening, authenticity, vulnerability and humility are all recurring themes in conversations about purpose but the common thread that runs throughout is being a fully feeling 'human'.[24]

At the heart of purpose-led leadership is an orientation to generate benefits – or what I call 'whole outcomes' – for the wider ecosystem in which we all live. The next chapter critically reflects on the business case for purpose-driven business and explores how an organisation can amplify its positive impact using evidence-based insights.

We can shape the future by our thinking, conversations and actions. It is up to us to choose – individually and collectively – whether we 'kick the can down the road' or forge a different path. As we stand at the edge of a fast-flowing river of increasing change, complexity and uncertainty, the bridge of purpose-led leadership stretches out before us. The rest of this book explores what it will take for us to cross it and create a better future for us all.

How to get started becoming purpose-driven

Before reading the rest of this book, spend some time reflecting on these questions:

1. What's a first step you could take to feel more energised in your work? For example, could you have more contact with your customers, engage your team members more fully or take a risk to share your ideas more widely? What will you do and by when? How will you know you've succeeded?

2. Think about a time when you experienced being led well. How did you feel? What results were created? What can you learn from this?

3. Have a conversation with your team about purpose. What difference would it make to them if you became more purpose-led? Ask them to identify three actions *you* could take to move your organisation closer to the following:

   Having a clear, compelling and authentic purpose that contributes to long-term well-being, guides day-to-day decision making, and engages and energises people to do great work.

4. Choose a critical external stakeholder. Ask them what you can do, within your sphere of influence, to become more purpose-led. Agree when you'll report back on the action that you've taken.

NOTES

1. Jaworski, J. (2011) *Synchronicity: The Inner Path of Leadership*, Berrett-Koehler.
2. Whyte, D. (2002) *Crossing the Unknown Sea: Work as a Pilgrimage of Identity,* Riverhead Books.
3. Nowek, M. and Highfield, R. (2011) *Supercooperators: Evolution, Altruism and Human behaviour, or Why we need each other to succeed,* Free Press.
4. *Better Business, Better World* Report (2016) The Business and Sustainable Development Commission.
5. UNHQ (2015) *Sustainable Development Goals*, UN Publications. See https://sustainabledevelopment.un.org/?menu=1300.

6. *On A Mission in the UK Economy* (2016) Advisory panel to mission-led business review: Final report Department for Digital, Culture, Media & Sport, UK Government publication.
7. Commitment to sustainability delivers even faster growth for Unilever, Unilever, 16 May 2015.
8. Global Corporate Sustainability Report (2015) Nielsen.
9. Hurst, A. (2013) *The Purpose Economy*, Elevate.
10. Mayer, C. (2018) The future of the corporation: towards humane business, *Journal of the British Academy*, 6(s1), 1–16.
11. Last, A. (2016) *Business on a Mission: How to Build a Sustainable Brand,* Routledge.
12. Enfield, H. (1988) *Loadsamoney,* Mercury Records.
13. EY Beacon Institute (2016) *The state of the debate on purpose in business*, EYGM Ltd. See https://www.ey.com/Publication/vwLUAssets/ey-the-state-of-the-debate-on-purpose-in-business/$FILE/ey-the-state-of-the-debate-on-purpose-in-business.pdf.
14. *2019 Edelman Trust Barometer* Daniel J. Edelman Holdings, Inc. See https://www.edelman.com/trust-barometer.
15. Craig, N. and Snook, S.A. (2014) From purpose to impact, *Harvard Business Review.* See https://hbr.org/2014/05/from-purpose-to-impact.
16. Harter, J. (2018) *Employee Engagement on the Rise in the U.S.,* Gallup, Inc.
17. Mind the Gaps: The 2015 Deloitte Millennial survey. See https://www2.deloitte.com/content/dam/Deloitte/global/Documents/About-Deloitte/gx-wef-2015-millennial-survey-executivesummary.pdf.
18. Corporate Perception Indicator, (2015) *Keeping it real – How authentic is your Corporate Purpose?,* Burston-Marsteller, Inc.
19. Hurth, V., Ebert, C. and Prabhu, J. (2018) *The What, the Why and the How of Purpose: A Guide for Leaders,* Chartered Management Institute and Blueprint for Better Business White Paper.
20. Pratley. N. (2017) Paul Polman: 'I could boost Unilever shares. But cutting costs is not our way', *The Guardian,* 20 May. See https://www.theguardian.com/business/2017/may/20/unilever-paul-polman-kraft-bid-market-deals-uk
21. Kouzes, J.M. and Posner, B.Z. (1995) *The Leadership Challenge: How to Keep Getting Extraordinary Things done in Organizations* (2nd edn), San Francisco, CA, US: Jossey-Bass.
22. Yukl, G.A. State University of New York, Alban, (2013) *Leadership in Organizations* (8th edn), State University of New York, Alban, Pearson.

23. Scharmer, O. and Kaufer K. (2013) *Leading from the Emergent Future: From Ego-System to Eco-System Economies,* Berrett-Koehler.

24. *The CEO Report: Embracing the Paradoxes of Leadership and the Power of Doubt (2015)* Heidrick & Struggles. See https://www.heidrick.com/Knowledge-Center/Publication/The-CEO-Report.

CHAPTER 2

THE BENEFITS OF BEING POWERED BY PURPOSE

Businesses that embrace social priorities perform better, reflect people's ideals and ambitions and so are primed for success.

On A Mission in the UK Economy report, 2016

'The world is changing, whether you like it or not. Are you?' Our speaker had hit his stride – and he was well qualified to speak. Loughlin Hickey, a former global head of tax at one of the big four accounting firms, had an air of confidence – and care – about him as he summarised the state of play about purpose-driven business.

It was the last afternoon of a two-day 'Immersion' workshop run by Blueprint for Better Business, a UK charity. On the folder laid out on the table, was their strapline – 'Uniting Corporate Purpose and Personal Values to Serve Society' along with sheets of yellow and blue sticky dots.

We'd used the dots earlier to place alongside household names – Barclays, Sky, Nationwide, Primark, GSK and others – to indicate which businesses we were proud to be associated with (blue) and which we felt dubious about (yellow). The overall pattern was mixed – blue and yellow stickers were clustered around the same brands to differing degrees. No business had been allocated dots of only one colour, creating a rich and complex picture.

As I looked through the window of the seminar room at the University of Cambridge, I could see trees bursting into pink blossom and daffodils standing tall in pots. Spring was in the air outside, which felt fitting for the palpable sense of renewal inside the room.

'Government, business and civil society are all saying the same thing,' Loughlin continued. 'Purpose-driven business is the right thing to do and now is the right time to do it. The Big Innovation Centre published a report in 2016 saying that the UK is losing well over £100 billion a year by not having purpose-driven business.'

I sensed a whole range of responses to this observation, from excitement and curiosity to scepticism. As a group of participants, we were a diverse bunch – a director of corporate purpose from a global PR organisation, an executive coach from a top business school, an author of a best-selling book on purpose, a founder of a social enterprise and a bishop from London, among others. Some had worked in organisations that had been founded with a compelling 'social' purpose while others were employees in organisations that were re-shaping their purpose. Our faculty too had a mix of backgrounds – an academic, a consultant and a tax specialist – all senior advisers to Blueprint.

'So what's next?', the director of corporate purpose asked, giving voice to the question that was on everyone's minds.

'Bridging where people are and where they want to go,' another of the Blueprint team responded. 'Many of the younger generation understand the concept. Some CEOs, who've been to Davos, know that purpose is the way forward. They've spoken with the external market about the changing role of business in society but when they go back to their organisation, there's some distance between them and the executive team. Not enough is being done to help bring others along. It's not so much a gap but a chasm!'

'There's a big prize waiting,' said Loughlin, 'But it's important we don't over-sell it. Leaders need to know about the pitfalls as well as the potential. An organisation can't force its values or impose its purpose on people. Research from the University of Sussex reveals that there's the risk of burnout if employees have to act as if their work is meaningful when it isn't. When staff sense that a purpose, even a 'purpose-beyond-profits', is self-serving rather than sincere, it can all start to unravel, there can be a lot of long-term pain.'

There was a pause while that sank in. Another voice came slowly into the dialogue – this time from someone who'd spent years working inside large organisations.

'What difference to strategy and operations will purpose actually make? One guy where I used to work, the one with the biggest mouth and the smallest brain, would mention maximising shareholder value at every turn. Shareholders come first: that's business as usual. In my next company the board of directors defined a purpose and some values, which were then discussed by senior management, but our input was not much appreciated. And worse, the values were often not respected. We could do nothing about it.'

As a knowing murmur rippled around the room, I was left thinking: 'What if leaders were to really see that a company's competitive advantage were to come from purpose? How do we do this?' As a practitioner I wanted to know how purpose-driven business can bring both financial success and societal gain – benefits not just for the lucky few but for us all. As I drove home west along the motorway with the sun setting behind the horizon, my heart was beating strongly. I felt determined to find an answer to the big question of 'How?'

WHAT THIS CHAPTER'S ABOUT

The tangible gulf between the dominant business logic and associated system 'lock-in' of today and the future possibility of a better world for us all is something that many of us can relate to. The free-flowing dialogue at the Blueprint meeting touched on many of the key themes of purpose-led leadership, which weave throughout this chapter:

- The groundswell of support for the benefits of purpose.
- Why purposeful leadership taps into our deeper human potential.
- How purpose-led leadership delivers wider benefits than profit alone.

Changing ingrained ways of thinking about people, business and leadership is a true paradigm shift. Purpose, not profit or personality, is unique in its ability to pull people together so that an organisation creates a vibrant economy, a true humanity and a sustainable planet – what I call 'whole outcomes'. Purpose is the difference that will make the difference in the longer term.

PURPOSE GOES MAINSTREAM

'The business of business is business' is the classic principle stated by Milton Friedman in 1961, the Nobel-prize winning US economist based at the University of Chicago. A corporation's sole purpose is profit maximisation to create value for shareholders. Any other corporate purpose is a distraction and unnecessary interference in the market that could lead to financial underperformance – the moral case being that this would in turn impact the economy and therefore societal welfare.

By making the moral case for shareholder value, Friedman increased the separation of business from society. He recruited and mentored several students and young professors at the University of Chicago who became leading economists, strengthening the model of profit maximisation. The long-standing belief that providing direct societal benefits could be a drag on profits has made business and society uncomfortable bedfellows to date. In the Epilogue, Dr Victoria Hurth delves further into why this is the case.

In recent years, however, thought leaders and business pioneers have challenged this model of shareholder primacy and leaving well-being to the state or the market – something that has been central to Anglo-Saxon capitalism for over 50 years. This was epitomised in the open letter 'A Sense of Purpose' that Larry Fink, CEO of BlackRock, the world's biggest investor, sent to the heads of FTSE100 companies and global leaders in January 2018. Fink warned leaders to expect more in-depth conversations about their 'social purpose' and 'greater scrutiny' about their strategic priorities as purpose-driven business gathers momentum.

One year later, Fink's letter was coined a 'catalytic text for a new era of purposeful capitalism'. This was not a statement by consumer activists, campaigners, academics or regulators; it was an observation made by the US business editor of the *FT*, Andrew Edgecliffe-Johnson. With his article, purpose hit the mainstream.[1]

In a world of corporate scandals, eroded trust and governmental failure, and over ten years after the major global financial crisis, business leaders seem eager to try something different. While a vocal minority objected to Fink's call to action, and some pointed out how BlackRock's actions don't match the rhetoric, it resonated with many more (Fink described this as a 10:90 ratio in favour). With a step-change in the number of companies spelling out their organisation's purpose in their annual report, the time was right, the conditions propitious and the marketplace ready for Fink's message.

The *FT* highlighted purposeful, inclusive capitalism as 'our best hope' for producing profitable solutions to the problems of people and the planet. This new worldview puts humanity at the heart of business, recasts the role of the company in society and rethinks corporate governance. It also calls for a radically different way of leading, as we shall see.

DON'T BUY THIS JACKET

The high impact ad posted by Patagonia (shown on the following page) is another signpost that points to purpose gaining ascendency through bold leadership. Published in the *New York Times* on Black Friday,

25 November 2015, Patagonia was probably the only retailer in the USA in the mainstream media encouraging people to buy less. By tackling consumerism head-on, Patagonia acted in line with its purpose of inspiring and implementing sustainable solutions to the environmental crisis, alongside providing customers with products they love to buy.

DON'T BUY
THIS JACKET

When I shared this ad at a 'Leading with Purpose' workshop that Dr Victoria Hurth and I co-led at the Division of Occupational Psychology Conference in January 2019, I was struck by participants' reactions:

- One woman thought it was reverse psychology. Similar to someone telling us *not* to think of a pink elephant and all we can do is visualise a pink elephant, she thought this ad was a clever way to get people to buy more.
- Another participant questioned whether the ad was for real or something I'd made up. As if!
- A further participant suggested that the poster had been designed to be provocative, without thinking that there was anything deeper at play.

This diversity of responses is understandable if we remember that the Friedman doctrine has held sway for over five decades, perpetuated by business schools across the globe. What is becoming increasingly clear is that this Anglo-American model of corporate governance needs a new blueprint. Not just because it's the moral or right thing to do, but because it reflects twenty-first-century leadership capacities and it makes good economic sense too.

In the case of Patagonia, the company's commitment to sustainability has been a big success. The company made global headlines in 2016 for pledging to donate 100% of its Black Friday profits to grassroots environmental groups working to protect our air, water and soil. The result was beyond their expectations, reaching a record-breaking $10 million in sales. Patagonia had anticipated $2 million and, when they beat this five times over, they attributed this success to the 'enormous love our customers showed to the planet' in what some called a 'fundraiser for the earth.'

A purpose-led approach unlocks people, performance and profit, making this movement different from corporate social responsibility (CSR) and sustainability that have come before. In this newly emerging model, the primary reason for an organisation to exist is not to make money as an end in itself. Profit is a condition for and a result of achieving a true purpose: to make a difference in the world.

THE RISKS OF NOT BEING DRIVEN BY PURPOSE

'Britain risks becoming an economic backwater if it does not foster purposeful companies' states the report by the Big Innovation Centre. 'Purposefulness' is worth up to 7% a year in performance terms. British companies are currently inadequately organised around corporate purposes that align all stakeholders around shared goals and values, costing the UK economy potentially £130 billion a year.[2]

There is increasing pressure on organisations to mitigate their negative impact and increase their positive impact on society. Facebook, which made $40bn in revenue in 2017, and its ability to manipulate public opinion was brought into question several years before the Cambridge Analytica story broke in 2018. As David Kirkpatrick says in *The Facebook Effect*, 'The reality is that Facebook could determine the winner of any election, in any democratic country.'[3]

There is, in addition, a growing backlash against a 'corporate giveaway', which supports the rich getting richer. In the case of the house-building giant Persimmon, when a huge bonus for the CEO of £100m plus was announced in December 2017, it was denounced by politicians, charities and corporate governance experts as 'obscene.' At a time when so many people struggle with housing in the UK, this lack of socially conscious leadership sparked many angry comments from many different quarters. Despite being an owner who has made actions to elevate stakeholders above profit, his leadership was off.

Further pressure for change comes from the reputational damage that results when a corporate scandal occurs and is amplified through social media. In the case of the VW emissions cheating scandal, we saw how the company risked alienating a whole future generation of car buyers who value the environment and who believed that they would be buying a car from an automaker who promoted itself as green.

While the leaders of VW were being true to their vision of becoming the world's number one producer by volume, this misguided vision without a meaningful basis meant their underhand approach caused their brand to take a huge hit in terms of customer loyalty. By VW not having a clear purpose and compromising the brand, this was a big risk to investors. Increasing transparency in our online world raises the stakes considerably for companies that act in ways that do not serve the greater whole.

For leaders to act differently, they need to see differently. Understanding the increasingly compelling business case for a purpose-led approach is one way to get started.

WINNING ON PURPOSE

The growing business case gives purpose-driven business solid foundations, making it something that is here to stay. Attracting many leaders is the benefit that a purpose-driven approach generates. To summarise, a purpose-led approach enables leaders to:

1. Engage team members as a compelling purpose pulls people together.
2. Enhance well-being among team members who find their work energising.
3. Increase team members' commitment to stay because their work is meaningful.
4. Build organisational resilience through stakeholders' trust in the organisation.
5. Generate higher rates of growth and innovation from a more inspired workforce.

6. Expand market share through deeper customer relationships and strengthened brand loyalty.

7. Navigate a disruptive environment by purpose acting as a North Star, a fixed point, for strategic decision making.

Research published in 2015 by the EY Beacon Institute and *Harvard Business Review* Analytic Services claims to have found the new 'genetic code' of a continuously evolving, successful twenty-first-century company. Their survey involved 474 executives, entrepreneurs and leaders from a diverse range of organisations, grades and geographies. They uncovered three categories of respondent, with the distribution as follows:

- **'Prioritisers'** – 39% had a clearly understood and articulated purpose.

- **'Developers'** – 48% were working to develop a clear and well-understood purpose.

- **'Laggards'** – 13% have not yet begun to develop or think about purpose.

Companies who had clearly articulated their purpose and aligned their organisation around it – the 'Prioritisers' – experienced three core benefits:

- They had higher growth rates, including an edge on revenue growth in the last three years, as well as greater customer loyalty and brand gains.

- They were more successful at transformation and innovation initiatives, such as a new product launch or expanding into a new market.

- They had more engaged employees who demonstrated more willingness to partner across functional and product boundaries.

'Purpose is a powerful lever in business', states the report. Companies that are able to harness purpose to drive performance and profitability have a distinct competitive advantage.[4]

Further evidence for purpose-driven organisations having an edge comes from the 2014 Deloitte Core Beliefs and Culture survey. This study found that creating a 'culture of purpose' builds business confidence and drives growth. Their online survey carried out in the USA with over 1,000 respondents found that:

- 82% of respondents who work for an organisation with a strong sense of purpose are confident that their organisation will grow this year (compared to 48% of those who do not have a strong sense of purpose).

- 81% of respondents working for organisations with a strong sense of purpose say that their stakeholders trust their leadership team (vs 54%).

- 74% of respondents working for purposeful organisations say their investors are confident in the company's growth prospects over the next year (vs 52%).

To achieve these benefits, 'purpose-beyond-profits' must, however, be the central driver of an organisation's strategy, not an optional 'bolt-on'. It needs to be strong enough that it becomes part of the organisation's operating model and inspiring enough that it unleashes people's energy.[5]

The proven commercial benefits are part of what makes a purpose-led approach distinct from previous attempts to make business 'a force for good'. Over a decade ago, in their seminal 2006 *Harvard Business Review* article, Michael Porter (the leading thinker on competitive strategy and of 'Five Forces' fame) and Mark Kramer stated that organisations could generate competitive advantage by addressing human and environmental challenges. By 'creating shared value' (the title of their article), companies could help bring business and society back together by opening up new markets in a way that produced value for society. This is not quite as deep as replacing profit-maximisation with purpose, but it set out the business case for serving society directly.[6]

Twelve years on, the financial results are emerging to support this proposition. Korn Ferry Institute compared the revenue growth of purpose-driven organisations with 500 consumer product group peers, including 71 publicly listed companies. They found that companies with a 'deeply rooted purpose' achieved a compound annual growth rate of 9.85% compared with a 2.4% for the wider consumer product sector.[7]

INVESTING IN OUR FUTURE

Alongside employees and customers, recent research shows that investors are also gravitating towards organisations that have a positive impact on the world. New acronyms are appearing that reflect this trend.

Boston Consulting Group (BCG) highlights that investment managers are paying increasing attention to integrating environmental, social and governance (ESG) issues into investment decisions. BCG calls a purpose-driven approach the 'next frontier in impact investing'. It estimates that global assets in socially responsible investing (SRI) were $23 trillion in 2016, up from $18 trillion in 2014, accounting for more than one-quarter of total managed assets.[8]

As robust ESG data become more readily available, we are, according to BCG, 'at the dawn of profound new developments' with regard to impact investing. They underline the 'tilt' away from investors focusing on financial metrics alone to considering how an organisation benefits society at large. BCG characterises this as a shift from maximising 'total shareholder return' (TSR) to creating 'total societal impact' (TSI).

BCG shares the results of a study that it carried out with 300 companies, across 5 sectors and with over 200 interviews. Overall it found that companies who adopt a TSI lens measurably improve their margins and shareholder returns. Even though the five different sectors it examined – consumer packaged goods, biopharmaceuticals, oil and gas, retail and business banking – operated in different margin environments, there was a consistent and clear link between ESG performance and company valuations.

This finding provides 'a much-needed shot of optimism for CEOs struggling with what may feel like conflicting goals'. In addition to meeting earning targets and transforming their business digitally, CEOs have to deal with the increasing demands of activist investors and customer challenge groups. Shaping a vision for shared growth and prosperity through having a compelling purpose that delivers TSI is enabling CEOs to enhance competitive advantage, manage risks and increase resilience in an environment of uncertainty.

FROM SIDESHOW TO SUSTAINED SHIFT

The investment landscape is changing as a result of millennial heirs to affluent parents coming of age. The US Trust, part of Bank of America Private Bank, estimates that $12tn worth of assets are slated to change hands over the next decade, making it the largest wealth transfer in history, roughly equal to three-quarters of US gross domestic product.

Research shows that the new beneficiaries of this wealth have different attitudes to how they will use it. If we place this in a historical context, it makes sense. Baby boomers made their money creating companies during a period of economic fragility after the two world wars and at a time when Milton Friedman was writing about the economy almost solely in terms of the profit incentive.

Various studies have found that a much greater percentage of millennials compared with baby boomers consider the ESG impact of companies when making investment decisions. A study by Fidelity that found that whereas only 30% of baby boomers and the older generation had made some kind of 'impact investment', this proportion had risen to 77% among affluent millennials and 72% among Generation X donors.

While some dismiss impact investing as the idealism of the young, others do not. Gillian Tett writing in the *FT* argues that these surveys point to a movement that is likely to have profound implications for the financial services industry:

'In the coming years, finance will need to start treating impact investing as a mainstream activity, rather than as a sideshow, and organise itself accordingly.'[9]

Is the game really starting to change or is this just an 'elite charade'? Andrew Edgecliffe-Johnson in his *FT* article highlighted how even Lehman Brothers had a page on sustainability in its 2007 annual report, claiming its role as an environmentally aware 'global corporate citizen'.[10] The desire to convince the world that business cares about more than the bottom line is nothing new. What is distinctive, however, is that that an 'unlikely alliance' of business leaders, employees, consumers, activists, academics and regulators are acknowledging that capitalism, as we know it, is breaking down and that an alternative approach is needed.

The move towards purpose where business exists not for profit maximisation but to serve a much greater set of stakeholders, profitably, is both excitingly possible and deeply challenging.

In the world of impact investing, Tett underlines that the transition to the new may not be easy. She points to lack of definitional clarity about SRI investing: is it avoiding 'sin stocks' such as tobacco, firearms and gambling or making a positive contribution through reducing carbon emissions or achieving gender pay parity? In addition, investors find it difficult to measure social returns in a transparent way. While work is being done to discuss how to define and measure impact investing by companies such as Aviva and Deloitte as well as the UN General Assembly and the World Bank, the approach remains untested as yet.

While definitional clarity and benchmarking are important hurdles to overcome, I believe that there is a much deeper set of forces at play. For purpose to be not a sideshow but a sustained shift, our whole mindset about leadership and our identity as human beings needs to change. This is where we turn next.

CHALLENGING THE DOMINANT PARADIGM

Our co-workers and customers in their 20s and 30s are sounding the clarion call of the future. They are telling us how work, business and leadership need to change. Without listening to them, there is a risk that companies fail to attract future customers and talented employees. As Buckminster Fuller said, 'In terms of the universe our children are our elders.'

Lisa Earle McLeod, author and business woman, expresses this desire for more meaningful work in her open letter to management on LinkedIn, with over one million views. She signs off with:

> *'I was raised to believe I could change the world. I'm desperate for you to show me that the work we do here matters, even just a little bit. I'll make copies, I'll fetch coffee, I'll do the grunt work. But I'm not doing it to help you get a new Mercedes. I'll give you everything I've got, but I need to know it makes a difference to something bigger than your bottom line.'*[11]

To make the shift to become purpose-driven, we will need the fuel of younger people's healthy anger and willingness to take a stand. We need to listen to their voices and understand both their passion and their pain in order to navigate a way forward.

A unique piece of research, *Millennial Voices* (2018) has captured what millennials working in ESG roles, as portfolio managers or analysts, have to say about working in the rapidly changing landscape of investment in their own words. Rob Lake is the founder of Authentic Investor, a not-for-profit initiative that seeks to cultivate the alignment of purpose, values and sustainability with day-to-day work in investment organisations, and a colleague with whom I run leadership programmes for those working in the investment industry. Here's a flavour of what millennials experience:

> *Maybe especially for millennials working in sustainability within the investment industry, it's challenging to, mmm ... I guess to just* be. *You're already seen as a naïve tree hugger by the very fact that you are a millennial, and even more since you work in sustainability – double softy! Do NOT use the words 'better world' in your organisation, because people will stop taking you seriously. When discussing my personal year plan with my manager, he asked me why I wrote down the words 'contribute to a better world' and told me to go do that before 9.00 am and after 5.00 pm.*

> (Asset owner, The Netherlands)[12]

In response to observations such as these, the report also contains reflections by investment industry leaders. Here's what Tim Hodgson, founder of Thinking Ahead Industry Institute, WillisTowersWatson UK, has to say:

> *My primary reaction to reading these accounts is anger. I want to take the words they have learned not to use, 'better world',*

*'doing good', 'positive impact' – and to shout them at our industry.
What else are we here for? Will our clients thank us for that return,
quoted to two decimal places, if we have cooked the planet? To say
that is not part of our role is to shirk the responsibility that goes with
our privileged existence.*

*My second reaction was apprehension. Will we have crushed these
spirits before they inherit the leadership of our industry? Have we left
things too late? My hope is that my generation will rise up and provide
genuine leadership so that these millennials, when it is their turn to
lead, will have some momentum to work with – and will thank rather
than curse us.*

We risk ignoring this younger generation with its differing consciousness
at our peril. Instead, we need to respond with maps, methodologies and,
crucially, models that serve them in their quest to become powerful leaders
of the future.

MOVING THROUGH RESISTANCE

Nothing is as dangerous as a bad model. Leaders and managers who
have the 'Chicago model' profit-maximisation at-all-costs mindset are
the 'hard-driving, strictly top-down, command-and-control-focused,
shareholder-value-obsessed, win-at-all-cost' business leaders that are very
familiar to us today.[13]

This 'gloomy vision' of corporate life is deeply embedded. The taken-
for-granted assumptions of the 'Chicago model' give rise to many of the
management practices and marketing activities we see in organisations
today, including:

- Employees are to be controlled, not trusted.
- Customers are to be sold to, not encouraged to make more conscious
  decisions.
- Shareholders are to be delivered maximum returns to, not consulted
  on more responsible ways of doing business.

If we take the view that purpose-driven business is truly a new paradigm,
this resistance is understandable. The US physicist and philosopher
Thomas Kuhn (1922–1996) identified a 'paradigm' as a framework that
contains the basic assumptions and ways of thinking that are commonly
accepted by the members of a scientific community. We can usefully apply

the concept of a 'paradigm shift'[14] – when there is a fundamental change in the basic concepts and experimental practices of a scientific discipline – to understanding the suspicion that surrounds purpose-driven business and how best to move forwards.

The movement towards purpose challenges conventional mindsets about business but, more crucially, about people. If we see it as a paradigm shift, we begin to understand why there is both acceptance and resistance – and to see that scepticism will gradually give way to support. A dominant paradigm in any discipline – science, economics or medicine – starts to fall away when it no longer fits the facts. When sufficient evidence emerges, as we are seeing in the case of purpose-driven business, a paradigm can no longer be defended. More accurate ways of thinking and new ways of acting start to appear.

We are seeing this paradigm shift happen in marketing. Hurth and Whittlesea (2017)[15] have outlined three major economic paradigms:

- **'Make-and-sell'** based on classical economics where the purpose of an organisation is profit-maximisation for shareholders through increasing sales and reducing costs.

- **'Sense-and-respond'** based on neo-classical economics, where the purpose of an organisation is profit-maximisation for shareholders through responding to consumer preference.

- **'Guide-and-co-create'** based on ecological economics, where the purpose of an organisation is to lead towards maximising long-term societal well-being for all through deep co-creative stakeholder relationships that transition what we think we need – and result in profitability over time.

Hurth and Whittlesea highlight that the first two paradigms have a view of 'the firm' and related behaviours that are incompatible with delivering long-term sustainable well-being for all. Only the 'guide and co-create' paradigm is compatible with creating long-term well-being for all. By recognising the characteristics of these paradigms, we can consciously move towards the third paradigm of 'guide and co-create' more easily. It requires businesses to recognise how they lead society at the deepest level of identity and culture. Think back to the 'Don't buy this jacket' message of the Patagonia ad to see some 'societal leadership' in action. If we see business through the eyes of 'make-and-sell' or 'sense-and-respond', the ad confuses people, as we saw in the reaction of the psychologists.

A new paradigm is often rejected at the outset. As we face the cynicism of the critics of purpose, we would do well to remember the wise words of Marshall McLuhan, the Canadian professor and philosopher:

> *Our Age of Anxiety is, in great part, the result of trying to do today's job with yesterday's tools and yesterday's mindset.*[16]

INCONVENIENT TRUTHS AND CONVENIENT UNTRUTHS

How do we recognise when we are thinking in the old or new paradigm? In terms of the broader context of business as a whole, according to Blueprint for Better Business, business-as-usual is beset with 'inconvenient truths' and 'convenient untruths'.

One of the inconvenient truths is that businesses have a very narrow view of the human being. We typically see a person, particularly the corporate version, as a self-interested, rational being who, with the right information, will make decisions to maximise their personal gain from choices offered in the marketplace. A 'human resource' is there to generate returns. 'Human capital' is there to maximise profit for shareholders.

The emerging field of behavioural economics, spearheaded by Richard Thaler, a US economist and professor at the University of Chicago Booth School of Business, has demonstrated just how flawed this model is. Thaler was awarded the 2017 Nobel Prize in Economic Sciences for his contribution to the growing field of behavioural economics, which studies finance and economics from a psychological perspective.

Thaler has shown how our emotions, impulses and gut instincts often trump our rationality in our economic decision making. 'Homo economicus' is a fictional character that suits the modelling of classical economics but has little to do with reality. We're less clear-headed and more emotional when we take decisions than the neo-liberal economic model would have us be.[17]

Politicians, policy makers and psychologists have applied this updated model of the human to 'nudge' people to change their behaviour. Thaler's insights have been credited for increasing British tax receipts through altering the wording of tax demands as well as persuading 20% more people to consider changing their energy provider. While we have to be careful in reducing our cultural and identity-based motivations to a series of in-the-moment behaviours, by disproving the previously accepted 'truth'

CHAPTER 3

INTRODUCING THE FOUR CAPACITIES OF PURPOSE-LED LEADERSHIP

You never change things by fighting the existing reality.
To change something, build a new model that makes the existing model obsolete.

Buckminster Fuller

* * *

There was tension in the air as the board members and I filed into the meeting room. Gone was the chattiness of the conversations over coffee that we'd just been having. People avoided looking at each other as they sat down. I noticed my own thumping chest and clammy palms. The rarefied atmosphere of the executive suite was, at that time, a new experience.

The ice thawed a little during the morning as my more seasoned co-facilitator gave some input. I stayed silent, appreciating the opportunity to be a fly on the wall. In line with the agreement we'd made in advance, I readied myself to swing into action in the afternoon by gathering my observations. Facilitating a dialogue about how this newly forming team could bring about positive change was a great opportunity to do the work I love.

My excitement was, however, soon zapped. As our morning session had overrun, the food for lunch had been placed on side tables. As I lifted plates onto the large table where the directors were sitting, one of them turned to me and said:

'So you've found a role then?'

By the cold glint in his eye and the stab in my stomach, I sensed this was more put-down than half-joke. Before I could make a wry or witty comeback, he continued:

'What are you doing here? Two facilitators but for the price of one, I hope?'

As I stumbled around setting down the plates, I did my best to compose myself to re-enter the conversation. I discovered, however, that I had no energy or enthusiasm to do so.

* * *

Looking back, this incident was a sharp reminder about how unhappy and unhealthy organisational life is for many people. Although I'd worked as an employee in large organisations a decade before, as a consultant I'd forgotten about the day-to-day reality of backbiting, bullying and 'macho' behaviour. Negativity, rivalry and a win-at-all-costs mentality all undermine performance and well-being, as many of us know first hand. All too often ruthless competition trumps healthy collaboration, and we all miss out.

The demands of the global economy for rapid decision making and an 'always on' mindset are overburdening leaders as well as employees, suppliers and customers. These pressures make unkind comments, backstabbing and selfishness, all of which have a negative impact on performance, more prevalent. To the extent that high levels of energy, an experience of being happily engrossed in one's work and a sense of purpose are missing, the organisations for which we work, we as individuals and the whole of society, lose out.

While the business case for purpose-driven business is strong (see Chapter 2), what is lacking is an in-depth exploration of the human leadership required to navigate this ambitious journey. This chapter addresses this shortcoming by introducing the critical missing piece: the *four core leadership capacities* that this new movement is calling for.

By developing these four capacities, leaders will be able to evolve a powerful purpose – for their organisation, team and themselves – and then deploy it effectively. This approach to leadership builds on, and is distinct from, the command-and-control leadership model (see page 38). To create a truly inspiring organisation, superior business results and wider social, environmental and human benefits, leadership styles need to evolve beyond the conventional into a more expansive space. This chapter covers the following territory:

- The critical shifts for leaders to make as they evolve their leadership style.

- The four capacities of purpose-led leadership, demonstrated by business leaders.

- How purpose creates a sense of belonging that enables people to do their best work.

THE SHIRTLESS DANCING GUY

I've been engaged in leadership development for nearly 20 years and there is one video that's up with the best. On YouTube, check out this three-minute clip, 'Leadership from a Dancing Guy' and enjoy![1]

We see in this video a typical scene from a music festival. People are sprawled about on a hillside, couples are chatting and laying out rugs at Sasquatch! Music Festival (George, Washington). The repetitive beat that's playing has got one chap, shirtless and with his arms in the air, dancing.

Soon we see another chap join him by waving his arms around in time. The 'leader' embraces him and they groove together, watched by a whole field of people. The first follower calls to his friends and shortly another, then two and three more followers join in. Over the next minute, more and more people jump in until it looks like the whole field is dancing together.

This short film, which became part of a TED talk, 'How to Start a Movement', got a standing ovation when it was given in 2010 and has had over 8 million views.[2] Derek Sivers provides the commentary on what it teaches us about how a movement can start in under three minutes! Here's what the video shows us about leadership:

- **Leadership calls for courage.** As a leader, you need to have the strength to stand your ground, do your own dance and risk looking ridiculous. There might be many others watching, judging and thinking you're a nutter and yet you keep moving by listening to the beat that gets you going.

- **Leadership is relational.** Without embracing the first follower, the shirtless guy would not have become the 'leader'. As soon as the first follower joins him, it is no longer about the leader as a singular individual; it's about the two of them, plural. As more and more followers jump in, it's the vibe that they co-create that attracts others. Leadership is inseparable from followership.

- **Leadership is systemic.** A leader is embedded in a social system. The bare-chested guy is not dancing in a vacuum but surrounded by others, watching. Even though there's a sense that others want to join in, they sit on the fence, holding back from making a fool of themselves. The pressure to conform – arising out of a 'field' of energy rather than a singular individual – runs high even at an indie-music festival.

Corporate leadership is, of course, much more complex than this video shows. Leaders in organisations are engaged in webs of relationships, power dynamics and hierarchical structures. The dancing man video does, however, demonstrate that leadership is not static and singular; it is systemic, fluid and participatory. And it is precisely this context that makes operationalising it such a challenge.

In the last 50 years, several new models of leadership, where leaders are viewed as stewards of the common good, have emerged. Servant leadership, transformational leadership, authentic leadership and ethical leadership all share some common ground with each other and with the model I propose here. Each of these four models is visionary, inspiring – and idealistic. Most of them point to the same exemplars – Nelson Mandela, Mother Teresa and Martin Luther King, Jr – and outline an illuminating list of characteristics and competencies for an individual leader to develop and demonstrate.

None of these leadership models has, however, taken off to the extent that they deserve.[3] As Jenny Wade argues in her article, 'Get off the mountaintop and back into the marketplace', while these models present the possibility that leadership can be a fulcrum for transformation beyond the egoic self, they all fall short when it comes to how leaders need to develop themselves on the ground. Moreover, each of these earlier models tends to focus on the singular leader rather than seeing how the systems in which they are embedded significantly shape their behaviour.

The critical piece that is missing from these earlier models are some powerful *'how-to'*s that take into account the systemic context of leadership. Leaders are hungry to dial up their productivity by becoming more purposeful, while still making a profit for shareholders. Many leadership teams want to know how to be at the top of their game as they interact with a broad array of stakeholders. Increasing numbers of organisations know that it is by becoming global stewards that they will best ensure their own survival but navigating this journey can seem overwhelming.

INSIGHTS FROM LEADERSHIP DEVELOPMENT RESEARCH

The good news is that research into leadership development shows how purpose adds a vital dimension that enables leaders to grow rather than get stuck at a certain stage of development. Purpose can play a pivotal role in helping leaders to deal with complexity and uncertainty so that their leadership fits the demands of our fast-changing world.

'Leaders are made, not born, and how they develop is critical for organisational change,' state David Rooke and William R. Torbert. In their classic *HBR* article, they outline how leaders evolve in predictable ways.[4] How leaders interpret and respond to their surroundings develops through a known sequence of stages.

Rooke and Torbert's model makes a distinction between three broad stages of leadership development. Their research found that:

- Leaders with a conventional leadership style are successful at delivering short- and medium-term objectives but become constrained by their inability to think outside the box. In fast-changing environments, this leadership style quickly becomes limited by rigid ideas about how things should be done (85% of the sample studied).

- Leaders who 'bridge' conventional and post-conventional styles of leadership start to break the rules and create the conditions where innovation can happen. Stability gives way to recognising uncertainty, re-evaluating previous ways of operating and trying out new approaches. They can, however, add to the uncertainty by their rule-breaking and willingness to experiment (10% of the sample).

- Leaders with a post-conventional style see the bigger picture, set the vision and are aware of their organisation as a whole and how their organisation is embedded in a wider ecosystem of stakeholders. They are keenly aware of multiple viewpoints and of the need to allow others to make mistakes in order to innovate. Others, who do not share their socially conscious business ideas, may reject their high moral standards and their focus on getting to the truth (5% of the sample).

It is not the case that leaders at post-conventional stages of development are inherently 'better' than leaders at earlier stages. In a fast-moving sales environment, leaders who operate in more conventional, opportunist ways might be the most effective in generating the most revenue. In a call centre where team members have limited interaction with one another, a leader with a conformist style might provide the social glue that's needed.

The earlier stages are a necessary foundation for what comes after. The later stages of development 'transcend and include' the previous. If a leader were a dancer, they would have more moves in their repertoire because they've learnt more choreography, enabling them to connect with a more diverse range of dance partners. The leaders of tomorrow will have the ability to 'style-flex' and adjust their dance to the music being played.[5]

In short, leaders at later stages of development are more agile in their thinking, have more systemic awareness and are better able to lead diverse stakeholders. They are also better equipped to deliver purpose, which requires several shifts in the ways leaders operate, from:

- meeting short-term goals to a long-term focus on societal well-being
- serving only shareholders to serving an expanded set of stakeholders
- maximising profit to putting people and a compelling social purpose first
- seeking power over others to empowering people to deliver great work.

Future leaders will increasingly embody these shifts. Going on this journey will both deliver purpose and draw on its power to draw people towards creating a better future for us all.

THE PULLING POWER OF PURPOSE

Purpose can 'pull' leaders to evolve the way they operate. This is significant because there can be many obstacles that get in the way. A leader might feel that things are unravelling and become confused about how to progress. There can be a strong instinct to pull back to the old and familiar as ingrained habits take hold. A leader might try to hold onto the 'tried-and-tested' and shut down alternative views that bring a wider perspective. For all these reasons, only a tiny proportion of leaders currently operate in post-conventional ways (5%).

Purpose can enable leaders to move with and not against the evolutionary impulse towards greater integration. It is the magnet that attracts leaders to grow into the next grandest version of themselves so that they don't get stuck in more conventional approaches:

- An organisational purpose breaks down barriers to engagement and helps a leader to build and sustain a culture of collaboration.

- A team purpose can light the fire between team members and so enable followership.

- A personal purpose gives a leader the conviction to stand their ground and overcome the pressure to conform.

To create a positive future and ensure organisational success, leaders developing their consciousness is crucial. As Frederic Laloux observes in *Reinventing Organizations:*

> *An organization cannot evolve beyond its leadership stage of development.*[6]

A leader's role in an organisation is not simply to create strategy or provide oversight but to engage and energise people around great work. Leadership models to date are incomplete and desperately need updating if we, as a global society, are to meet the significant systemic challenges we face and organisations of today are to remain viable in the future.

The evolution of consciousness will also help leaders to embrace the new paradigm of purpose-driven business. Leaders need to move beyond dualistic thinking and polarised debate by understanding that purpose and profit can work together in a dynamic way. This 'non-dual' consciousness includes profit *and* purpose, people *and* performance, power *and* empowerment, material prosperity *and* spiritual well-being. This inner change is highly significant. Without it, outer change is not possible. At the heart of the movement towards business becoming a force for good in the world is this shift in consciousness.

CREATING SUSTAINABLE CHANGE

Leaders are typically rewarded for their drive, determination and decisions. While achieving external results such as sales targets and profit margins are important, they are not sufficient to lead in 'high change' contexts where a deeper shift in consciousness is needed.

In her 2017 book *Still Moving: How to Lead Mindful Change,*[7] Deborah Rowland shows how leaders need to develop awareness of the 'whole system' as well as their 'whole self' in order to create change that sticks. Rowland contrasts this style of leadership, which she calls 'still moving' with leaders 'busily acting'. When leaders rush into action without attending to the whole system and their inner state, they ultimately 'moved nowhere'. Her research, which included interviewing 65 leaders along with a statistical analysis to investigate leadership effectiveness, revealed three 'Big Messages':

- In times of complex change when many people are impacted, some leaders are significantly more successful than others. Leaders who integrate two sets of skills – attuning to their 'whole self' and attending to their 'whole system' – create change that sustains itself (statistically, this combination of skills accounted for 52% of the variance between success and failure).

- The more senior a leader is, the more important it is for them to leverage their 'whole self'. By generating a relaxed 'field' or an 'affirming and non-anxious' presence around them, they create an environment where others can air their concerns, express their authentic selves and focus on what's important.

- The inner capacities precede the outer capacities. Rushing into action often means that dysfunctional dynamics repeat themselves. Effective leaders 'lead from their source' instead of getting stuck into doing straight away: 'Stillness is first required in order to move well.'

While leading with purpose calls for many capacities, this research helps to distil the essence of what's needed.

THE FOUR CORE CAPACITIES OF PURPOSE-LED LEADERSHIP

As Buckminster Fuller said, to change something, we need to build a new model that makes the existing model obsolete. For leaders to move away from old style 'command-and-control' leadership, they need something to replace it. Purpose has the unique potential to help leaders unleash a positive flow of energy in their system by removing obstacles and giving their people a North Star to orient towards. Purpose needs leadership and leadership is, in essence, about purpose. With this focus, a new model of leadership becomes possible.

Central to a new model of purpose-led leadership are four capacities. When a leader embodies these four capacities, they are able to go on the journey from being a conventional leader who seeks power over others, to becoming a transformational leader, who inspires others to achieve their best through being powered by a compelling purpose.

These four core capacities of purpose-led leadership, which are set out in the following figure, arise from various sources. Along with the research cited are over 15 years, international consulting experience and numerous conversations with CEOs, colleagues and change-makers, including the purpose 'pracademic' Dr Victoria Hurth (who has written the Epilogue) and leadership expert Dr Alison Miles. Ed Rowland and I developed an earlier model of six capacities in a paper we co-wrote with our colleague Scott Downs that I have refined in the light of further research, coaching and consulting work.[8]

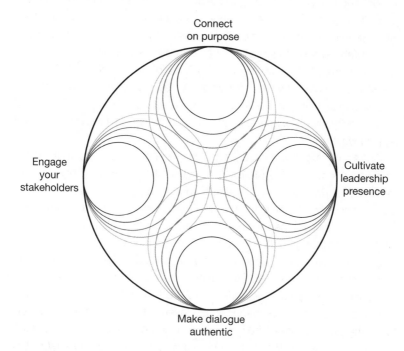

Purpose-Led Leadership: Four Core Capacities

Taken together, these capacities enable leaders to bring their 'whole self' to their work, unlock the potential of the 'whole system' and create 'whole outcomes' including competitive advantage and radical social change. They enable a leader to support each team member to have a sense of belonging and to see the connection between their individual purpose and the shared purpose the organisation commits to.

Developing these four interrelated capacities enables leaders to uplift their people and their performance. There's a circular and cumulative impact of the four elements as they spiral together rather than them being a linear construct or discrete entities. The four chapters in Part II of this book delve into each of these capacities in turn, showing how you, as a leader, can strengthen your ability to be powered by purpose. For now, here's a brief introduction.

THE FIRST CORE CAPACITY: CULTIVATE LEADERSHIP PRESENCE

Cultivating leadership presence is about becoming self-aware, whole-hearted and attuned to what wants to happen. While presence is 'beyond words' and can be challenging to convey, it is fundamental to leading with purpose. Presence enables a leader to bring their whole self, see their whole system and deliver 'whole outcomes'. To understand how this works, let's switch contexts to sport and then come back to business.

Top sports players are 'in flow' by bringing presence to their game. 'Flow', a term coined by the psychologist Mihály Csíkszentmihályi in 1975, is also known as being 'in the Zone'. This state refers to being fully immersed in an activity with a sense of relaxed concentration, energised focus and real enjoyment.[9]

Csíkszentmihályi has described the flow state as the 'optimal experience' as it leads to deep feelings of satisfaction as well as high performance. While we can enter a state of flow during any activity, we need to be fully engaged. Passive activities like watching TV do not take us there. We do not, however, need to be at the top of our game to experience flow, although cultivating our presence might get us there!

Johan Cruyff, the Dutch professional football player, who is widely regarded as one of the greatest players in football history, is an exemplar of presence. He led the Netherlands to the final of the 1974 FIFA World Cup and received the Golden Ball as player of the tournament. Referred to as 'the total footballer', he had a genius for timing shots, seeing passes that no one else could see and being aware of the ebb and flow of the whole game.

Cruyff understood what it was to be fully present. He once said, 'You have to be in the right place at the right moment, not too early, not too late.'[10] For him the purpose of the 'beautiful game' was not just to win but to win in the 'right' way. Victory was only meaningful when it captured the hearts and minds of competitors and spectators. Joy and entertainment were as important as the results achieved, as he said: 'Quality without results is pointless. Results without quality is boring.'[11]

Although Cruyff's physical stature and strength were not particularly impressive, his reading of the game was exceptional. 'We discussed space the whole time. Cruyff always talked about where people should run, where they should stand, where they should not be moving. It was all about making space and coming into space', said Barry Hulshoff, who played with

Cruff in the 1970s.[12] Cruyff's appreciation of 'space' enabled him to be a prolific goal scorer and team player; he played to the strengths of others around him with his deep awareness of his teammates' positions as an attack unfolded. His style embodied participation, simplicity and fluidity – qualities associated with presence.

Being present and 'open for business' is a great state for corporate leaders to be in. In his review of Mihály Csíkszentmihályi's book, *Good Business: Leadership, Flow, and the Making of Meaning,* Coert Visser builds on the notion of 'good work' in which you 'enjoy doing your best while at the same time contributing to something beyond yourself.'[13] Because purpose provides this higher-order context, individuals and teams in purpose-driven organisations are more likely to experience flow and higher levels of achievement.

Leadership presence (as I call it) applies at the three levels that leaders work at. In an organisation, our presence expands our ability to let go of outdated ways of working and be open to new ideas and directions. In a team, with presence, we are open to others' ideas and do not feel threatened by others' input and genius; we stay grounded when triggered. On a personal level, we stand in our own authority without needing external validation with a clear sense of what life is calling us to do.

It is only by building leadership presence that a leader will stop operating in more self-absorbed ways. In her article, 'I covered the city for 20 years – and here's what I learnt' Sarah Gordon, business editor at the *Financial Times*, highlights how the failures that led to the financial crisis of 2008 were less about financial processes and more to do with the behaviour and character of leaders. She writes:

> *There was one element to the crisis that I have seen repeated in many different forms: overweening power. In the business world this breeds all sorts of crises, from the personal to the systemic.*[14]

Martin Sorrell's 33 years at WPP, the advertising company he founded, ended in controversy in part because he treated the people who worked most closely with him with contempt. At Lehman Brothers, the final chairman and joint CEO, Richard Fuld, had accrued such power that he was not held to account by his board members whose job it was to do so. Sarah Gordon gives examples of other CEOs that did not like to have their judgement questioned and who, particularly with a long tenure, lost self-awareness, encouraging irresponsible leadership behaviour and poor business decisions.

In our increasingly interconnected world, we need leaders who bring wholehearted presence to their leadership more than ever. As thought leader Richard Barrett observes:

> *The performance of the business is determined by the unmet emotional and egoic needs of the founder or CEO.*[15]

Developing presence utterly changes our notion of leadership and power. Instead of seeing leaders as people who occupy certain positions, we recognise that anyone can take a lead from within any role. Instead of seeing power as hierarchical, we start to see that true power is within us. A leader's primary motive changes from seeking control over others to serving others by contributing to something larger than themselves. They no longer seek *power over* but *power with.* Power is seen as a dynamic that is both within us and between us, creating a vibrant exchange of energy, which brings a real sense of aliveness.

THE SECOND CORE CAPACITY: MAKE DIALOGUE AUTHENTIC

To become purpose led, authentic dialogue is a central mechanism. An organisation must become what Catherine Turco, associate professor of work and organisation studies at MIT Sloan, calls a 'conversational firm'.[16] Her proposition arises from spending 10 months inside a software company where she documented day-to-day activities, observed hundreds of meetings and interviewed employees. Free-flowing cross-hierarchical, cross-boundary dialogue contributed to high levels of success.

In a conversational firm, all employees are encouraged to speak up on major business issues, not just on issues to do with their own patch. Leaders share with the entire workforce detailed business information and trust that the collective wisdom will be greater than what can be deciphered in the C-suite alone. Often the best ideas are hidden away in corners of the organisation that leaders don't consult. By working across the traditional, hierarchical structure, leaders unlock the deeper potential of their organisation through inviting others to join the conversation.

To make a free flow of dialogue across the corporate hierarchy a reality, Turco observed how it is important to separate out 'voice rights' from 'decision rights'. Whereas the former are delegated broadly, the latter are still organised in a more hierarchical way. This creative tension – between the democratic and the more autocratic – enables clear decision making without too much disruption. The formal leader remains the single point of accountability for the co-created outcome. If roles are not clearly defined, it's possible that people will engage in more 'social loafing' and not pull their weight as they would in a more traditional, hierarchical structure.

The ground-breaking leader, Herb Kelleher, the founder of the hugely successful airline company, Southwest Airlines, demonstrated a core aspect of this capacity: listening. When Kelleher introduced $15 flights in 1971, he broke the US airline cartel. Southwest Airlines is USA's most successful carrier, carrying 120 million passengers a year. While many of the company's early competitors such as Pan Am and TWA no longer exist, Southwest Airlines has been profitable throughout its 45 years.

The company founding purpose – to connect people with what's important in their lives through friendly, reliable and low-cost travel – remains at the heart of the company. Kelleher (who died on 3 January 2019) had an approach to business and people that inspired many. He was shaped by the ruthless behaviour of his competitors and, having survived various injunctions to kill off Southwest Airlines during its very early days, the company became his worthy cause. The hostile behaviour of his competitors offended the sense that his mother had instilled in him to treat all people equally and with respect.

A signature of Kelleher's leadership was to put his employees first, ahead of his customers. He was very clear about the order of priorities: as CEO he was responsible for his people, and they were responsible for the customer. Central to Southwest's way of operating is looking after its people so that they are happy to serve its customers. There is a 'flow' of positive energy moving through the system: from senior leaders to staff to customers. People are truly seen as their single greatest strength and most enduring source of long-term competitive advantage. As Herb Kelleher once said, 'A company is stronger if it is bound by love rather than by fear.'[17] I wholeheartedly agree.

Because this mindset is real and not rhetorical, employees interact with customers with a sense of warmth, friendliness and pride that many organisations would find hard to beat. Herb Kelleher's leadership also inspired many other leaders. Doug Parker, CEO of American Airlines, acknowledges that the most important lesson he ever learnt about leadership came from observing Herb Kelleher.

'Every conversation he was in was, he was really engaged, really listening,' Parker said in an interview for *Business Insider.* 'And what

I realized is that was incredibly important to how he led because he learned and he took it back to his work and it made that company better and stronger.'[18]

While listening is a skill that many leaders find counter-intuitive to their usual inclination to be the person talking and giving direction, it is integral to success. By listening intently to the people around them and their issues, leaders can ensure that they have the tools they need to bring purpose to life.

THE THIRD CORE CAPACITY: ENGAGE YOUR STAKEHOLDERS

There is increasing recognition that leadership is systemic: leaders operate as part of a team, a team is part of a network of teams in an organisation, and an organisation is an interconnected part of a whole ecosystem of stakeholders. Purpose-led leaders collaborate with a wide field of stakeholders – staff, customers, activists and suppliers – to generate society-wide transformations.

This was brought home to me at an event I attended where Richard Walker, CEO of Iceland, was interviewed at the city-based agency OneHundred. With the expansive London skyline in the background, the benefits and challenges of being purpose-driven were openly discussed with questions and comments from the audience of 50 corporate change agents.

Richard Walker talked passionately about how the company has removed palm oil from all Iceland products, as well as its commitment to reduce plastic packaging and food waste. Their planned 'Rang-Tan' Christmas ad (developed in collaboration with Greenpeace), which highlighted the plight of the orangutan as huge swathes of tropical rainforest are cut down to make way for palm oil plantations, achieved more than 60 million views online and over a million people signed a petition to have it shown on TV.[19] Since the ad appeared, the palm oil industry has made significant new zero deforestation pledges, showing the power that corporate activism can have.

In the cynical atmosphere that pervades much of business and the media, it is all too easy to dismiss Iceland's removal of palm oil as yet another marketing gimmick. An article in *The Telegraph* declared that Iceland's palm oil campaign had 'failed' because it did not translate into sales.[20] In his response to the article by James Frayne on 12 May, Walker argued that the objective was never increased sales but an expression of the company's long-standing commitment to 'Doing It Right'.[21]

The fact that it didn't boost our sales was of absolutely no consequence – and I write that as one of Iceland's shareholders.

'Doing it Right' has been the company's motto for over 50 years.[22] Malcolm Walker, Richard's father, had founded Iceland in 1970 with a single, small shop in Oswestry, Shropshire selling loose frozen food. During a visit to the USA in the 1970s the slogan for Marriott Hotels, along with their reputation for great customer service, caught Malcolm's eye: 'We do it right'. Since then, Iceland has taken a lead in the UK by removing artificial colours, flavours and preservatives from its own label food in the 1980s, and a lead globally by banning GM ingredients and taking action against environmentally damaging refrigerants in the 1990s. More recently, a survey revealed that 82% of Iceland's customers agree with the company's stance on palm oil.

During his interview, Richard Walker talked openly about 'walking the tightrope' of turning a profit while creating positive change in the world. The needs of many different stakeholders hang in a super delicate balance. As a long-term supporter of Greenpeace, Walker is committed to doing the right thing and 'democratising environmentalism' rather than pursuing growth by opening more stores. His ability to engage stakeholders – his board, staff and customers – has been critical for the success of his leadership and to Iceland raising awareness of environmental issues among their five million weekly customers – and beyond.

THE FOURTH CORE CAPACITY: CONNECT ON PURPOSE

A compelling organisational purpose is unique in its ability to focus people on serving something 'beyond self'. Aligning a system by connecting people with an inspiring 'why' is at the heart of purpose-led leadership. When a business has a broader purpose than the profit motive, people have a sense of belonging to something significant.

Emanuel Faber, CEO of Danone, a large French food company, which owns brands such as Activia yoghurt and Evian, rejects the long-standing Anglo-Saxon idea of profit-maximisation for shareholders, orienting Danone around pursuing a more meaningful purpose: to get healthy food to as many mouths as possible so that everyone, from suppliers to consumers to owners, benefit. In *The Economist* (9 August 2018) Faber is quoted as saying: 'People are willing to walk out of brands that they've been consuming for decades', preferring to shop locally, where suppliers are often smaller producers and the products more likely to be organic, plant-based or GM-free.[23]

Danone does appear to be walking the talk. It has sold subsidiaries that produce unhealthy products such as biscuits, chocolate and beer. Evian is aiming to become carbon neutral and Danone is working on making recycled plastic, which has a grey look, attractive to drink from. The company runs a large-scale, not-for-profit 'social business' in collaboration with Nobel laureate, Muhammad Yunus, providing high-quality yoghurt to Bangladeshi school children.

Rose Marcario, CEO of Patagonia, is another leader who connects strongly with a purpose-beyond-profits. In 2015, under Barack Obama's presidency, Marcario was singled out for her efforts to protect the environment. Not afraid to challenge corporate convenience, she takes a stand for business becoming an agent of societal change and to speak out about why business matters. Marcario also puts her money where her mouth is. Under a new corporate tax code in the USA, Patagonia found itself paying a lot less in federal taxes. In a letter posted on LinkedIn on 28 November 2018, Rose Marcario, CEO, wrote:

> *Based on last year's irresponsible tax cut, Patagonia will owe less in taxes this year—$10 million less, in fact ... Instead of putting the money back into our business, we're responding by putting $10 million back into the planet. Our home planet needs it more than we do.*[24]

Marcario referred to the US Government's own recently published report on climate change, warning that unless significant changes are made, we could be facing catastrophic changes to our planet by 2050. She pointed to the 'woefully inadequate' political response to climate change so far and how 'taxes protect the most vulnerable in our society, our public lands and other life-giving resources'. Whereas many companies will do anything to pay less tax, Patagonia treated a tax windfall in a purpose- and stakeholder-driven way.

A compelling purpose generates a deep culture that is unique to the organisation, which in turn creates a source of competitive advantage and sustainable profitability. A distinctive culture – whether it's the friendliness of Southwest Airlines or the buzz of Patagonia – is the one aspect of an organisation that competitors cannot copy. Structure, process and goals can all be imitated but a culture of purpose can't. Southwest Airlines has been profitable every year for 45 years in a low-margin business where competitors frequently go bust. The results of purpose-led leadership speak for themselves.

OUR LONGING FOR BELONGING

What these four capacities of purpose-led leadership have in common is that they enable leaders to meet a fundamental human need: our longing to belong. Many leaders overlook this vital dimension of human life, particularly those who are more task- than people-focused. Becoming purpose-led helps leaders to address this oversight by making work meaningful for people and giving them a sense of their 'right place'.

Our desire to belong is a universal human need. While many aspects of our working lives have been transformed by changes in technology, this essential dimension remains the same. While the technological revolution in the workplace has changed 'how' we work, it hasn't changed *why* we work.[25] From an evolutionary perspective, this makes sense. If we didn't belong to the tribe, and instead were on our own, we would soon be food for sabre tooth tigers.

No matter what changes a digital transformation brings about, a sense of belonging remains essential for our well-being. One of the great humanistic psychologists of the twentieth century, Abraham Maslow, put belonging into his widely cited hierarchy of needs in 1943. Several thinkers have, however, challenged Maslow's thinking by arguing that our need for belonging is primary rather than secondary.

The award-winning Chilean economist Manfred Max-Neef has proposed an alternative to Maslow's model, in which needs – including our need for belonging – are complementary rather than hierarchical (apart from the basic need for subsistence or survival). Real needs are seen as few, finite and ontological (stemming from the condition of being human) rather than created desires, which are infinite and insatiable.[26]

Purpose therefore taps into the deepest levels of human motivation. Belonging is not a 'nice-to-have' but essential for our well-being. As the Afrikaner author, farmer, political adviser and philosopher Lauren Van der Post wrote:

> The Bushmen in the Kalahari Desert talk about the two 'hungers'.
> There is the Great Hunger and there is the Little Hunger. The Little
> Hunger wants food for the belly; but the Great Hunger, the greatest
> hunger of all, is the hunger for meaning ... Once what you are
> doing has for you meaning, it is irrelevant whether you're
> happy or unhappy. You are content – you are not alone in your
> Spirit – you belong.[27]

By developing the capacities of purpose-led leadership, leaders have a unique opportunity to create a sense of belonging by focusing people on serving the well-being of others. This, in turn, provides well-being to those who serve. Purpose can become part of this virtuous circle by engaging and energising all team members in the pursuit of great work.

IN CLOSING

Becoming purpose-led enables a leader to bring about exceptional results for an ecosystem of stakeholders. This is, however, only possible if a leader leads in a way that genuinely implements an impactful purpose. At the heart of the purpose-led leadership is a deeper orientation towards well-being, love and right action:

- **Well-being** because when we bring our wholehearted presence, our circle of care extends to include everyone – including future generations – not just ourselves.
- **Love** because when we engage in authentic dialogue and creative collaboration, we reach out to one another and honour our shared humanity.
- **Right action** because when we connect with the wider field of people around us, we want to be part of a healthy organisation that creates positive change in the world.

When we lead from love, we operate from an expansive place of opening up, sharing and caring about others' well-being. Instead of the meeting room being a place where we put people down, it becomes a place where we lift people up. When we lead with a truly compelling purpose, we ignite other people's excitement, energy and enthusiasm to make this planet a better home for us all.

How to shift your leadership to become more purpose-led

Take a pause to reflect on these questions:

1. Identify the person in your team who might feel least clear about their contribution or place of belonging. What's one action you could take to help strengthen their sense of belonging? When will you do this by?

2. Identify someone you admire who leads in an inspiring way. Choose one behaviour they demonstrate that you would like to embody. Commit to

enacting this behaviour over the next month. With whom you will try out this
new behaviour?

3. Reflect on a recent time when you saw power being used badly. What did
   you experience? Reflect on a time you saw power being used well. How did
   this feel? What can you learn from this?

4. Review the descriptions of the four capacities of purpose-led leadership in this
   chapter. Which of the capacities do you most need to develop? Ask a trusted
   colleague for their ideas about how you can expand your leadership in this way.

NOTES

1. See https://www.youtube.com/watch?time_continue=4&v=
   hO8MwBZl-Vc.
2. See https://www.ted.com/talks/derek_sivers_how_to_start_a_
   movement?language=en.
3. Wade, J. (2019) Get off the mountaintop and back into the marketplace: Leadership as transpersonal psychology's highest calling,
   Transpersonal Psychology Review, 21, 22–39.
4. Rooke, D. and Torbert, W.R. (2005) Seven transformations of leadership, *Harvard Business Review,* April, 66–76.
5. Genovese, M.A. (2015) *The Future of Leadership: Leveraged Leadership in an Age of Hyper-Change*, Routledge.
6. Laloux, F. (2014) *Reinventing Organizations: A Guide to Creating
   Organizations Inspired by the Next Stage of Human Consciousness,*
   Nelson Parker.
7. Rowland, D. (2017) How to Lead Mindful Change, Wiley-Blackwell.
8. Rozenthuler, S., Rowland E. and Downs, S. (2016) *Leading Systemic
   Dialogue: Unlocking Collective Intelligence for Purpose-Led Performance* (self-published).
9. Csíkszentmihályi, M. (1975) *Beyond Boredom and Anxiety: Experiencing Flow in Work and Play*, San Francisco: Jossey-Bass.
10. Winner. D. (2012) *Brilliant Orange: The Neurotic Genius of Dutch
    Football*, Bloomsbury Publishing.
11. Reported by Leo Messi on Twitter, 24 March 2016.
12. Winner, D. (2012). *Brilliant Orange: The Neurotic Genius of Dutch
    Football*, Bloomsbury Publishing.
13. See https://web.archive.org/web/20131110043540/http://
    articlescoertvisser.blogspot.com/2007/11/good-business-
    leadership-flow-and.html.

14. Gordon, S. (2019) I covered the City for 20 years – and here's what I learnt, *Financial Times*, 8 March.
15. Barrett, R. (2013) *The Values-Driven Organization: Cultural Health and Employee Well-Being as a Pathway to Sustainable Performance*, Routledge.
16. Turco, C.J. (2018) *The Conversational Firm* (2nd edn), Columbia University Press.
17. Quoted in *The Economist, 12* January 2019, Obituary: Herb Kelleher died on 3 January.
18. Zhang, B. (2019) American Airlines CEO reveals the most important lesson he learned from the legendary founder of Southwest Airlines, *Business Insider*, 23 May. See https://www.businessinsider.com/american-airlines-ceo-learned-lesson-from-southwest-airlines-founder-2019-5?r=US&IR=T.
19. See https://www.youtube.com/watch?v=JdpspllWl2o.
20. Frayne, J. (2019) 'It's no good companies being "woke" when their customers are all Brexiteer Tories', *The Sunday Telegraph*, 12 May.
21. Walker, R. (2019) Palm oil was all about Doing The Right Thing, not a marketing gimmick, 20 May. Available at: https://about.iceland.co.uk/2019/05/20/palm-oil-was-all-about-doing-the-right-thing-not-a-marketing-gimmick/.
22. See www.sustainability.Iceland.co.uk.
23. Choosing plan B (2018) Danone rethinks the idea of the firm, *The Economist*, 9 August.
24. Marcario. R. (2018) Our Urgent Gift to the Planet, *LinkedIn*, 28 November.
25. Psychology at work: Improving wellbeing and productivity in the workplace. Report published by the British Psychological Society, October 2017.
26. Max-Neef, M. (1989) *Human Scale Development: An Option for the Future, Development Dialogue*, Dag Hammarskjöld Foundation.
27. van der Post, L. (1958) *The Lost World of the Kalahari*, Vintage Publishing (2002 edn).

PART II

THE FOUR CAPACITIES OF PURPOSE-LED LEADERSHIP

CHAPTER 4

CULTIVATE LEADERSHIP PRESENCE

*Through presence and stillness we can activate emerging future
possibilities in the midst of a new kind of conversation.*[1]

Otto Scharmer

I n our rapidly changing world, where everyone and everything is becoming
connected, new pressures are emerging. To navigate an acute distrust of
business and more demanding customer expectations, leaders need to let
go of outdated assumptions and ways of operating. Cultivating leadership
presence is foundational for this to happen. With deeper presence, a leader
is able to remain centred when facing unexpected disruptions, be open to
new directions and build trusting relationships. People follow people. Leaders who are grounded in who they are, what they stand for and what really
matters take others with them on the journey to become purpose-driven.

* * *

There were five of us gathered round the table in the high-tech meeting room
of a world-class engineering company. The state-of-the-art glossy walls
doubled up as white boards for writing and there was a large screen where
decks of slides and people in other places could be projected. As we'd
entered the room, one of my colleagues had pointed out the newly opened
innovation lab across the corridor – the jewel in the crown of the company.

Be here now
The letters of a poster – large, colourful and vibrant – caught my eye from
outside the window. I could see into the office next door where the poster
was pinned to the wall. There was no logo or website, the poster was
simply a call to be present.

I smiled as I saw the words. They reminded me of a book I'd read 25 years ago that still intrigues me today. *Island* by English writer Aldous Huxley was published in 1962 as the utopian counterpart to his most famous work, the dystopian novel *Brave New World* (1932). It's the story of a cynical journalist who finds himself shipwrecked on the fictional kingdom of Pala, gaining entry to this otherwise 'forbidden island'. He awakens on the island with a leg injury to the sound of a local bird saying 'Attention!' The islanders are so committed to staying connected with the present moment, they taught the birds to say 'Attention!' as they fly around to remind people to stay focused.

Be here now

The irony of the moment suddenly hit me. With my mind slipping away to other times and places, I was neither here nor now with the people I was sat with. This meeting had taken over four months to land and needed my full attention.

Memories of our previous encounter with this client flooded back. A moment of magic when the chief information officer (CIO) had acknowledged in public his newly appointed deputy with warm words and a firm hand on his back so that he could step up into his new role fully 'authorised' to do his best work.

Be here now

The poster landed me back in the present moment once more. Reminiscing, even about the good times, was stopping me from being fully present to what was happening right now. As I listened to the deputy CIO and his HR manager describe their current leadership challenges, I found myself wondering, what's the work to be done now?

Be here now

As soon as I noticed my attention had slipped away (again!), I was present once more. The deputy CIO was now up at the whiteboard sketching out his 'leadership ecosystem'. As he mapped out this intricate web of relationships across the length of the room, I realised I would need all my attentiveness to support this leader. To have the 'breakthrough year' that the organisation wanted, I would need all my presence – as would he.

* * *

Presence is a concept that is difficult to describe and largely unexamined in the leadership literature. This is a real oversight as leaders who actively cultivate their presence are better able to engage and energise the people around them to do great work. People's attention is one of the scarcest resources in organisations due to constant distractions from unexpected interruptions to an endless stream of emails. Mindfulness practices such as meditation, ritual and silence are increasingly being incorporated into leadership development activities to improve perspective taking, deepen empathy and promote calmness. Our presence is a precious resource that can be consciously mobilised to create positive outcomes.

Becoming more present is not about becoming qualified to enter a Zen monastery, Taoist temple or Shinto Shrine, but about staying in touch with the reality of the present moment. It helps to reduce 'attention residue'[2] – continuing to think about one issue when you need to pivot to the next. When we switch tasks, our full focus doesn't follow straight away as some part of us remains engaged with the original issue. Attention residue has been shown to have a significant adverse impact on performance, unless we find ways to consciously manage it (more on this below).

In *Deep Work,* Cal Newport argues that knowledge workers who develop the ability to carve out focused chunks of time in which to produce high-quality, meaningful work will be the 'winners' in our increasingly distracted digital age.[3] Constantly checking our emails, rushing from meeting to meeting and incessantly scrolling social media all stand in the way of us doing truly valuable work.

Recent research reveals that presence is a capacity that we can develop. The results of a quantitative survey and in-depth interviews with 196 CEOs, MDs and other senior leaders from organisations such as Google, KPMG and HSBC found that while only 39% had met more than 10 leaders with 'executive presence' in the last 10 years, the majority believed that leaders are able to expand their presence through mentoring, role modelling and coaching.[4]

In *Good to Great* Jim Collins found that the most successful leaders were not charismatic extroverts but those with 'extreme humility coupled with intense professional will'. The words used by those being led to describe their leaders included quiet, humble, modest, gracious, self-effacing and understated. It is people who are grounded in who they are rather than those focused on their own self-aggrandisement that lead the best organisations.[5]

Ignoring our interiority is what Otto Scharmer calls the 'blind spot' of leadership. When we focus our attention on what we do rather than the 'inner place' from which our leadership flows, we limit what can happen. When Scharmer asked Bill O'Brien, the late CEO of Hanover Insurance, to summarise his most important insight from leading transformational change in his company, Bill O'Brien shared this observation:[6]

> *The success of an intervention depends on the interior condition of the intervener.*

Read that sentence again. It is profound. Take a moment to become still and reflect.

Scharmer calls this shift towards including our inner reality in our responses 'presencing'. He combines the words 'presence' and 'sensing' to reflect the heightened state of awareness that, when evolved, can bring an open mind, heart and 'will' to our leadership. During this 'Age of Disruption' while our civilisation of consumerism and narcissism is dying, an 'emerging future' is starting to be born. Scharmer, with Katrin Kaufer, writes:

> *It is a future we can sense, feel, and actualize by shifting the* inner place *from which we operate ... This inner shift, from fighting the old to sensing and presencing an emerging future possibility, is at the core of all deep leadership work today. It's a shift that requires us to expand our thinking from the head to the heart. It is a shift from a system awareness that cares about the well-being of oneself to an eco-system awareness that cares about the well-being of all, including oneself.*[7]

Deepening presence is at the heart of Scharmer's 'Theory U' model of generating profound change. This model moves through three broad stages of letting go of what we think we know, sitting in the unknown and 'letting come' by allowing new insights to emerge. Key to each of these 'movements' is slowing down and allowing spaciousness.

For leaders to deepen their presence, it helps to have role models, success stories and 'how-to's. With this in mind, this chapter covers the following:

- What leadership presence is.
- Why developing leadership presence matters.
- How to develop presence.

WHAT LEADERSHIP PRESENCE IS

When was a time that you became so immersed in what you were doing that you lost a sense of time? You might have been reading a novel, talking with a colleague or writing a report; any activity that requires focused concentration can take us there. Already you've had a taste of this capacity.

When we operate from a sense of our presence, we are in a state of absorbed relaxation. There is a feeling of spaciousness or 'Flow' inside us (see page 52). Afterwards, when we look back, we realise that we'd been totally 'there' and in touch with our best self.

When we have a 'felt sense' of our presence, we are right here, right now. All our attention is focused in this moment. If we're in a meeting, we're attentive to other people; we're not thinking about our emails, 'to do' list or other distractions. We stay in contact with what's happening in the room, as well as what's going on inside us.

When we're absorbed by our own preoccupations, we're not available to others. People around us, even young children, can sense this disconnectedness. I learnt this one December afternoon when I looked after Orla, my niece who was one year old at the time. As it was too cold to go outside, we spent many hours in my home. Whenever my attention went to my smartphone instead of her, she noticed straight away. It was a striking reminder of how exquisitely attuned we are to one another, before we learn not to be.

When I think of the people I've met who are truly present, there is something magnetic about interacting with them. Their eye gaze is confident, their conversation is engaging and they have a sense of ease about them. Patsy Rodenburg, author, voice coach and theatre director, underlines how, when we are present, there's an exchange of energy between us and other people. There's a sense of mutuality, a flow back and forth.[8]

Rodenburg contrasts this with two other 'non-present' states. In one, your energy 'falls back into you'. There's a contraction, a closing down, a movement inwards. Our voices become tight, our bodies rigid, our shoulders stiff. Our breathing is shallow or there might even be a sensation that we've forgotten to breathe. When our deeper vitality is cut off, it's almost impossible to inspire other people, no matter how compelling a purpose is on paper.

In the other state, our energy is 'pushed out.' Our voice becomes strident, our chin juts out, our eyes are haughty. When we're in this puffed-up place, other people turn away rather than towards us, and we might not even notice. Motivating stakeholders to align around a purpose becomes mission impossible.

By contrast, when we discover our presence, we are neither deflated nor inflated. We feel relaxed and trust how things are unfolding. We don't try to control or manipulate others but allow them space to be themselves, just as we are being ourselves. We feel supported by a larger intelligence flowing through us. Other people are attracted by this expansive energy and want to draw closer. Aligning others around a shared purpose becomes much more possible when we are in this state.

OUR TWO SELVES

To cultivate a deeper sense of presence, it helps to understand how we're wired inside. Since it was first published in 1975, Timothy Gallwey's book, *The Inner Game of Tennis,* has become a classic because it offers a valuable tool for inner exploration.[9] As a tennis coach, Gallwey identified that the biggest obstacle to playing tennis was self-criticism, which led to lapses of concentration and nervousness. By thinking too much and trying too hard, players became tense, impeding their ability to play the game spontaneously, shouting 'Idiot!', 'Rubbish!' and worse at themselves and others.

By contrast, Gallwey found that players who cultivated relaxed concentration progressed more quickly. Students who focused their awareness on their breathing or on listening to the ball bounce performed better than those who followed the traditional method of learning techniques to swing their racket, position their legs or bend their knees. By attending to the 'inner game' of tennis rather than only the outer technicalities, students tapped into their natural abilities and played with greater ease.

As a way to understand this pattern, Gallwey developed a model of two inner selves that we all have inside us. He drew a distinction between our conditioned self (which he calls Self 1) and our true or spontaneous self (which he named Self 2). Most of us are all-too-familiar with our Self 1, also known as our inner critic, with its judgmental voice that interferes with our present moment experience. On the tennis court when Self 1 gets the upper hand, we grit our teeth, make rigid swings and awkward movements. This tightening process leads to us feeling jittery and frustrated, which further meddles with how we play.

Whereas Self 1 tries to make the game happen, Self 2 lets the game happen. Self 2 is the instinctive, dynamic part of us that is effortlessly alert. We are aware without over-thinking; we are attentive without being anxious. We are in a free flow of action, which feels exhilarating and energising. The following diagram gives the key features of Self 1 and Self 2.

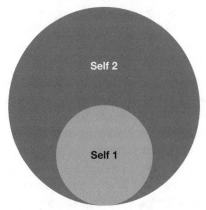

Self 1 – Conditioned Self
Judgemental and critical
Over thinking
Feels tense

Self 2 – True Self
Present and spontaneous
Effortlessly alert
Feels at ease

Cultivating Leadership Presence

There are two ways to cultivate presence. The first is to quieten Self 1 and the second is to trust Self 2. To the extent that we are able to let go of the punitive judgements of Self 1 and come from the inner knowing of Self 2, it strengthens our leadership. We engage and energise others when we're in an accepting and expansive place ourselves.

WHY DEVELOPING LEADERSHIP PRESENCE MATTERS

There are several benefits to cultivating presence and building trusting relationships is chief among them. Marc Benioff, CEO of Salesforce, attributes the sustained success of the company to its operating principle of 'values create value'. Known for being a great place to work, Salesforce has four values – customer success, innovation, equality and, most importantly, trust. In an interview for *Fortune*, Benioff states: 'If trust isn't your highest value, the employees will walk out ... Customers will walk out, investors will walk out and leaders will walk out, and you're seeing more of that everyday.'[10]

The runaway egos of top leaders create havoc in organisations. In their 2011 book, MPs Matthew Hancock and Nadhim Zahawi highlight the behaviour of Fred Goodwin, former CEO of the Royal Bank of Scotland, as one example. 'Fred the Shred,' famous for his cost-cutting – and for leaving the UK taxpayer with a £45 billion bailout bill – was well known for his outbursts of rage when he didn't get his own way. In an email titled 'Rogue Biscuits', he threatened catering staff with disciplinary action after they offered pink wafers to executives in his boardroom instead of his favourite fare.[11]

Deepening presence reduces the risk of 'acting out': demeaning, yelling at or humiliating others. When a leader behaves in this way, it hurts others and it hurts them too. Emotional retrenchment after the event can lead to feelings of shame or, at the other extreme, stubbornness that 'I was right!' Wasted energy and lost potential are the result.

Dealing with reactivity is key. Lashing out at others does not engage team members or anyone else. While it provides a short-term release of pent-up energy, it pollutes the atmosphere. No one wants to work for a leader who 'throws their toys out of the pram' or withdraws into a sulky silence, no matter how inspiring their espoused purpose is.

When a button inside of us gets pushed, it's an opportunity to pause, reflect and search inside ourselves so that the button loses its charge. In *Where Did You Learn to Behave Like That?* Dr Sarah Hill provides coaches and leaders with a powerful set of tools to dig into personal history rather than sweep it under the carpet.[12] We are all shaped by our childhood and if we don't do the work to uncover this, it is much more likely that our reactivity continues to harm others. Integrating our early conditioning – through talking with a coach, therapist or trusted friend – is core to deepening presence.

SENSING INTO FUTURE POSSIBILITIES

An expanded presence enables leaders to become aware of out-dated ways of thinking. In his new book, *Trailblazer,* co-authored with Monica Langley, Marc Benioff reflects that although he has been a lifelong champion of technology, he's become aware of the dangers by taking time to listen to his employees, customers and other stakeholders. Their message was simple: The world is changing, and the purpose of a business, and how it operates, needs to evolve to meet the challenges of the future.[13]

Benioff tells the story of a moment of disruption at Davos in January 2018 when he was on the keynote panel. On the back of data breaches at Facebook and even voter manipulation in the USA, the widespread distrust of tech industry had become the hot topic. Benioff made a comment that compared social media to cigarettes and sugar – a harmful product that is highly addictive and damaging to people's health if left unregulated.

When he got back from Davos, his phone kept ringing with tech leaders telling him that he'd betrayed them. Despite receiving so much scorn, he went on to write his book about business leaders re-building trust by using technology to improve the state of the world – not least because in business school, 'stakeholderism' was not the education he'd been given. He reflects:

On that snowy weekend in Davos in 2018, I finally realized that the tables had turned. Salesforce, the company I'd led for almost twenty years, was guiding me in a new direction.

Presence is the capacity that enables leaders to hear the future calling. Without presence, we risk holding onto assumptions and becoming stuck in the old way of doing things. At Salesforce, Benioff has created meditation rooms throughout their offices. When asked in an interview for *The New York Times* (published in June 2018) how meditation influences his leadership, Benioff said that cultivating a 'beginner's mind' is key.

'I'm trying to listen deeply, and the beginner's mind is informing me to step back, so that I can create what wants to be, not what was,' Benioff said. 'I know that the future does not equal the past. I know that I have to be here in the moment.'[14]

When we become present, our minds become more expansive. A.H. Almaas, a Kuwaiti American author and founder of the Ridhwan school of personal development (where I am a student) teaches that this spaciousness feels very different from deficient emptiness, which many of us might associate with 'stilling' our mind. In his book, *The Unfolding Now*, Almaas describes how presence is not 'a mental construction dredged up from my past ... I am experiencing this moment completely, directly, without anything intervening. I am the very awareness, the very consciousness, that is present, that exists, in this very moment.'[15]

Some of the most influential CEOs, executives and celebrities credit practices for becoming more present for contributing to their success.[16] In an article for *Everyday Health,* Oprah Winfrey, Jeff Weiner (CEO LinkedIn) and Arianna Huffington (co-founder of *Huffington Post* and Thrive Global) all acknowledge the part that meditation plays in their ability to be their best selves.

NAVIGATING ETHICAL DILEMMAS

In leadership, actions have a huge multiplier effect, impacting the lives of many people. In the 2017 report 'Tomorrow's Leadership and the Necessary Revolution in Today's Leadership Development' by Peter Hawkins, Professor in Leadership at Henley Business School, highlights that twentieth-century 'industrial age' thinking is no longer adequate for the new challenges that viral social media, online tracking and big data bring.[17]

The digital world is ushering in an age of 'radical transparency'. Apple's tax avoidance, Sport Direct's employment conditions and Facebook's data harvesting practices have shown how corporate scandals are quickly and visibly played out on the world stage. Hawkins suggests that leadership, when facing a moral conundrum, ask themselves:

> *How will this be seen by our customers and stakeholders when our systems are hacked into or the news gets out?*

By taking the time to truly engage this question, there would be fewer disastrous fallouts. If leaders listened to what their own inner guidance and their stakeholders were telling them – brought greater leadership presence – better decisions, stronger reputations and trusting relationships would be the result.

A recent study by The Chartered Institute of Personnel Development, 'Purposeful leadership: What is it, what causes it and does it matter?' (June 2017) highlights the importance of leaders developing their 'moral selves'. When followers rated three different aspects of their leader's behaviour – their vision for their team, commitment to stakeholder groups and their 'moral self' (behaviour that reflected personal qualities such as integrity, fairness and kindness) – the only one that showed a significant correlation with employees' ratings was a leader's 'moral self'. If a leader doesn't attend to this aspect of their development, they are unlikely to take their people with them.[18]

Organisations who help their leaders to develop their leadership presence will have a competitive edge. Their leaders will expand their ability to inspire others, have the courage to take 'right action' and the willingness to be publicly accountable for their decisions.

HOW TO DEVELOP PRESENCE – QUIETEN SELF 1

Once we find a deeper impulse inside – the desire to serve others or to lead a purpose-led team – we will need all the support we can muster to deal with our Self 1. This critical, judgemental voice inside causes us to contract. Otherwise known as our inner critic or 'superego', learning to address its admonitions is a core challenge facing leaders (and, indeed, any of us).

Our superego is a structure of consciousness that's been built up over many years through identifying with the judging, critical and blaming attitudes of the environment in which we grew up. Imagine the punitive side of your parents', teachers' and other authority figures' voices playing in surround sound in your mind – that's your superego. Its job is to maintain the status quo and to protect us from making reckless mistakes.

Growing up, it was important for us to internalise a sense of caution – our survival depended on it. However, what was adaptive then might be dysfunctional now, particularly when we hear the call to adventure and need to develop our intuitive contact with life. Our superego is therefore both an old friend as well as a formidable foe.

The modus operandi of the superego is often one of attack. Our superego is a harsh judge that keeps us, and our dreams, in check. At other times, the superego can appear as a more subtle and yet still judgemental voice, as if we had a controlling parent stood on our shoulder, watching our every move.

The exacting energy of the superego can also be outwardly directed towards others, whom we look at with a harshly critical eye. Unless we bring this coercive inner force into the light of awareness, it will run the show and keep us stuck. As a leader, unless addressed, it will sabotage our interactions as no one likes to feel in the firing line of judgement.

How to disarm your inner critic

To deal with the superego, there are three key steps: detect, describe and disengage.[19]

1. To detect your superego, notice when you go tense. The inner critic, when it takes over, often feels heavy or harsh, and our body contracts. Next time you're in a meeting, observe when and where your body tightens (in your jaw, stomach or chest?).

2. Describe your superego. When you observe this critical voice, explore it rather than push it away. Take a moment to explore if your inner judge is around right now. You might find it making a running commentary in your mind as you read this:

   - 'I should be doing something useful not just reading.'
   - 'I can't believe I'm sitting here with a book when I have so much to do.'

▶

- 'No wonder I'm overlooked when I spend all my time naval-gazing.'
- 'I'm such a slacker! I'll never reach my potential.'
- 'I really should be out there earning more money at my age.'
- 'No one will give me a break if I carry on like this.'

Are the statements you hear mildly corrective, downright aggressive or somewhere in-between? What words would you use to describe the feel or texture? You might have an image of an animal or another entity that embodies the energy of your superego.

3. Disengage from the superego. You might use humour to make light of it. You could use assertion to tell it to back off. You might change your physical posture as a way to 'stand up' to your superego. Experiment and see what works for you.

Becoming aware of our superego sends the message that there are different parts of you interacting. Author Byron Brown suggests challenging the superego by putting the voice into the second person as if your inner critic were addressing someone else. For example, instead of saying, 'I'm such a failure', it becomes, 'You're such a failure.'[20]

Amplifying this voice of judgement helps to send the message to your psyche that there are different parts of you interacting. The part of you who is judging (Self 1) is not the totality of you (Self 2). By doing this, the parts inside us rearrange themselves to create a different inner atmosphere. We might notice that we become more spacious, less tense, more relaxed. We loosen our grip on what we need to have happen and instead let what wants to flow through come through.

HOW TO DEVELOP PRESENCE – TRUST SELF 2

Senior leaders typically spend up to 80% of their time in meetings. This calls for 'black belt mindfulness'[21] or advanced attentiveness, as there can be so many demands on our attention. The following are some simple things that will help you while interacting with others so that you can connect with your fuller Self (Self 2). Many of them include using your body and breathing. We are embodied beings, moving through space and time. Effective leaders physically move in line with their presence and this is seen very clearly by their people.

How to become more present

Here are some things to try before, during and after a meeting or conversation.

Before a meeting

Take a few moments to become present. Find a quiet space where you can close your eyes, scan your body and notice what you're feeling. Pay particular attention to any signs of stress that you sense. Breathe into this part of your body to help to release any tension.

Put your phone, laptop and other devices away. Keep them out of sight so that you're less likely to swivel your attention in their direction. The people you're with will feel more valued if they're not competing for your attention.

During a meeting

Stay in touch with your own body as you interact with others. Feel your feet on the ground, your backside in the chair and your spine sitting upright.

Place your attention in your belly and notice yourself breathing in and out. If you're able to, lightly place your hand on your stomach to help you to stay connected with this 'belly breath'. When you notice that you've 'jumped' out of yourself or lost touch with your sense of self, focus again on your breathing.

Maintain eye contact when another person is speaking. This helps to keep your mind from wandering. It communicates to the other that they have your full attention. Hold off from interrupting so that you can discover what the other is thinking and feeling.

At key moments during a meeting, stay close to how you're feeling. If a decision is being made, notice any sensations that arise. Pay particular attention to how your gut is feeling. Notice if your heart lifts or sinks. Observe whether a decision makes you feel more or less alive. If you can appropriate, share what's going on for you with others.

If you're not able to give other people your full attention, say so. It is better to say, 'I know you need to talk with me and I'm interested, but I want to give you my undivided attention' than to be in a semi-distracted state. Take care of what you need to and then return to the conversation.

After a meeting

Carve out whatever space you can between meetings rather than rushing from one to the next. Even a short break of a few minutes helps to clear your mind and reduce 'attention residue'. If it's possible to stand outside or open a window, even for a few seconds, the fresh air will help to keep your attention focused in the here-and-now.

At the end of a meeting, jot down any actions or key decisions that were taken so that these don't remain as 'open loops' in your mind. Incomplete items have been shown to consume a disproportionate amount of psychic energy. Close your 'loops' from one meeting before you head to the next.

While deepening your presence in meetings can be challenging, the results can be transformative. When we are present, we are in touch with what's really happening. When we're fully in the moment, we can access the inner knowing of our true self (Self 2). When we're attentive, we see opportunities and risks that we miss when we're only half there.

When we turn within ourselves, it's possible that we become aware of a new direction to fall in with. In a state of active receptivity, we might feel a nudge that prompts us to reach out to someone, start a conversation or make a new connection. These small movements become the apertures through which new possibilities unfold and your true self emerges.

HOW TO DEVELOP PRESENCE – CULTIVATE A PRACTICE

Leader presence builds over time with conscious practice. Having coached hundreds of leaders over the years, one of the most reliable tools that I've seen leaders use to deepen their presence is to develop a regular practice.

It is vital to make this manageable. Better to practise consistently for a few minutes a day than to aim for 20 minutes and repeatedly miss it. The important thing is to do your practice rather than try to achieve anything in particular. The value is in the doing, not in the result.

How to cultivate a practice

To deepen your presence as a leader, develop a regular practice. There are four key dimensions to an effective practice – make a *DATE* with yourself!

■ **D = Daily.** Commit to doing one specific thing every day. One leader decided that instead of checking his email first thing, he would take a few minutes to breathe deeply as soon as he woke up to help him to be more purposeful and feel more in control as he stepped into his day.

- **A = Accountable.** Find an ally to help you keep your focus. Share your intended practice and ask them to 'hold your feet to the fire'. One leader emailed his buddy with a simple progress report each week, stating how many days he had done his breathing practice. Several months later he noticed how he was able to sit in even high-stakes meetings and feel a sense of serenity.

- **T = Targeted.** Tailor your practice to develop your presence in a context that matters. One leader cultivated her ability to stay present during a meeting by stopping taking notes and summarising the key points on paper after she'd left the meeting. Over time she noticed that her retention of key points improved.

- **E = Edgy.** Challenge yourself to move into new territory. One leader, who had received some feedback that his pattern of interrupting others was frustrating, practised consciously allowing others to finish their sentences and express themselves before he gave his opinion. A year later the ratings on his 360-degree feedback report significantly improved.

BEYOND MINDFULNESS

While the movement towards 'being here now' brings many benefits from clear thinking to better relationships, it does, however, have its critics. 'McMindfullness', with its associations of fast food that isn't nourishing, is a label that's been given to the application or 'mutation' of contemplative practices, mostly from Buddhist traditions, to the workplace. The 'de-spiritualising' of contemplative practice can be problematic in several ways:[22]

- Developing an attitude of 'non-judging' and 'non-striving' by simply allowing what's unfolding to unfold could lead to extreme passivity among employees. Mindfulness training could actually weaken people's capacity to resist or object where taking a stand might be called for.

- Mindfulness training, for example, for nurses in a stressful work environment, could deflect responsibility away from managers and politicians. As nurses are encouraged to 'better manage' or adapt to their unhealthy work environments, this might make systemic changes that would benefit everyone less likely to happen.

- Secular mindfulness practice risks losing its power to truly transform individuals and society without the accompanying training in ethics, which would typically take place in a Buddhist context. More worryingly, greater mental sharpness could generate more negative outcomes if, for example, people in the military kill with more accuracy but less discernment about whether or not this is right action.

While the risks outlined above are valid, there are also ways to address them. Cultivating presence is only one of the vital capacities needed in order to lead with purpose. Making dialogue authentic includes equipping leaders with the skills to speak out when they need to. Engaging stakeholders enables leaders to see the bigger picture and include a greater range of beneficiaries in their decision making. Connecting on purpose makes it more likely that leaders will create a vibrant culture of right action by encouraging everyone to move forward in line with the organisation's 'why'.

The four capacities are inter-related and each is inseparable from the others. That said, to lead with purpose, developing your full presence is the first capacity to focus on. While it might seem challenging, the boost to your sense of self-worth is very significant. By cultivating our presence, we create solidity in ourselves. We know that we exist without reference to anything outside. This 'substance' enables us to step away from boardroom dramas, office gossip and hubristic posturing. Our greater vitality draws others to us, not because of our charisma, but because we are living life at the centre of our own experience.

Our presence – so simple, so basic and yet so rare – is what creates the most impact when someone walks into the room. Great leaders have it and you can too. Presence is available to us each moment and cultivating presence will greatly enhance the quality of your life and your leadership.

NEW WAYS OF WORKING

Returning to the story that this chapter began with, my colleague and I co-facilitated a meeting for the CIO and his extended leadership team. Instead of tackling business issues straight way, we took time to become present. We started by inviting people to respond to:

'What's the energy you're stepping in with?'

We encouraged them to be honest. 'It doesn't matter whether it's enthusiasm, scepticism or exhaustion, what matters is that you say it as it is for you right now.'

'I feel scattered,' said the CIO, when it was his turn to speak. As soon as he'd said it, various heads nodded. I had a sense of his energy – and the energy of the group – becoming more settled. Noticing when we're not present is a powerful way to become more present.

As the rest of the circle spoke, it was like watching a black-and-white film turn into colour. By communicating his felt sense in the *now*, the CIO's honesty reverberated around the room. Others started to participate more wholeheartedly because their leader had been willing to show up authentically.

By the end of the two days, the team had crystallised and committed to six new ways of working to unlock the fuller potential of the team. When people bring their presence, purpose comes to life too.

SUMMARY

- Leadership presence is a critical capacity to develop even though it is often overlooked in the literature and challenging to define.

- Presence arises when we are totally 'here', operating out of our best self. Our relaxed presence puts others at ease, engaging and energising them to do great work. Our felt sense of 'rightness' helps us to discern which actions to follow.

- The benefits of cultivating leadership presence include building trusting relationships through not 'acting out'; navigating ethical dilemmas through better discernment and letting go of outdated ways of operating to make way for the new.

- To quieten our 'Self 1' (inner critic or superego), we need to notice when we go tense. To disarm our inner critic, detect, describe and disengage from the judgemental and critical voice inside us.

- Being in the moment expands our experience of our 'Self 2' or True Self. This spontaneous, relaxed, effortlessly alert part of ourselves is always there within us but often blocked off through our conditioning.

- Developing a regular practice helps us to stay in touch with our True Self. Making this a DATE – Daily, Accountable, Targeted and Edgy – enables us to make more conscious choices about how act and interact with others.

- Cultivating leadership presence is necessary but not sufficient to lead with purpose. The other three inter-related leadership capacities are also needed.

NOTES

1. Scharmer, O. (2009) *Theory U: Learning from the Future as It Emerges*, Berrett-Koehler Publishers.
2. Leroy, S. (2009) Why is it so hard to do my work? The challenge of attention residue when switching between work tasks, *Organizational Behavior and Human Decision Processes*, 109(2), 168–81.

3. Newport, C. (2016) *Deep Work: Rule for Success in a Distracted World*, Piatkus.
4. Potter, A. (2018) Investigating the critical characteristics of an inspirational leader, *Assessment and Development Matters,* Psychological Testing Centre, British Psychological Society, Spring.
5. Collins, J. (2001) *Good to Great: Why Some Companies Make the Leap ... and Others Don't,* William Collins.
6. Scharmer, O. (2013) *Uncovering the Blind Spot of Leadership,* The Daily Good, 9 July, www.dailygood.org.
7. Scharmer, O. and Katrin Kaufer, K. (2013) *Leading from the Emergent Future: From Ego-System to Eco-System Economies*, Berrett-Koehler.
8. Rodenburg, P. (2009) *Presence: How to Use Positive Energy for Success in Every Situation*, Penguin.
9. Gallwey, T. (2014) *The Inner Game of Tennis*, Pan Books.
10. Leaf, C. (2019) Salesforce Founder Marc Benioff: What Business School Never Taught Me*, Fortune, Inc*, 15 October.
11. Hancock, M. and Zahawi, N. (2011) *Masters of Nothing: How the Crash Will Happen Again Unless We Understand Human Nature,* Biteback Publishing.
12. Hill, S. (2017) *Where Did You Learn to Behave Like That?: A Coaching Guide for Working With Leaders*, Dialogix.
13. Benioff, M. and Langley, M. (2019) *Trailblazer: The Power of Business for the Greatest Platform for Change*, Simon and Schuster.
14. See https://www.nytimes.com/2018/06/15/business/marc-benioff-salesforce-corner-office.html.
15. Almaas, A.H. (2008) *The Unfolding Now*, Shambhala Publications Inc., 2nd edn, p. 136.
16. See https://www.everydayhealth.com/meditation/highly-successful-ceos-celebrities-who-practice-meditation/.
17. Hawkins, P. (2017) *Tomorrow's Leadership and the Necessary Revolution in Today's Leadership Development*, Henley Business School.
18. Chartered Institute of Professional Development (2017) *Purposeful leadership: What is it, what causes it and does it matter?*, 13 June.
19. I am grateful to Claus Springborg for this framework about the superego. Claus is a colleague and author of (2018) *Sensory Templates and Managerial Cognition – Art, Cognitive Science and Spiritual Practices in Management Education*, Palgrave Macmillan.

20. Brown, B. (1998) *Soul Without Shame: A Guide to Liberating Yourself from the Judge Within,* Shambala Publications Inc.
21. Chade Meng Tan (2012) *Search Inside Yourself: The Unexpected Path to Achieving Success, Happiness (and World Peace),* HarperOne.
22. Cohen, E. (2017) Cutting the Buddha's body to fit the Neoliberal suit: Mindfulness – from practice, to purchase, to Praxis, *Annual Review of Critical Psychology,* 13.

CHAPTER 5

MAKE DIALOGUE AUTHENTIC

Change happens by listening and then starting a dialogue with the people who are doing something you don't believe is right.

Jane Goodall

For an organisational purpose to contribute to the sustainable success of a company, authentic dialogue is needed to uncover what the organisation is really about. When leaders are able to talk – and, more crucially, listen – to one another, a compelling purpose can be agreed. The organisation's 'why' will then be able to guide day-to-day decision making, create alignment around future work and resolve ethical dilemmas. To take dialogue to this level, people need to feel safe to speak out, be willing to accept diversity of perspective and navigate any conflicts that a purpose-driven approach stirs.

Let's look at the challenge facing one leadership team to have a 'big conversation' about purpose in order to take their business forward.

* * *

'To have some fun and hopefully make some money along the way!'

As soon as the partner of the design agency said it, I saw smiles spread across the faces of the other two partners who had co-founded the business. It was a purpose that had served them well for 25 years. While they had never formally agreed their company's purpose, it was easy to see looking back that this is what they'd been about.

fst is a strategy-led design agency that solves business problems to build the brands of the future. For them, design always serves a higher purpose: to solve their client's problems using creative thinking and beautiful design in order to deliver solutions that work. The partners were particularly proud of the people who had hopped from one client to the next and then the next – their 'triple jumpers' – taking fst and its 'challenge, change, make better' approach with them.

Crunch time had come, however. While revenues were in the several millions, profits had flatlined. In addition, the three partners wanted to step back from full-time leadership of the business and hand over the baton to a new team of three leaders that they'd been developing, who were keen to take the business on.

'The question of purpose is critical,' continued Otto, who had joined the agency as a graduate over two decades ago. 'What's got us to where we are today is not going to work going forwards. If we want to create a solid platform and a global footprint for the next 25 years, we need to revisit our purpose.'

Listening to the three partners talk, I became aware of both the common ground they shared and the different perspectives they held. There was a mutual desire to find a way for the agency to flourish, as they had agreed to hand the business over to the new leaders. Beyond that, there were some significant differences.

Otto talked enthusiastically about the new articulation of the company's purpose that the 'transition team', who'd been commissioned to take this on, had come up with. His question was how the new purpose could be a real differentiator so that they created positive change in the world *and* became an agency that new clients proactively sought out.

Craig, a co-founder, shared that when he'd tried out this new purpose statement with a client, it had fallen flat. He spoke of the need to feel confident about the new purpose with frontline staff and in a business-to-business setting – and he was a long way from that.

Mark, the other co-founder, stayed silent and I wondered whether he was engaged with the purpose question at all. When he did eventually speak, he sounded more focused on what the next chapter of his life would look like as he'd given so much of his time, energy and passion to the business.

What became clear was the need for the partners to have an authentic dialogue to explore all their different perspectives. The question was: How could they stay curious long enough for new insights to surface? To what extent would they be willing to risk saying what really needed to be said even though it might cause discomfort? How could they 'hold' the tension of their different views so that a new expression of their purpose could emerge?

As I sat there listening, I became aware of the need to steady myself for what might be an emotional rollercoaster. Talking about what really matters, particularly about purpose, makes a conversation challenging and catalytic. I placed my feet flat on the ground, sat up a little straighter and took a deeper breath – became more present – ready to go on the journey with them.

* * *

Becoming powered by purpose involves leaders grappling with big questions: Why are we here? What are we about? What do we offer that truly engages our stakeholders? While this is not easy territory to navigate, it is hugely rewarding when we do. As a consultant, I have seen many times across numerous settings how leaders who engage in meaningful conversations about purpose start to shift their perspective on what they are here to do.

Creating the conditions where questions about purpose can be explored is a critical skill. Many leaders want to leverage the benefits of being purpose-driven but will only do so when they are able to engage in effective dialogue with their stakeholders. If leaders simply do more of the same – restructuring, reviewing targets, refining processes – nothing significant will change.

Transforming an organisation to become more purpose-driven requires business-as-usual to be interrupted and disrupted in many ways. Meetings need to go beyond the typical dynamic of one or two people dominating the conversation. A purpose-led approach is about diverse team members each contributing to bring purpose to life and dealing with the inevitable messiness of conflict along the way.

The good news is that creating an environment for a deeper dialogue is easier than many leaders think. There are several practical steps and tools that make a real difference, and I'll come to these shortly. To give you an overview, this chapter addresses these vital areas:

- What dialogue is and isn't.
- Why authentic dialogue matters.
- Three ways to generate real dialogue.

WHAT IS DIALOGUE?

Not every exchange of words is a dialogue. A shouting match is not a dialogue. A debate in Parliament is not a dialogue. A presentation with a short question-and-answer session tacked on at the end is not a dialogue. Two people talking over each other and not listening is not a dialogue. As it has been said, 'Two monologues do not make a dialogue.'

One way to understand dialogue is to explore how it differs from other forms of conversation. Understanding these different types of verbal interaction, which are laid out in the Conversation Continuum below helps leaders and teams to carve out the time that true dialogue calls for.

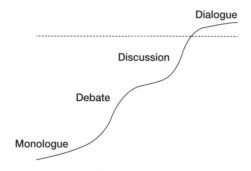

The Conversation Continuum

Moving from the simplest form of verbal interaction (monologue) to the most skilled (dialogue), the four different types of communication are:

- **Monologue.** One person speaks and the other/s listen. A leader holding a 'townhall' to transmit a message to a large audience can be an effective way to communicate. The risk is, however, that the other people aren't fully engaged. The speaker is often 'downloading' information that they already know and others switch off.

- **Debate.** An exchange where one person puts forward an argument to support their point of view and another challenges it with a counter-argument. While this can be lively as people 'nail their colours to the mast', it often results in people taking fixed positions and becoming entrenched. The combative atmosphere limits learning.

- **Discussion.** A conversation where people analyse options and try to decide on a way forward. The root of the word 'discussion' is the same as 'percussion' and 'concussion' and means to 'shake apart' or 'break down'. While a discussion can be a useful way to explore the respective pros and cons, it rarely leads to fresh thinking.

- **Dialogue.** A meaningful conversation where people think together about new possibilities. Coming from the Greek, *dia,* meaning 'through' and *logos* meaning 'word', the essence of dialogue is the flow of meaning that comes through an exchange of words. When people slow down and speak about what is moving through them in the moment, new ideas and deeper insights emerge.

You'll see that there's a dotted line on the Continuum. While many teams know how to have a monologue, debate or discussion, there is typically a threshold to cross in order to have a dialogue. Without getting across this line, leaders will continue to do what they've always done. New outcomes only emerge when leaders think and talk together differently.

There is a risk that we might think a real dialogue is about us sharing our every thought, judgement or feeling. It is not. Shooting from the hip (or the lip) will not take us there. I share a few observations below about what I've learnt over the years looking back upon want makes an *authentic* dialogue actually take place. Before you read these, you might like to explore your own experience, to see what's true for you. Think about a time you spoke with someone when there was a difficult issue to discuss and you were able to speak your truth as well as listen to the other person's truth. How did you feel during the conversation? How did you feel after the conversation? What does this tell you?

An authentic dialogue might not feel 'nice' at the time but it does feel true. The overall state it leaves you in is clearer, more lucid; it might even feel revelatory. You may, however, have experienced some discomfort along the way to arrive at this place.

These are the key elements I've observed that help a team to have an authentic dialogue:

- **Participation.** Everyone who is present participates. For some this might involve being very vocal; for others it might mean that they say less. What matters is that each person feels engaged and energised, whatever their level of contribution.

- **Honesty.** Individuals speak about what's in their hearts and minds. They say it as it is for them. They are willing to be vulnerable and risk others disagreeing with them. People stay in touch with their own experience.

- **Respect.** When someone says what's true for them, everyone else listens. Different points of view are acknowledged as being legitimate, even if there is disagreement. People welcome diversity of perspective as the best ideas emerge from synthesis.

- **Not knowing.** There is a willingness to sit with 'not knowing' what the way forward is. A leader may need to guide people through uncomfortable moments, so that the group doesn't go back into politeness or even silence, as this is often where the transformative learning is.

- **Co-creation.** No one tries to control the conversation. People understand that everyone has a piece of the puzzle. The dialogue flows where it goes. People 'trust the process' and allow the unexpected to come through.

Unlike monologue, debate or discussion, dialogue opens up new possibilities. By talking with one another, a leadership team can agree who they are, what they're about and why they exist. A group of thoughtful, committed individuals can change the world when they are able to talk and think together about their purpose and how to bring it to life.

WHY TALKING ABOUT PURPOSE MATTERS

Including purpose in a dialogue helps to create several shifts in mindset. While shifting mindsets takes time and skill, it enables a business to move forward. As Einstein famously said, we cannot solve a problem at the same level at which the problem was created.

Having a purpose-centred dialogue shifts the conversation onto another level of thinking. Addressing the wider context of 'why' helps to unify participants (who might be from competing departments) beyond their individual demands to a higher-level goal. This stops a team 'fire fighting' or 'feeding the beast' (as they called it in one organisation where leaders spent all their time preparing reports and presenting to the executive committee). When purpose is included in the conversation, the following themes are covered:

- **A longer-term focus.** The typical strategic plan has a five-year window. A CEO is often in place for around four years. Purpose-driven business is, by contrast, not a short-term endeavour; it is about creating value for the business, wider society and future generations.

- **Bigger issues.** Instead of focusing on empire building, being purpose-driven calls on leaders to attend to how their organisation will contribute to a sustainable future by making a difference (see Chapter 6).

- **People- rather than process-centred.** Caring about relationships is critical for purpose-driven leaders who need to connect with a broader set of stakeholders than in the world of shareholder primacy.

THREE WAYS TO GENERATE AUTHENTIC DIALOGUE

In my experience, there are three key ways that leaders can deepen a dialogue about purpose, which I cover in the rest of this chapter. These are:

1. Create a 'container' or 'safe space' in which people can talk and think together about what really matters.
2. Engage in deep listening in order to surface a way forward that serves the whole system.
3. Recognise the different 'fields' that a conversation moves through in order to navigate conflict and generate fresh insights about purpose.

CREATE A 'CONTAINER'

To shift common stuck patterns of talking tough, talking nice or not talking at all, leaders need to attend to not only the words that are spoken but to more subtle aspects of communication. Our tone of voice matters, as does the quality of our presence and the clarity of our intent.

For team members to be meaningfully engaged with purpose, it helps to create a 'container' for a different kind of conversation. Container comes from the Latin *con*, meaning 'with', and *tener,* meaning 'to hold'. The essence of a container is, therefore, the sense of being held. Our attention is held, our energies are engaged, and our minds are open.

Typically, however, many meetings fall flat at the outset because the container is deficient. Board members sit stiffly around a table, one or two team members dominate the conversation or a deck of PowerPoint slides takes centre stage. Such meetings can quickly be dismissed as yet another 'talking shop' where views are apparently exchanged but nothing really changes.

Bringing purpose to life will not happen unless unhelpful rules of engagement – people defending their positions from opposing trenches, macho posturing, puerile point-scoring – are perturbed and disturbed. Without a container, the conversation is unlikely to drop into a deeper space where authentic purpose can come into view.

A container is created when people bring their full presence to the room (as we explored in the previous chapter). As people feel safe to voice their half-formed ideas and discover new meanings, their energies gather together. The atmosphere starts to deepen. This shift in the shared 'field' allows a flow of new ideas – for example about bringing a compelling purpose to life – to move through the room.

Global thought leader (and former working colleague) Bill Isaacs has popularised the concept of a 'container' for productive dialogue. In his article 'Conversations that Change the World',[1] Bill describes the remarkable breakthroughs that occurred when he facilitated dialogue at steel plants where the issues to be discussed were hot, conflict was rife and the atmosphere was tense.

The steelworkers were familiar with physical containers. Large cauldrons, where molten metal was mixed with oxygen and chemicals, were used to contain a dangerous and potentially explosive process. Bill saw a parallel on the human level: a holding environment was also needed to manage the highly charged energies between the executives and union leaders. After several months of bi-weekly meetings, both sides began to collaborate and work together towards a common set of goals. They had gradually created a 'container' that was able to stand – and transform – the heat of human exchange.

Having worked myself as a dialogue facilitator at oil refineries, I have seen how re-patterning relationships results in better business performance. In my previous book,[2] I shared the story of how, during a fierce fight between management and union side, a moment of human connection became a critical turning point. Respect, curiosity and authenticity catalyse a different kind of conversation.

With a strong container, our creativity goes to the next level. A team is able to attune to their collective purpose that no one could have come up with by thinking alone. A vibrant purpose statement 'pops' effortlessly into view. The conditions in which a conversation takes place matter. A purpose statement written in a rush won't stick. As the quality of the container expands, so does the possibility of creating a purposeful organisation.

START WITH A CHECK-IN

To create a container, there is a simple and practical thing that you can do. At the start of a meeting, instead of getting down to business straight away, take some time to meet as fellow human beings. Make sure that this is a meaningful, not a cursory exchange, otherwise it will put people off more than engage them.

Invite everyone who's present to say something in response to a prompt that creates a respectful, friendly and informal tone (more on prompts below). Setting a pattern of full participation early on makes it more likely that people will stay energised throughout.

How to create a container

1. Think about an important conversation you have coming up. What's a question you could use as a check-in at the start of the meeting? For example:

   - 'What's your best outcome for this meeting?'
   - 'What most energises you about becoming more purpose-driven?'
   - 'Which stakeholder do you think this meeting could most benefit? Why?'

   At the meeting itself, write up the check-in question (or questions) on a flipchart. This helps people to keep on track when anxiety levels might be running high.

   If needs be, follow the check-in with a second short 'round' of people sharing their name, role and any other more formal information. But go for the human touch first!

2. Be willing to go first in the check-in, if needed. Reflect on how you can show up as authentically as possible. To help you to gather your thoughts, ask yourself:

   - What is it that I most want to communicate? What does this conversation mean to me?
   - If I were to share a vulnerability around the topic of this conversation, what might it be and how could I share it?
   - Imagine someone you respect encouraging you to be brave. What would they want you to say?

   This is not about rehearsing a word-perfect check-in but setting an intention to be real. The more present and vulnerable you are, the more quickly you'll create a container.

3. Explore other ways to encourage conversational turn-taking. For example:

   - Take a short time-out half way through the meeting to reflect on how it's going. Say, 'Let's take a pause here and see how we're doing.'
   - Do a quick 'go-round' after a break. Say, 'Let's hear one word from each person so we have a sense of how the meeting's landing so far.'
   - End a meeting with a 'check-out' to bring a sense of closure. Ask, 'What do you need to say in order to feel complete?'

> Overall, aim for a strong start and a strong finish. Keep in mind the big difference it makes if everyone participates. As the conversation progresses, notice who's *not* speaking. At an appropriate moment, invite the people who've been quieter to share some thoughts.

Starting a meeting with a 'check-in' might be the single, most powerful change you can make to improve the quality of your dialogue. Give each person the chance to speak and be listened to. Help those who struggle to find their voice to make a contribution early on as it's easier to speak again after having spoken once.

ENGAGE IN DEEP LISTENING

Another critically important element that a leader can bring to purpose-based conversations is better listening. To stay attuned to purpose, leaders need to be sensitive to the wider environment as well as to the people they lead, who often know more about local matters than they do. Deeper listening enables new insights to emerge, whether these are about where an organisation wants to go, what customers are waiting for or disruptive shifts happening in the marketplace.

Will Butler-Adams, CEO of the hugely successful, purpose-driven Brompton Cycles, demonstrates this more responsive way of leading. In 2018 Brompton reported that commuters switching from public transport to pedals helped power a 15% jump in annual turnover – to £33m – after they moved to a new factory in London. Butler-Adams recognises that solutions to problems are to be found everywhere in an organisation. His job is to give others the space to pioneer and to listen to their ideas. He's clear that although he's the boss, he doesn't tell people what to do. He gives them direction and encourages them to meet others outside the organisation for new inspiration.[3]

To be an effective propagator of purpose, it is essential that a leader learns to listen well. The Listening Spectrum tool is a powerful tool that improves listening by raising awareness of habits that get in the way. Dik Veenman, founder of The Right Conversation, introduced me to this model, which I have adapted for my own work (shown in the following figure). Exploring this continuum not just conceptually but experientially has led to some great results. Following some team dialogue, I lay out the spectrum on the floor and invite leaders to stand at the point that best represents where they were during the time we talked.

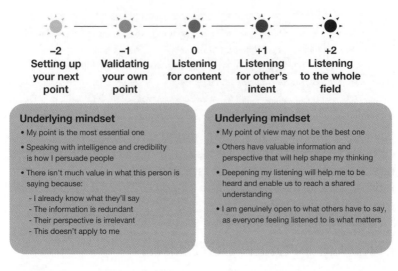

The listening spectrum (adapted from The Right Conversation)

When leaders stand on the spectrum, they quickly 'get' that being at different points feels distinct in their bodies. They report feeling much better towards the 'mutual learning' (+1 or +2) end of the spectrum than at 'unilateral control' (−2 or −1):

- −2: body tight and tense, shoulders hunched, eyes glaring, chest puffed up.
- −1: body has a sense of 'holding on' or 'gripping', arms folded, chin jutting out.
- 0: body is neutral, neither leaning in nor leaning out.
- +1: body starts to relax, jaw unclenched, arms unfolded.
- +2: body has a sense of ease, chest opened, shoulders dropped, back straight.

When we make a habitual pattern of action – such as listening – conscious, an invisible phenomenon starts to show itself. We start to notice what feels good and what doesn't. We become aware of what relaxes us and what makes us go tense. We wake up to the impact that a habit, such as setting up our next point, has on us and others. When we become aware of what feels better, we are more likely to move in that direction.

NAVIGATE CONFLICT TO ARRIVE AT 'FLOW'

Many leaders – in organisations, politics and civil society – struggle to talk about big issues. Recent research shows that avoiding tough conversations is the number one obstacle that stops organisational effectiveness. In her most recent book, *Dare to Lead,* Brené Brown, best-selling author and top TED talker, reports that more than half of the leaders identified the cultural norm of 'nice and polite' as the main block to having difficult conversations.[4]

To encourage more healthy exchange, it helps enormously if leaders have an understanding of how dialogue moves through a sequence of conversational 'fields'. Understanding this rhythm helps a team to settle into talking together as a full picture around purpose does not happen in the first hour of a meeting. It takes time – and a willingness to navigate conflict – for deeper insight to come through.

At the heart of purpose-led leadership is being willing to take a stand for what we believe in and to reach out to talk with diverse stakeholders. We need to stay curious, be generous and stick with the messiness of emergence. We take a break when needed and circle back, if necessary, to arrive at a deeper understanding of what our purpose is. Dialogue is not, however, a linear process to get there and teams often need some tools to help them find their way.

Understanding that there are four 'fields' of conversation to move through equips leaders to have more generative dialogue. Drawing on the work of Otto Scharmer,[5] the flow of dialogue unfolds as follows:

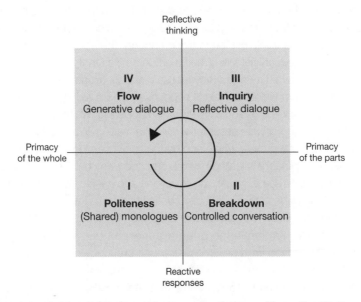

The four fields of conversation: navigating conflict effectively

- **Field I – Politeness/Shared monologues.** People say what they think they're expected to say. Talking is superficial and clichéd responses are common. The atmosphere is stiff. Rather than listening fully to one another, there is a series of individual monologues.

- **Field II – 'Breakdown'/Disturbance.** People start to say how it really is. Differences of opinion come in as people begin to express what's actually on their minds. As conflict starts to surface, the energy in the room increases and the atmosphere intensifies.

- **Field III – Inquiry/Reflective dialogue.** People listen to one another without interrupting. They slow down and become curious about their own and others' thinking. They respect others' perspectives even when they don't agree with them. The atmosphere is reflective rather than reactive.

- **Field IV – Flow/Generative dialogue.** People start to talk together and think together in creative ways. New insights emerge. There might be a sense of the group speaking with one voice, as a flow of collective intelligence moves through the room. The atmosphere is enlivening, energising and, for some, even sacred.

The move from Field I to Field II is a critical moment. When someone speaks their truth, even though it might be uncomfortable, it takes the group out of being 'nice and polite' to one another and into a more authentic space.

Many teams get stuck in a loop between Fields I and II – politeness and breakdown. When someone starts to disturb the pattern of being nice by speaking a hard truth, asking a provocative question or asserting a dissenting opinion, if the container isn't strong enough, the conversation swings back into more superficial talk. When a group senses that a topic is too hot to handle, they avoid it unless they feel safe enough to go there.

The move from Field II to Field III happens when we stop giving opinions and stay curious. We inquire into what's really happening. We might ask others how they're feeling or what assumptions they're making. We might express a desire to understand more where another person is coming from. We might acknowledge someone's feelings, which don't go away but fester if ignored, and ask people to say more. Asking questions with genuine curiosity and no judgement is our best ally when a disturbance has come into the room.

Moving into Field IV – generative dialogue – is what will really bring purpose to life. I'm reminded of an experience I had with a group of bankers who moved from politeness, through breakdown into inquiry and then flow, when they talked about their organisational purpose. I share this story later (see page 159) to show that while the Four Fields model is elegant on paper, it is even more powerful as an embodied experience.

I've walked teams with as many as 60 members through the four fields by laying the two dimensions on the floor using masking tape and labelling the four quadrants with coloured pieces of card. As we stand together in the different fields, I invite team members to notice what they feel, sense and intuit as they become present to the four atmospheres.

The rich sensory data that comes through helps people to face their fears and galvanise their energy to have authentic dialogue. When people have the chance to physically stand in the field of 'breakdown', they often notice that they feel energised and alive. This phenomenological data helps to counter prior assumptions that conflict always feels tense and should therefore be avoided.

'I'm thinking with my body', as one leader put it.

The challenge is not that there are sometimes difficult issues to discuss, but that people feel unable to talk about them. By developing their ability to navigate the Four Fields, leaders are more likely to hear unfiltered bad news, tune into untapped ideas and get comfortable with being uncomfortable.

For a team to talk meaningfully about purpose, or any other hot topic, they need to turn conflict into a more generative conversation. By understanding that 'the only way out is through' (as the saying from therapy goes) disagreement becomes a less scary space to be. To arrive at a place of deeper insight or 'flow', a team needs to navigate its way through a field of friction and into a more creative space.

Given the lack of authentic dialogue, organisations are currently working at a fraction of their capabilities. Many people prefer to remain silent rather than risk their sense of belonging, need to fit in and career prospects by speaking out. As ever-increasing competitive pressures call for harnessing collective intelligence to bring purpose to life, developing the capacity for better dialogue has never been a more pressing imperative.

How to navigate conflict

Identify a challenging conversation that you've had. This could have been with a client, in your own team or in another setting. It may have been face-to-face, on video conference or on the telephone, with one other person or several others. It might have involved:

- dealing with criticism/negative feedback
- an unresolved conflict among team members
- a discussion about a contentious issue.

1. Think back to some of the key things that the other person/s said. Imagine you're back in the conversation. Practise some active listening as if you were speaking to the person for real:

   ■ 'What I'm hearing you say is ...' or 'It seems like you're saying ...'

   ■ 'It makes sense to me that you ... given that ...'*

   ■ 'I imaging you might be feeling ...'

2. Reflect on what the other person *didn't* say that might have been significant. What can you recall of their facial expression, tone of voice and body language? What does this reveal to you? What might have been different if you'd found a way to include the unspoken in your conversation?

3. Think about your team or a group that you are regularly in conversation with. Look at your conversation through the lens of the Four Fields:

   ■ What's been your experience of moving from 'Politeness' into 'Breakdown'? What have been the trigger/s? Who said or did what?

   ■ What's happened after a disturbance? If the group went back into Politeness, how could you have intervened for a different outcome?

   ■ What would helpful 'Inquiry' look like? What would you say? How might you enable others to stay curious and deepen their understanding?

---

*For example, you might say 'It makes sense to me that you want to sell 10,000 more packages this month given that our shareholders' biggest concern is that we make a bigger quarterly sales number.'

USE INQUIRY TO DEEPEN A DIALOGUE

For leaders to have more authentic dialogue, we have seen that questions are a valuable ally. Research shows that while low-performing teams get stuck in asserting opinions without seeking to understand where others are coming from, high-performing teams bring their curiosity.[6] Top teams have a healthy balance between 'advocacy' and 'inquiry'. They operate in the top right-hand quadrant of the following figure, where as many questions are asked as opinions given.

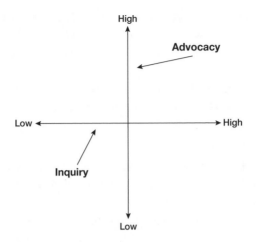

Advocacy – To say, voice, promote, announce, suggest, advise
Inquiry – To ask, inquire, probe, explore, learn, listen, find out

Advocacy and inquiry: two key dimensions of dialogue

For a leadership team to become more purpose-driven, there are several key questions to explore together. I have adapted these questions from a piece of research carried out by *Blueprint for Better Business,* an independent UK charity. The focus of their study was: How can an investor tell the difference between a company that is authentically pursuing a purpose beyond profit and a company that has undergone a slick communications exercise?

Blueprint found that there were eight crucial questions for investors to ask a CEO, chair or other senior executives. These arose out of a conversation they convened among leading investors from a range of asset management companies, whose combined assets under management were worth over $8 trillion.[7]

A PURPOSE-REALITY CHECKLIST

1. In simple terms, what is our organisation in business to deliver and for whom? How does that differentiate us? Why do we even exist?
2. What does success look like and how do we measure and review it?
3. How does our pay policy link to long-term success?

4. What's the quality of dialogue like in our leadership team? How are our conversations connected with our purpose as an organisation? Can we give examples of how our corporate purpose has changed our decisions?

5. What positive and negative impacts does our organisation have on society? How are we maintaining our 'licence to operate'?

6. How are our people feeling? Can we give examples of how we've responded to specific concerns?

7. Which external relationships are most important to achieving our purpose (e.g. customer, supplier, regulatory)? What key measures do we use to assess the strength of these?

8. How do we, as a leadership team, know that we're doing a good job?

Using inquiry about purpose and identity is a powerful move to make in a conversation. My colleague, Rob Lake, has some powerful stories to share. He tells of the difference it makes when questions about identity, along with purpose, are brought into the room. Rob is the founder of Authentic Investor, a not-for-profit initiative that seeks to align purpose, values and sustainability with day-to-day work in investment organisations.

Rob and I run leadership programmes for leaders who have designated RI (responsible investment) or ESG (environmental, social and governance) responsibility. These often-unacknowledged change agents face real challenges as they seek to influence their stakeholders to make investment decisions that include sustainability.

In his insightful article, 'Is this who we really are? The power of quiet questions',[8] Rob includes two real-life stories that involved members of investment committees – one at a pension fund, the other at a New York private equity firm – who had discovered the positive impact of using inquiry about purpose and identity with committee members.

In the stories are several things that are common in many organisations when people face difficult decisions and ethical dilemmas:

- **Avoidance of the real issues.** Voicing concerns openly makes many of us feel shaky, particularly when the stakes are high. Better to stay silent, we tell ourselves, than to rock the boat and risk derailing my career.

- **'Corridor conversations'.** People discuss how they really feel outside the meeting room. 'Elephants in the room' remain unless they are openly addressed in a forum where people feel able to speak freely and explore 'undiscussables' together.

- **Pressure to conform.** Even though team members have misgivings, they decide to toe the line. They carry on with a standard process rather than push back on a partner's or senior leader's request that they know is misguided.

Asking questions about purpose and identity is a powerful way to interrupt these disabling patterns. By including something beyond the numbers on a spreadsheet, the protagonists enabled their colleagues to have a much richer dialogue than the usual business-as-usual discussion. As a result, the decision was taken not to pursue investments that would have been ethically questionable and potentially damaging to the organisation.

How to shift a conversation onto another level

Here are some questions that will help you prepare to convene an authentic dialogue:

1. What is your typical communication style? To what extent do you balance asking questions with giving opinions? How can you bring more curiosity to your conversations? For example, you could say:

   - 'What interests me most right now is ...'
   - 'Help me to understand x ...'
   - 'What am I missing here that might make all the difference to my understanding?'

2. What issues lie 'beyond the spreadsheet' or the technicalities you're dealing with? What questions can you ask so that your team talks about what really matters? You might try the following:

   - 'What are your biggest concerns about this situation?'
   - 'What's at risk if we do make a change? What's at risk if we don't?'
   - 'Who do we choose to be as an organisation? How will our decision about x reflect that?'

3. Revisit the Purpose Reality Checklist on page 99. Think about your team and notice the question that jumps out most at you. What new insights might a dialogue about the stand-out question generate for your team?

THE HOME OF THE BRAVE

Returning to the story that this chapter began with, the three partners at fst agreed a way forward. They explored, rather than ignored, their differences and found some common ground. Through dialogue and a 'constellation' (see page 136) brilliantly led by Ed Rowland, they saw that a more potent organisational purpose than the one they'd lived but never really articulated was possible.

In order for their new purpose to aid day-to-day decision making and generate confidence among their clients, the partners agreed that it needed to be 'sticky' and co-created with the three future leaders of the business.

When Otto and I caught up a year later, he shared how the 'big conversation' around purpose had been pivotal to the 'legacy deal' they'd agreed to enable fst to flourish. Without the new purpose (backed up with a mission, vision and value proposition), the three new leaders wouldn't have felt comfortable taking on full ownership of the business.

It had taken the six of them several months to arrive at a new articulation of fst's purpose so that their employees would continue to feel they're making a positive difference, while developing their careers, and their clients would strive to do the unexpected rather than do the same things over and over again, which would eventually bring any organisation down.

'We don't need a cravat and a pocket full of buzz words to be good at what we do', Otto said. 'But having an ongoing dialogue about our purpose – 'to create a world less expected' – has been emotional, fulfilling and team-binding. Our purpose underpins all our decisions – the clients to go after, turn down or do pro bono work with. And, as 'the home of the brave', it keeps us true to the energy that we founded the business with'.

SUMMARY

- Dialogue differs from monologue, debate and discussion. Authentic dialogue is about talking and thinking together about what matters most.

- Including purpose in a dialogue enables a team to make several shifts in mindset: a focus on the longer term and the bigger issues beyond the spreadsheet.

- Creating a safe and energising 'container' is essential for people to talk. Using a 'check-in' at the start of a meeting encourages people to participate fully.

- Deeper listening supports the exploration of purpose. Each person will contribute their best ideas when they feel valued and heard.

- A dialogue that unfolds through four conversational 'fields' – 'politeness', 'breakdown' 'inquiry' and 'flow' – makes a deeper exploration of purpose possible.

- To make dialogue authentic, stay curious and ask questions that focus people's minds on purpose, such as *'Who do we choose to be as an organisation? How will our decision about* x *reflect that?'* Balance asserting opinions with genuine inquiry that comes from a place of not knowing.

- Questions about purpose and identity encourage people to talk about what their organisation is really about and helps to resolve ethical dilemmas.

NOTES

1. Isaacs, W. (2017) Conversations that change the world, *Strategy+Business*, 8 February.
2. Rozenthuler, S. (2019) *How to Have Meaningful Conversations,* Watkins: London.
3. Spotlight: Keeping Pace with a Changing Workplace, *New Statesman*, May 2016.
4. Brown, B. (2018) *Dare to Lead: Brave Work, Tough Conversations, Whole Heart*, Penguin Random House.
5. Scharmer's model of the Four Fields appears in Isaacs, W. (1999) *Dialogue and the Art of Thinking Together*, Bantam Doubleday Dell Publishing Group.
6. Losada, M. and Heaphy, E. (2004) The role of positivity and connectivity in the performance of business teams: A nonlinear dynamics model, *American Behavioural Scientist*, 47(6), 740–65.
7. Adapted from Blueprint for Better Business (May 2018) *How can investors identify purpose-led companies?* See http://www.blueprint-forbusiness.org/wp-content/uploads/2018/05/Blueprint-how-can-investors-identify-a-purpose-led-company-May-2018.pdf.
8. Lake, R. (2018) Is this who we really are? The power of quiet questions, originally published on *LinkedIn,* 5 July.

CHAPTER 6

ENGAGE YOUR STAKEHOLDERS

Leadership is becoming less about being the smartest in the room and much more about how we collaborate, work with diverse stakeholders, inspire and bring the best out of others.[1]

Professor Peter Hawkins

An organisation has much more to offer the world than just its products and services. It has its intellectual property, financial resources and industry expertise, along with a community of talents and a field of stakeholders. It is an energetic entity with a voice. All of these assets can deliver a great service to customers, sustainable returns to shareholders and advance society's well-being. At the heart of becoming purpose-driven is looking beyond the limited landscape of traditional stakeholders to serve a broader array of beneficiaries.

Let's see what this means for one leader.

* * *

'What a beautiful afternoon!'

Jen Morgan, the executive director of the Psychosynthesis Trust (an educational charity), had called me on the dot of 4pm, as arranged. It was good to hear her bright hello.

'I'm sitting here looking out of the window,' she continued. 'The London skyline is glinting in the September sunshine, although I'd rather be out walking in the woods.'

Jen had asked to have a chat about fine-tuning the organisation's strategic narrative. I'd felt energised from the moment I'd read her email but, right now, I too could feel the lure of the warmth outside.

'I want to re-invigorate our purpose,' Jen shared. 'The Trust was founded to benefit individuals and society through teaching, therapy and personal development. Fifty years on, we're now at a critical stage of development. Our founding purpose – to bring the soul back into psychology – still feels important but we now want to scale our work and make a greater contribution to shifting human consciousness during these turbulent times.'

I felt a flutter of excitement move through me.

'Why do you think that crystallising a more potent purpose will help?'

I was genuinely curious. While clarity of purpose will strengthen any organisation, I was aware of the risk of 'chunking up' to purpose to avoid more primary matters. Were people feeling excluded? Was there any long-standing conflict? Was morale low? A so-called 'spiritual bypass' is as possible in a corporate setting as it is in a personal one.

'What's the core issue that you think a re-invigorated purpose will address?'

'Our business model is unique in that our Programme Delivery Team trainers have work and projects outside of the Trust. Partly because of this a deeper sense of togetherness is missing. We need a new articulation of our shared purpose that is true to what we teach – going beyond personal self – so that all our stakeholders can align around it. Our purpose needs to express what we care about and the positive impact that the Trust wants to have. It needs to have more of a … "feeling" dimension to it.'

'What do you currently think is the essence of your purpose?'

'Helping people to become more of who they are.'

I noticed that I felt flat as she said it. The purpose did indeed need some more life force.

'Anything else you'd like the purpose to be about?'

'I'd like it to provide a strategic direction. Some staff are fearful of growth. Several of the trainers have been around a long time and have really been the lifeblood of the organisation. And there's also a risk of their habitual ways of doing things limiting the organisation's evolution.'

There was a thoughtful pause.

'I want to lift the organisation. The "living being" of the Trust deserves to have greater visibility and voice. We do some amazing work – and I want it to reach more people.'

Jen continued to speak slowly, as she spoke about what really mattered to her.

'I'm driven to help human systems evolve and align with natural systems. I see myself as a "horse whisperer" for the organisation, tuning into where it wants to go. I'd like us to arrive at a re-articulated purpose that will really light up *all* our beneficiaries.'

'Sure,' I said, smiling.

As I looked out of my own window, I watched a couple of bright orange autumn leaves fall slowly to the ground. I also became aware of how, as Jen had spoken, I could feel the energetic field of the Trust swirling around: the excitement and fear, enthusiasm and resistance, caring and hurt. When I put the phone down, I decided it was time for an afternoon walk of my own.

* * *

A report, 'People on a Mission' (2016), by the Korn Ferry Institute, part of the global executive search firm, found that although the purpose-driven companies they studied have a strong external image, vibrant brand and customer engagement, it is their commitment to their people and wider set of stakeholders that fuels their success.[2]

The Korn Ferry Institute carried out interviews with 30 leaders from 20 different organisations. The companies, which included Etsy, TOMS and Chobani, had to meet several criteria: a visible and authentic purpose, engaged employees, a customer-oriented culture and strong financial results. They found three key conditions that gave rise to superior performance:

- People are the top priority and are encouraged to bring their 'whole selves' to work.
- Senior leaders make decisions based on the organisation's purpose and values.
- Enabling practices to bring purpose to life – such as sharing success stories – exist across the whole organisation.

Korn Ferry also found that, because a potent organisational purpose is larger than the organisation itself, purpose-led leaders actively enlist others. They maintain a 'laser-like focus' on serving all stakeholders, not just shareholders. They mobilise the support of their boards by talking with them about how purpose creates sustainable competitive advantage with its unique ability to unite employees, customers, suppliers, shareholders and investors in a way that few other things can.

Returning to the definition of organisational purpose researched by Dr Victoria Hurth and colleagues (see page 15), a key component of a potent purpose is that it energises and draws together relevant stakeholders. When an organisational purpose feels flat, it is likely that there will be a felt-sense among staff and other stakeholders that the organisation is missing something. A sense of belonging, buoyancy or 'buzz' is often absent. These intangibles might not be visible or even fully known but they can certainly be felt.

To re-invigorate an organisational purpose, leaders need to connect with the hearts and minds of their people, *in that order*. An energising purpose, which has the magnetic power to 'pull' people in the same direction, will never come from our minds alone. We cannot 'think' our way to a potent purpose – we need to harness its energy by feeling it.

To set hearts alight to create positive change, purpose-led leaders need to integrate thinking and feeling, the seen and the unseen, the known and the unknown. To uplift people and performance through a powerful purpose, leaders have to be plugged into the energetic field of their whole system, as well as their whole self (see Chapter 4 on leadership presence) and the meeting room (see Chapter 5 on authentic dialogue). Their antennae detect what vibrates – and drains – these energetic fields.

This is a radically different perspective from the conventional view that sees a leader as a rational, objective and logical part of a bureaucracy. This perspective, which dates back to the rationalists of the eighteenth century, views the organisation as a machine. The dominant mental model for organisations still comes from this mechanical mindset: leaders pull levers, tamper with teams and people are 'cogs' in a machine. This metaphor is consistent with, and gives rise to, a more transactional, command-and-control approach to leadership (see page 38). Purpose-led leadership is a new paradigm, calling for new leadership behaviours and a decidedly different mindset where stakeholder engagement is key.

This chapter covers the following territory:

- What is a stakeholder?
- Why it matters to connect with stakeholders.
- How to connect with stakeholders to re-energise an organisation's purpose.

WHAT IS A STAKEHOLDER?

A critical difference between business-as-usual and business-making-a-difference is the shift from serving shareholders to connecting with a wider set of stakeholders.

There are many definitions of a stakeholder. The one that I have found most helpful is by Mike Clayton in his (2014) book, *The Influence Agenda,* where he offers the following:

> *Stakeholder: Anyone who has any interest in what you are doing.*

A stakeholder could be an individual, a group, a team or another organisation. The word 'anyone' encourages us to cast our net wide. 'Any interest' suggests that they can be interested in what you are doing, how you are doing it or its outcome (intended or unintended). It is also worth noting the alternative definition that Clayton offers, which is just as wide and just as true: a stakeholder is 'anyone who can ruin your day'![3]

The term 'stakeholder' has grown in popularity in the last 50 years. It originally appeared in gambling culture in the early eighteenth century to denote someone who was holding a wager. In the USA and UK, 'stakeholder' became more commonplace following the publication of a seminal business book that focused on business ethics, *Strategic Management: A Stakeholder Approach* (1983) by R. Edward Freeman.[4] The British Prime Minister Tony Blair popularised the term further when he floated the idea of a 'stakeholder economy' in his speech in January 1996 rejecting Margaret Thatcher's idea that 'there's no such thing as society' and replacing it with the idea that we are all stakeholders in our society.[5]

A purpose-driven organisation sees all the people who are impacted by its activities as stakeholders. This turns on its head Milton Friedman's free market view that serving only shareholders through profit maximisation is the business of business. Instead, the purpose movement sees business as being there to serve humanity and the planet, profitably.

Stakeholders include those on the inside and outside of a company. In some organisations, distinct groups make up the company profile: employees and partners or founders and staff. Internal stakeholders might also include family members of a family-owned business if they are actively working inside the organisation.

Those outside the organisation – suppliers, investors, competitors and regulators – are also part of the stakeholder landscape. We might also include future generations who will be impacted by an organisation's actions and decisions. Even though they are not yet directly involved in the delivery of the outcomes, they have an investment in the organisation's performance and outcomes.

External stakeholders also include non-human entities such as animals, nature and the wider environment. NGOs campaigning to protect the planet might be their representative by giving voice to an entity that cannot speak for itself. It is important to include those who might be negatively impacted by a company's actions or products, even though these parties might take time to come to mind. As Mike Clayton writes: 'Projects and change would be easy if it were not for the people involved.'

In *The Influence Agenda,* Clayton tells story of Brent Spar, the oil platform owned by Shell and Esso. In December 1994, the UK Government approved the deep-water disposal of the 137-metre tall platform. Shell, which had responsibility for the decommissioning, explored options, carried out impact assessments and commissioned reports. It finally sought approval from regulators and the UK Government for its plan to tow it into the North Atlantic and use explosives to sink it. Analysis suggested damage to the marine environment would be minimal.

In February 1995, Greenpeace heard about the plan and organised an international campaign in protest. Following widespread boycotts of Shell service stations and the occupation of Brent Spa by 23 activists and journalists, Shell changed its plans for disposal with its decision to use on-shore disposal options, as favoured by Greenpeace and its supporters. Shell put the eventual cost of disposal at £60 million, but this would be much larger if loss of business and reputational damage were included.

Decades of research have found that early engagement of a broad array of stakeholders improves organisational decision making.[6] Around half of organisational decisions fail to achieve their goals. Cognitive biases affect our judgements (such as confirmation bias where we seek information that proves we're right). Where information is ambiguous or limited, we often rely on easily available information such as past practices or 'hippos': the highest-paid person's opinion. Including a diverse range of stakeholders creates a better understanding of the problem and the issues of implementation, including of purpose.

IDENTIFYING YOUR STAKEHOLDERS

While a compelling organisational purpose needs to be driven from and by top leadership, it has to energise the whole ecosystem of stakeholders. When team members feel excited, they accomplish together what they could never achieve separately. When customers feel inspired by a company's products or services they keep coming back for more. When investors are confident that a business has a sustainable future, they choose to take a stake in it. How a leader casts their net wide to include all these different stakeholders in the purpose discovery, articulation and activation process is where we turn our attention next.

How to engage your stakeholders

1. Review the list of stakeholders below. Add any stakeholders that are missing in the blank lines of the column marked 'Stakeholder category'. Take your time to reflect. Some stakeholders who are ultimately affected by your organisation might not immediately come to mind. Ask yourself:

   ■ Who, besides our customers, do we reach or are we involved with?

   ■ Whose needs do we meet or aspire to meet?

   ■ Who might our products and actions unintentionally impact?

2. Identify your key stakeholders. Write a few words to describe the challenges and opportunities they bring. Consider the needs of those on whom the survival of your organisation depends. Are your customers changing their expectations in ways that might impact your future sales? To what extent do staff go the extra mile? Are investors starting to ask questions about purpose-beyond-profit? Is an activist group lobbying for a change?

Stakeholder category	Key challenge and opportunity
Employees	
Shareholders	
Customers	
Suppliers	
Investors/providers of finance	
Communities in which company operates	
Interest groups/activists	
Founder/s	
Board of directors	
Non-executive directors	
Employees' families	
Government/regulators/law makers	
Competitors	
Partners	
Other influencers/the media	
Future generations	

3. Identify three things you can do that will create better stakeholder engagement, for example have a dialogue with a group of activists. What will be your measure of success? Perhaps you agree to re-articulate the purpose of your organisation in a way that satisfies them?

Stakeholder engagement activity	Measure of success
1.	
2.	
3.	

WHY ENGAGING STAKEHOLDERS MATTERS

Recent research by Boston Consulting Group (BCG) has found that companies 'with high purpose scores' enjoy higher than average ten-year total shareholder return (TSR). To deliver this attractive outcome, however, purpose needs to be embraced vigorously by all the participants in a company's broader ecosystem.[7]

In the tech sector – with its unprecedented potential to impact our future – BCG notes that purpose is not living up to its promise. Despite iconic Silicon Valley companies having ambitious ideas of purpose – for example, '[To] organize the world's information and make it universally accessible' (Google) – there has been a growing backlash in response to consumer privacy breaches, antitrust fines and concerns about company culture, reflecting the view that these companies have strayed from their purpose.[8]

BCG's own data reveal a significant and worrying disconnect between having a strong purpose and living it. In a survey carried out in June 2018, they explored perceptions of purpose among employees and management in 15 leading USA-based technology companies. Although 87% of employees surveyed agreed their company has a clear and compelling purpose, only 65% agreed their company would turn down a profitable opportunity if it conflicted with their purpose. Among those who 'strongly' agree that their company has a clear and compelling purpose, this gap was even greater (54% difference).

This disconnect means bringing purpose to life is often incomplete and unclear. To reset purpose, in tech companies and in organisations more broadly, BCG highlights that organisational purpose has two distinct aspects:

- **Aspirational.** An organisation's 'why' needs to engage and energise employees to do great work.
- **Realistic.** Leaders and employees make decisions that align with the organisation's purpose. It is actions that bring the 'why' to life.

A more expansive and grounded view of purpose is needed. Instead of purpose being narrowly defined by referring only to the products or services that a company sells to its customers, the true purpose of a company recognises that shareholder returns are a vital part of a company's existence but they are only one part.

Salesforce is living proof that 'stakeholderism' works, as CEO Marc Benioff calls it. Founded 21 years ago, Salesforce has become a $131bn company, delivering a 3,500% return to its shareholders since becoming a public company in 2004. To create a more equal, fair and sustainable way of doing business, Salesforce focuses on shareholder return and stakeholder return hand-in-hand. It has pioneered the '1-1-1 Model' giving 1% of its product, 1% of its equity and 1% of employee time to philanthropic causes. 9,000 companies have adopted this model of valuing all stakeholders and many more have adopted its principles such as volunteerism, including Apple and PayPal.[9]

On the other hand, it is important that an organisational purpose does not become inflated. Lofty ambitions that are not backed up with decisions and actions that align with purpose, leaves a company open to its products being used and abused by others seeking to cause harm. BCG recommends that technology companies consider a form of 'white hat hacking' of their products to better understand how they can be misused. They note that civic leaders and social commentators are becoming impatient with the response from tech leaders when unanticipated bad outcomes arise that 'we had no idea this could happen'.

None of us wants to look naive or neglectful. Stakeholder engagement and right action is our best bet to mitigate this. When Swedish teenage climate activist Greta Thunberg chastised world leaders for failing to take sufficient steps to stop climate change, she amped up the anger that many people feel with business leaders.

'You have stolen my childhood and my dreams with your empty words,' she said at the United Nations Climate Action Summit in New York on 23 September 2019. 'You're failing us, but young people are starting to understand your betrayal. The eyes of all future generations are upon you.'

Her courage and call for focused action resonated for many around the world. As younger people increasingly find their voice about the future of the planet being at stake, the urgent need for business leaders to engage a broader array of stakeholders has never been greater.

MAP YOUR STAKEHOLDERS

To spur business performance and win trust, leaders need to balance these two aspects of purpose – the inspirational and the 'guard-railing'. This requires leaders to be deliberate in their decisions about who their stakeholders are and how to engage them. With the right stakeholders on board, leaders can evolve their organisation's purpose and ensure that it is properly articulated and embedded.

Connecting with stakeholders is a strategic activity. It requires an ability to see the bigger picture and a mindset of proactive engagement. Drawing a stakeholder map to explore how purpose can unify different groups and strengthen relationships is a great way to start.

To give you a sense of the activity that follows, the following figures are the output that Jen Morgan of The Psychosynthesis Trust created. Don't worry about the detail; what matters is seeing how a leader can quickly see the big picture of how their stakeholders currently relate to one another and the organisation's purpose. There are two maps – the current reality and the desired future – and the differences between them gives insights into actions that are needed to engage stakeholders around purpose.

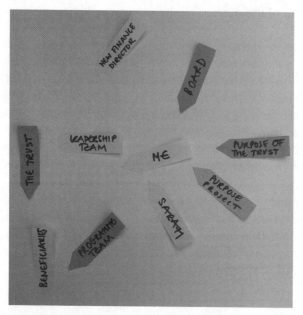

Jen's map of the current reality

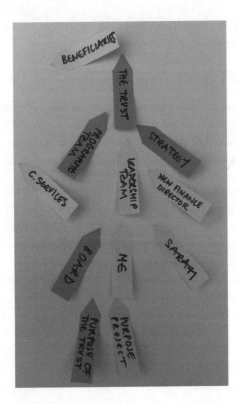

Jen's map of the desired reality

This 'desktop' mapping exercise brings several benefits. It enables a leader to make sense of a complex ecosystem of stakeholders, which might otherwise seem overwhelming, in a creative and even playful way. It helps a leader to see stakeholders who are at risk of being overlooked or ignored or who might be leaving the system. The mapping also reveals where the 'acupressure' points for change are in the stakeholder ecosystem. Rather than becoming entangled or taking things personally, mapping brings a detached clarity so that a leader can see their system more clearly.

I'll say more about the discipline of systemic coaching and constellations, which inspired this exercise later (page 136). In the meantime, seeing which stakeholders need to be energised and engaged is a powerful way to bring purpose more clearly into view.

How to map your stakeholders

Before you begin this activity, gather together some materials. You'll need:

- a pen
- small sticky notes (ideally these are arrow shaped but oblong ones will do)
- a large sheet of blank paper (a sheet of flipchart or A3 paper work well).

Part 1 – Current reality

1. Write your name on a sticky note. Next, identify your six to eight key stakeholders and write each on separate sticky notes (you might find it helpful to review your responses to the previous exercise in this chapter). On each sticky note draw an arrow so that the stakeholder can face a certain direction.

2. Write on an additional sticky note 'Purpose'. This represents your organisation's current purpose. Include an arrow on this sticky note.

3. Place yourself on the 'map' by moving the sticky note with your name on it onto the blank sheet of paper. You might be in the centre or close to the edge. Go with what intuitively feels right, without thinking about it too much.

4. Before you place the other elements, reflect on the current reality that exists between you, your stakeholders and your organisation's purpose. Don't pretend that things are better than they are or ignore any 'hard truths'.

5. Place 'purpose' where you sense it best sits. Next, place each stakeholder on the map (the sequence doesn't matter), tuning into the whole picture as it unfolds. You might need to adjust elements as you go. Pay attention to:

   - **Distance** – the stronger the relationship between stakeholders, the closer you place the sticky notes.
   - **Direction** – the more aligned stakeholders are, the more they go in the same direction.

Part 2 – Desired future

6. Reflect on what the map is telling you. Tune into how the whole field of stakeholders feels. Notice which relationships feel engaged and energised. Take note of where the map feels flat or lifeless.

7. Explore what will strengthen the whole map. This is not about making it better just for you or any other single stakeholder. Your focus is on

▶

energising the whole field by noticing what feels better. You might experiment with the following:

- **Reposition yourself** – place yourself closer to a stakeholder that needs more support or where you find it easier to have a wider perspective on where all stakeholders stand in relation to purpose.

- **Add a stakeholder** – introduce a new element if someone significant or some group is missing.

- **Alter the distance** – bring two stakeholders closer together or further apart if they've become too close.

- **Change the direction** – create greater alignment with the purpose by moving a stakeholder to go in the same direction as the purpose.

8. Reflect on the key differences between the current reality and the desired future. Identify one or two concrete actions that will strengthen the whole stakeholder landscape. You might decide to engage a stakeholder that you've overlooked, invite two stakeholders with competing interests to talk through their perspectives or re-set your purpose through a multi-stakeholder dialogue.

FEELING THE FIELD

Purpose-led leaders are not 'king pins' in a machine but rather, to use Jen Morgan's phrase, 'horse whisperers' who are attuned to energetic fields. As Laloux writes in *Reinventing Organisations,* we can best view organisations as '... an energy field, emerging potential, a form of life ... pursuing its own evolutionary purpose'.[10]

Connecting with the energetic field makes more sense if we tune into how an organisation itself has a life of its own. Walk into a UK hospital and you can feel the spirit of the NHS filling the corridors. Enter the colourful office of a Virgin company and you can sense the stardust that's sprinkled over the brand. Go into the reception area of a financial company headquartered in St James's Square, London and the rarefied atmosphere surrounds you.

Creating a systemic map helps a leader to feel into the energetic field of their organisation. Without a leader using this sensitivity, an organisational purpose will lack power. How to 'feel the field' is something that we can all learn to do. Did you notice during the mapping exercise the vibes stakeholders were giving off? Did your antennae detect how energised different people are? Were you able to tune into the atmosphere? Paying attention to our felt-sense is a potent source of information.

When we draw on our somatic intelligence rather than rely only on our analytical mind, we start to unpack what's going on. When we notice that a stakeholder is energised, a new market is exciting or an evolved purpose statement feels inspiring, we activate our organisation's best future possibilities, based on the best possible data.

The space between us is filled with energy. The stiffness in the boardroom at the start of a meeting is palpable. The air in an office after an argument has taken place feels 'thick'. Humour cracks the static during a speech and we sense the relief. We can feel, in a physical way, what is going on in the energetic field, even though it is unseen, silent and subtle.

The energetic field is a matrix of intertwining, interwoven 'vibes' that people emit. We all transmit energy and we all receive the incoming vibes that others give off. These emanations form a constantly changing, invisible weave that we each feel and feed. From a quantum perspective, the crisscrossing, intermingling energetic field is powerful because it holds physicality together. In a corporate setting, this matrix of interwoven 'vibes' holds an organisation together. Without this energetic 'mesh', things literally fall apart.

We are all connected to this combined energy field through a 'pipeline' of energy exchange. The closer we are physically, the more intense we feel the energy; the further way, the finer is the sense of connection. We are never totally disconnected from anything. We can, however, stay stuck in the illusion of separation. We might appear as individual forms and see the world in terms of objects or individuals, but, ultimately, we're all part of a singular consciousness. The ultimate reality is unity, not separation.

To the extent that a leader 'comes from' the perspective that we are all connected, the more they will be able to shape the future. When a leader 'charges' the field with a compelling purpose that truly serves others, they send positive energy along the 'pipeline'. As we become aware that we are part of a larger force field, an organisational purpose can really light up the whole field of stakeholders.

EXPLORE THE FOUR TYPES OF PURPOSE

When an organisation connects with its true, most compelling purpose, this serves as a powerful energetic wellspring for its people, customers and other beneficiaries. At Lego, the founding purpose – to encourage play and to inspire and develop children – has been the star on its horizon for 85 years. At Plastic Whale, its commitment to generate solutions for plastic-free waters by showing that economic value can be created from plastic has attracted corporate partners and volunteers worldwide. In 2017, its fleet of boats, made out of recycled plastic, took 6,000 people fishing for plastic in the canals of Amsterdam. Their purpose is clear and future-focused. 'We exist to solve a problem,' says Marius Smit, who founded the Dutch social enterprise in 2011, 'We want to go out of business.'[11]

In other organisations, however, leaders can be caught up in the past. Being wedded to the founding expression of an organisational purpose that no longer energises staff or customers is problematic. With Henry Ford's purpose of democratising the motorcar, it is clear to see how this purpose needs updating, given the environmental pressure to reduce carbon emissions.

The founding purpose of an organisation needs to be honoured, but also continually evolved to meet the changing needs of the marketplace. To connect people, performance and profit, an organisational purpose also has to be authentic. Despite good intentions, many 'espoused' expressions of purpose are some distance away from the 'actual' purpose that the organisation embodies, as we saw in the tech companies. If you've ever worked for an organisation that claimed to be about saving the world or improving sustainability but was really about making money, you'll know about the cynicism of the corridor conversations, the suspicion that leaders are only there to line their own pockets and the muted energy of the mission statement pinned to the wall.

To enable leaders to reconcile these different dimensions of purpose, a great tool is at hand. When leaders understand that there are four different types of purpose (outlined in the following figure), they are able to think and talk more effectively about how to articulate, activate and embed a purpose that engages and energises a broad array of stakeholders.

This framework of four types of purpose enables leaders to discover and uncover purpose. Edward L. Rowland (founder of the Whole Partnership) discerned the four levels of organisational purpose and created the original version of the Organisational Purpose Diamond (see the following figure). In our work together, we have used it as a catalyst for dialogue to reveal aspects of purpose that have been hidden from sight and to generate insights about how to evolve the organisation's 'why' in a way that energises stakeholders.

The founding purpose, the espoused purpose, the actual purpose and the most compelling purpose of an organisation are often not the same thing. In

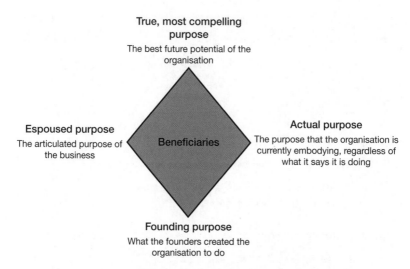

True, most compelling purpose
The best future potential of the organisation

Espoused purpose
The articulated purpose of the business

Beneficiaries

Actual purpose
The purpose that the organisation is currently embodying, regardless of what it says it is doing

Founding purpose
What the founders created the organisation to do

Organisational Purpose Diamond: the levels of purpose
Organisational Purpose Diamond by Edward Rowland and Sarah Rozenthuler (www.wholepartnership.com) is licensed under the Creative Commons Attribution-ShareAlike 4.0 International License.

our work, we have discovered three key insights that lead to organisations being powered by purpose:

■ The founding purpose of an organisation needs to be respected and, at times, updated. It provides insights into the uniqueness of the organisation, which is a source of competitive advantage, as the founding energy cannot be replicated.

■ When the actual purpose aligns with the espoused version, the decisions and actions of leaders and employees are consistent with the organisation's 'why' and this strengthens performance.

■ Including beneficiaries in the dialogue about the four different types of purpose enables the organisation to evolve its purpose to become the true, most potent purpose.

For an organisation to be authentically purpose-driven, its purpose must provide a clear motivational frame for the whole organisation. This is not just about poetic words or high ideals; it is about leaders creating the conditions where people can form a meaningful emotional connection with the purpose and work together to bring it to life. Purpose is not a statement; it is a guiding energy we feel in our body. When purpose no longer provides energy or power, it needs to evolve otherwise an organisation risks becoming irrelevant. To engage stakeholders in a dialogue to evolve organisational purpose, see the following box.

How to create a purpose dialogue

Invite a diverse group of stakeholders to have a dialogue around the following transformative questions. Include in your circle:

- the founder/co-founders
- current beneficiaries
- future leaders
- 'critical friends' who will bring alternative perspectives.

Explore the following questions together. Start with a focus on the past, then move to the present, and finally tune into the future.

Past: founding purpose

- What was the founding purpose of our organisation?
- What have been our authentic and distinctive strengths as a company?
- What need (human or non-human) have we fulfilled, or aimed to fulfill, in society?
- Who would miss us if we didn't exist?

Present: espoused and actual purpose

- What is the currently espoused or stated purpose?

- To what extent does the organisation 'live' this stated purpose? Any gaps?
- To what degree do employees, customers and other stakeholders make decisions in line with purpose of the organisation? To what extent does it light up the ecosystem?

Future: true, most potent purpose

- How much does the organisation's purpose resonate with you personally (or not)?
- What success stories would bring a compelling purpose to life?
- What do our feelings tell us about the true purpose of our organisation?
- What are the next key steps to bring purpose alive in our organisation?

Integration

Now reflect together on the following questions to move forwards:

- What have we learnt about our organisational purpose?
- How does this dialogue leave us feeling?
- What do we sense *is* the true potential of our organisation?

Be as open and as honest as you can. For example, if there are feelings of discomfort about the gap between the 'espoused' and 'actual' purpose, it is important to include these. If there are shared feelings of excitement about the organisation's true purpose, you might have struck gold!

BUILD ON THE FOUNDING PURPOSE

We have a deep hunger for purpose. From 150 interviews and questionnaires carried out with leaders for their book, *The Power of Purpose,* John O'Brien and Andrew Cave found that while the majority of respondents (81%) saw themselves as very 'purpose-powered', only 60% described their organisations in the same way.[12] Given this gap, more leaders need to tune into the true, most potent purpose of their organisation and bring this to life.

In *The Power of Purpose,* it becomes clear that unearthing the energy with which the founders created the company reveals insights into the company's uniqueness. Exploring how this differentiation is still relevant today is a source of meaning and motivation. Let's look briefly at a couple of examples.

At Boots Opticians, Ben Fletcher, the former managing director, describes how they used the purpose with which the larger Boots Group was founded in the nineteenth century as a guide to evolving the organisation's current purpose. Jesse Boot, the founder, had had the simple idea that healthcare should be accessible to everyone regardless of their means.

By revisiting this founding purpose, Boots Opticians were fired up to add to it by crafting purpose statements such as 'We commit to enrich the life of every person' and 'We are a health-led optician and care about a whole lot more'. Having got some clarity about their purpose and what it meant, they then asked themselves, 'What would the business look like if we lived this in every way?'

At TSB, CEO Paul Pester describes how they looked at the history of the bank and talked with customers to evolve their purpose. They explored why there was such vitriol towards banks in the UK following the financial crash in 2008 and what they wanted from banks moving forwards. The clear message from customers was to return to their original purpose of helping communities to thrive and helping hard-working local people to help themselves.

Learning about the bank's heritage was key to crystallising the bank's updated purpose. Henry Duncan, a Scottish vicar, founded TSB in 1810 to help his poorest parishioners. The purpose of the Trustee Savings Bank (as it was called) was to help local labourers out of poverty by giving them access to a bank account. At that time, workers needed £100 to open a bank account, which was roughly the same amount as they earned in a year. TSB, which began in a local church hall, decided that they would, once again, serve the local community of which it is part and nothing else. They have no investment banking, no derivatives trading and no overseas investments. Purpose clarifies what an organisation does *and doesn't* do.

Although a founding purpose can be a source of inspiration to re-set purpose, this is not always the case. The origins of Facebook provide a note of caution. (Full disclosure: I have a Facebook account although it's no longer on my smartphone.) Prior to founding Facebook, Mark Zuckerberg wrote the software for its predecessor, Facemash, when he was in his second year of college. The Facemash website, which opened in 2003, allowed visitors to compare two female student pictures side by side and let them decide who was 'hot or not'. As I watched the Cambridge Analytica debacle unfold in 2017, I found myself reflecting on how the founding energy of an organisation can cast a long shadow if it does not evolve into a more compelling version that the organisation truly lives.

ALIGN THE ACTUAL AND ESPOUSED PURPOSE

The hugely successful outdoor clothing and gear retailer Patagonia is an inspiring example of an organisation where the leaders have worked to bring the actual and espoused purposes of the organisation into alignment. The purpose of Patagonia was defined in 2012 to be: 'Build the best product, cause no unnecessary harm, use business to inspire and implement solutions to the environmental crisis.'[13]

Instead of this being laminated to the wall, it is lived by the whole organisation. Following their visit to Patagonia's headquarters in Ventura, California (and a surfing lesson to boot), Corporate Rebels observed that what's striking about the company is that everything seems to revolve around this purpose.[14] The place has a buzz about it. Each team member is passionate about the product and the societal impact that Patagonia is aiming to have.

Whether they're in social media, the labs or HR, employees consciously contribute to Patagonia's purpose.

Leaders demonstrate their commitment to the purpose – and helping their people to live the purpose – in tangible ways. The founder, Yvon Chouinard, and his wife Malina set up a high-quality on-site childcare centre in the early days to support employees who wanted to start their own families. As a result, the vast majority of women are able to return to work after having children, which helps the company to achieve gender equality.

In the 1990s, the company critically examined its own supply chain and decided to switch from using conventional to organic cotton. Following visits to cotton farms and seeing the impact of chemicals poisoning the soil, air and groundwater, leaders prioritised reducing environmental harm. Even though clothing made from conventional cotton was responsible for 20% of the company's total business, and sales of around $20 million were at stake, the leaders went ahead and communicated their decision transparently to the rest of the team.

More recently, in December 2016, Patagonia donated its entire 'Black Friday' sales to environmental organisations around the globe, about five times above what the company expected. Supporting grassroots nonprofits to take care of our air, water and soil for future generations is in line with their purpose of being a business that implements solutions to the environmental crisis.[15]

Corporate Rebels concluded that the authenticity with which team members lived Patagonia's purpose was unlike anything they'd experienced before. There is no progressive organisational structure or charismatic CEO creating a highly engaged workforce. The purpose is so vibrant that all the Patagonia people are connected with it. Performance is strong and profits are bountiful – the true power of leaders walking the purpose talk.

UNCOVER THE TRUE, MOST POTENT PURPOSE

To crystallise a compelling purpose that inspires positive change, leaders need to be alert to the world around them through communicating with their stakeholders. They need to be attuned to the change they intend to make and to understand their place in the world.

Returning to the story of the Psychosynthesis Trust, Jen Morgan and her leadership team did arrive at a more compelling version of their organisational purpose. Going on this journey took over a year and involved four key phases:

- Firstly, the Organisational Purpose Diamond was used to explore the four levels of purpose, which helped the team to see that a new articulation of the true organisational purpose was needed.

- Secondly, Jen and I mapped the Trust's key stakeholders using the constellating method to ensure that everyone who needed to be included was included and to feel into the energetic field of the organisation.

- Thirdly, highly skilled purpose practitioner Emma Ashru Jones worked in partnership with Jen and the Trust, interviewed key stakeholders and carried out multiple creative workshops revealing dimensions of the new purpose that they would find energising. Emma used these to craft four possible new purpose statements and crystallised their final purpose statement in collaboration with the leadership team.

- Finally, I led a constellations workshop for the leadership team to explore which of four statements was most vibrant by looking through the eyes of the staff, the customers and the alumni (people who'd been through their training programmes).

The final articulation of the Trust's purpose – Bringing about Wholeness in a Fragmented World – felt refreshing, distinctive and inspiring not only to them as a leadership team but to the broader array of stakeholders that they serve.

SUMMARY

- A stakeholder is anyone who has an interest in what an organisation is doing. Stakeholders are internal and external and include nature and the environment, future generations and those who might be adversely affected by the decisions and actions of an organisation.

- Stakeholder engagement is a strategic activity. Leaders need to see the bigger picture of their whole ecosystem in order to uncover an organisation's niche and 'right place' in the world.

- Involving key stakeholders early on in the purpose discovery process reduces bias in decision making and unintended consequences such as reputational damage.

- Mapping stakeholders enables a leader to identify which stakeholders they might be overlooking and where to strengthen relationships in order to activate purpose. It also highlights missing stakeholders who might be critical to bring purpose to life.

- There are four different types of purpose: the founding purpose, the espoused purpose, the actual purpose and the organisation's true, most potent purpose. A multi-stakeholder dialogue to explore these different purposes helps evolve a compelling future purpose and align the espoused and lived purpose.

- Tuning into an organisation as an energetic entity enables a leader to bring purpose to life more fully. Using this sensitivity enables a leader and their stakeholders to form an emotional connection with the organisation's purpose and activate an organisation's best future possibilities.

NOTES

1. Hawkins, P. (2017) *Leadership Team Coaching: Developing Collective Transformational Leadership*, Kogan Page.
2. Korn Ferry Institute (2016) *People on a Mission*, Korn Ferry Ltd.
3. Clayton, M. (2014) *The Influence Agenda: A Systematic Approach to Aligning Stakeholders in Times of Change*, Palgrave Macmillan.
4. Freeman, R.E. (1984) *Strategic Management: A Stakeholder Approach*, Cambridge University Press.
5. Tony Blair quoted in Davies, G. (1996) Tony Blair puts meat on the stakeholder bones, *The Independent*, 16 January.
6. Rousseau, D.M. (2018) Making evidence-based organisational decisions in an uncertain world, *Organisational Dynamics.* See https://www.cebma.org/wp-content/uploads/Rousseau-2018-Organizational-Dynamics-Evidence-Based-Decisions.pdf.
7. Hemerling, J., Swan, J., Kreisman, C.C. and Reed, J.B. (2018) *For Corporate Purpose to Matter, You've Got to Measure It*, Boston Consulting Group Publications, 16 August.
8. Kennedy, D., Hemerling, J., Norton, K., Kreisman, C.C. and Reed, J.B. (2019) *Solving the Tech Industry's Purpose Problem*, Boston Consulting Group & Brighthouse Publication, June.
9. Leaf, C. (2019) *Salesforce Founder Marc Benioff: What Business School Never Taught Me,* Fortune, Inc, 15 October.

10. Laloux, F. (2014) *Reinventing Organizations: A Guide to Creating Organizations Inspired by the Next Stage in Human Consciousness,* Nelson Parker.
11. See https://www.theguardian.com/travel/2018/feb/28/ fishing-for-plastic-amsterdam-canal-tour-with-a-difference.
12. O'Brien, J. and Cave, A. (2017) *The Power of Purpose*, Pearson.
13. See https://www.patagonia.com/company-info.html.
14. Minnaar, J. (2016) The power of purpose: How Patagonia walks the talk. *Corporate Rebels*, 7 December. See https://corporate-rebels. com/patagonia/.
15. See https://www.patagonia.com/100-percent-for-the-planet.html.

CHAPTER 7

CONNECT ON PURPOSE

No one can whistle a symphony. It takes a whole orchestra to play it.

H.E. Luccock

Collaboration is fast becoming a premium capacity for organisations in our interconnected world. It lies at the heart of a purpose-driven business where everyone feels engaged and energised to pull in the same direction. Team members will only be willing to go the extra mile if their environment is supportive. In order to release a free flow of positive energy in their system, leaders need to create a sense of belonging, attend to dysfunctional dynamics and connect their people with a compelling purpose.

Let's take a look at the challenge facing one leader striving to do exactly this.

* * *

Dear Sarah,

A colleague recommended you. I'm the CEO of a large CIC (Community Interest Company), providing health and care services to 350k people and employing 3000 staff. We are amalgamating with a similar organisation in our local area and need to strengthen the cohesiveness and resilience of our senior leadership team (SLT). I would welcome an early conversation about your possible role in this. When could we talk?

Regards,
Adam

When I received this email, I noticed a feeling of both excitement and trepidation. The leadership challenges of today are often, at first glance, chockful of both opportunity and overwhelm. What, I wondered, was the unwritten request here? What was the real work to be done? It is not enough for an organisation to have a compelling purpose; people need to connect with it.

Challenges such as merging with another organisation can create difficult dynamics that might upend even the most robust purpose.

'It's a moment of great uncertainty,' the CEO said, when we met several weeks later. We were sitting in a small meeting room of an office building that had seen better days. The glass atrium overhead was in need of a good clean. More opaque than transparent, it let limited light in. Was that symbolic in some way, I wondered?

'It's a ticking time-bomb,' Adam continued. 'The merger with the other organisation is creating a lot of concerns for my directors. There are no guarantees of transfer of employment so there are real worries about what happens to them. Relationships in the team are strained and, when behaviours become difficult, tribalism sets in.'

I watched as his brow furrowed and his eyes lost some of their shine.

'It's also a time when we need to be on best game. We deliver over 80 services and there are blurred lines between portfolios. The directors cut across one another because they're finding it difficult to trust one another, which creates even more tension. And that's before we join forces with the other organisation.'

'So what do you want?'

'I want us to move from being a group of talented individuals to becoming a high-performing, indivisible and visible team. We need to break out of stuck patterns of finger-pointing and work through these challenges together.'

'Anything else?'

'As a new CEO I'm struggling to make sense of it all. At the moment my brain is a very busy place!'

As our conversation progressed, I'd heard an almost constant stream of email notifications pinging in. I couldn't see his device but guessed that his rapidly filling inbox was also a very full space.

'The technical knowledge that I used to apply to solve problems isn't helping any more,' Adam continued. 'Nor is this a case of who's right or wrong – it's much more complex than that. I'd like us to come together as an SLT to agree how we can be a collective that really serves the people we're here for.'

An hour later, when I walked out of the building, I noticed that my own head was 'busy' with the many issues we'd discussed. A neglected pond in the courtyard caught my eye. The water looked dull, murky grey. Dried out, yellowy plants floated on the surface. No fish swimming here, I thought.

The 'fishtank' metaphor of Dr William Tate from The Institute for Systemic Leadership flashed into my mind. His call for leaders to move beyond focusing on individuals (the 'fish') and see problems as residing more in the quality of the whole 'fishtank' in which they are swimming felt pertinent. When a systemic approach is absent, team members are more likely to fall into the trap of blaming others, taking things personally or fighting their corner.

What would it take to 'clean the fishtank' and release a clear flow of sparkling energy into this system? How could I help this CEO to make sense of the complex world he was trying to navigate? How could he connect his leadership team and growing ecosystem of stakeholders with the 'why' of the CIC – to deliver quality healthcare services and improve patients' well-being – so that the purpose really came to life? As I walked out into the bright sunlight, I sensed it would be a stirring adventure to go on.

* * *

DEVELOP SYSTEMIC INTELLIGENCE

Many CEOs and leaders are feeling overwhelmed. They want to move forward in a way that strengthens the whole system and themselves, but they don't know how. All-too-familiar are the seemingly intractable problems that exist in many organisations:

- Poorly performing teams as a result of difficult and unresolved dynamics.
- 'Turf wars' between ambitious leaders who compete rather than collaborate.
- Unsuccessful external hires who struggle to fit into their new roles.
- In-fighting and conflicts between teams, departments or work groups.
- Failed mergers and acquisitions as the different cultures of the organisations clash.
- An obsession with targets, numbers and metrics as a way of keeping control.
- A lack of strategic direction, as there is no compelling organisational purpose.

Common to all these challenges is the failure of leaders to take a systemic approach. Attempts to 'modernise' the NHS by successive governments, creating untold problems, illustrates this well. The issues in the NHS stem from no one in government having their eye on the whole as they made changes. The 'marketisation' of the NHS, which was intended to increase collaboration between different parts of the system, has had the unintended impact of increasing fragmentation and subverting the energy of improving of people's health and well-being – the true purpose of the organisation.

The NHS is suffering, like many organisations, from silo working, low morale and high turnover. Instead of working together to provide integrated systems of care for patients (particularly for those with multiple diseases), hospitals, GP surgeries, community nursing, the ambulance service and walk-in units are being forced to compete with one another. As each entity tries to protect its budget and ensure that its own performance will meet the benchmarks by which it will be measured next time its contract comes up for renewal, 'perverse and protectionist behaviour ricochets round the system'.[1]

To address unhelpful behaviours, leaders need to remove obstacles impeding the flow of positive energy in a system. In order to do this, leaders need to develop their 'systemic intelligence': the ability to understand a system and intervene skilfully. Purpose will only motivate higher levels of performance, guide day-to-day decision making and become a unifying force for relevant stakeholders when leaders attend to the quality of the environment (or 'fishtank') in which people work. As Dr Victoria Hurth and colleagues state:

> *Without the ownership of purpose by the governing body, and without appropriate cultural leadership and system-wide oversight, the move to purpose is ultimately unsustainable.*[2]

When leaders develop the capacity to connect people with a compelling 'why', purpose can become a lodestar for inspired action and is felt throughout the whole system to be 'right'.

This chapter covers the following:

- What a system is.
- Why it matters to take a systemic approach.
- How to align a system.

WHAT IS A SYSTEM?

A useful and graphic illustration of a system is the image of a child's mobile suspended from the ceiling. When one part of the mobile moves the rest of the mobile moves too. If one part of the mobile is taken away, the remaining parts must find a new balance. The different parts of the 'system' are in an ever-changing, mutual dance with one another.

An organisational system hangs in a delicate balance. Flexible, strong bonds between the constituent parts promote a flow of vibrant energy around the system; brittle bonds limit the onward flow and might break under pressure, leading to system collapse.

A systemic view sees a continuously shifting matrix of relationships. We don't just focus on the 'objects' hanging on the mobile (such as individuals or teams), we pay attention to the whole human relationship system and how the organisation is embedded in its wider environment.

The diagram below shows how various stakeholders co-exist in a constantly changing, interdependent web of relationships. The mobile could also include other groups or individuals such as future customers, previous employees, families of employees as well as activist groups, nature and future generations.

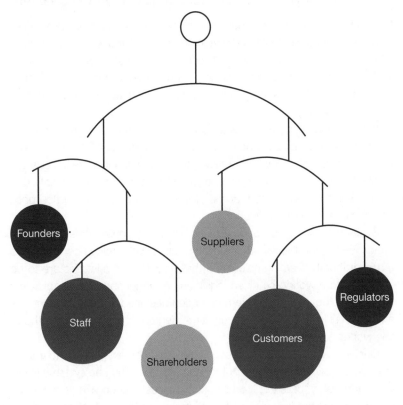

An organisational system, made up of all these different stakeholder groups, is a living organism that often behaves in ways that are different from the sum of its parts. Think of a leadership or sports team that is made up of star performers but functions poorly as a collective. A system has a life of its own.

With the rise of social media, instant communications technology and an expanding global consciousness, it is becoming impossible for organisations to sustain an isolationist view. Consumers and other stakeholders are increasingly able to create powerful feedback loops between the organisation and its environment (see page 160). No longer can an organisation decide, on its own terms, when and how to engage with others. In order to survive in the global marketplace, organisations will have to adapt by seeing themselves as part of dynamic environments that they affect and that affect them.[3]

WHY IT MATTERS TO ENERGISE A SYSTEM

Recent research concludes that leaders need to develop their ability to see how the different elements in a system interrelate. Who feels empowered? Who feels excluded? How can 'followers' and not just leaders be included in decision making? Leaders will increasingly need to cultivate a systemic mindset or their 'ripple intelligence' in order to navigate complexity, without artificially reducing it.[4,5]

When repeating patterns persist such as stuck teams, high staff turnover, or broken working alliances, it is a real opportunity to dig underneath the surface to find out what's really going on. When leaders include the whole system in their strategic analysis, they can illuminate, clarify and resolve systemic issues so that the organisation can truly live its purpose and maximise its performance.

Systems thinkers such as W. Edwards Deming highlight the importance of acknowledging the part that a system plays when things go wrong. As a rule of thumb, Deming calculated that only 15% of mistakes are to be attributed to a workforce or an individual. A staggering 85% of mistakes are the result of how the system has been designed. The performance of an individual is influenced to a very large degree by the system that he or she works in.

Our pervasive tendency to overlook the wider context gets us into trouble in a number of different ways. Author and pioneer of human systems thinking, Barry Oshry, calls this 'contextual blindness'. Recognising that we are not just people but 'people-in-context' makes us less likely to grandstand, withdraw or pull rank. We find ways to make others feel less burdened, oppressed or 'torn' and are able to align a system to live its true purpose.[6]

HOW TO ALIGN A SYSTEM

A systemic approach, while transformative, does require a profound change in orientation. We tend to zero in on the specific details of a situation rather than see the wider context. Overcoming this widespread tendency is a crucial leadership challenge. The good news is that there are some cutting-edge tools that go beyond reductionist ways of thinking. When leaders use a 'wide-angle' lens to look at their organisation and create a healthy system, people will be much more likely to pull together and deliver a true organisational purpose.

Drawing inspiration from psychology, organisational development and the growing discipline of systemic coaching and constellations, three 'how-to's follow. These focus on creating a sense of belonging, cleaning the 'fishtank' and fostering a resilient culture.

CREATE A SENSE OF BELONGING

The famous – and notorious – 'Robbers Cave' experiment gives leaders some powerful insights about how to set up a human relationship system for success – and failure.

The psychologist Muzafer Sherif was born in 1905 and developed his social psychology in the context of war and ethnic conflict in Turkey. A Muslim who had attended a Christian school, Sherif later became a political activist as well as an academic and psychologist. He ran his experiments, together with his wife Carolyn, in the USA between 1949 and 1954.

A group of 24 10- to 12-year-old boys were carefully selected and taken to a camp in Oklahoma for 3 weeks. They were divided into two groups and put through a series of competitive games that were intended to create conflict. It worked: the groups clashed, hostility grew and suspicion increased. Many 'spontaneous frustrations' arose, when the boys vandalised the property of the other group and had 'garbage wars' using food as a weapon against the other group. Tents were pulled down and flags were burnt.

Given their vicious behaviour, it would be easy to conclude that the boys were violent by nature. The studies revealed, however, how conflict unfolded over time due to the animosity that arose as a result of a sense of belonging to one group and not the other. The competitive games were deliberately designed to reward one group, for example with pocketknives, while the other group got nothing.

Sherif showed how even boys who were the 'cream of the crop' back in their local communities could behave anti-socially in a competitive context. We typically don't see how where we are in a hierarchy and the group loyalties we hold invisibly and powerfully shape our behaviour. As thought leader, engineer and author W. Edwards Deming put it:

A bad system will beat a good person every time.

Across a series of three studies, of which Robbers Cave was the third, an important pattern emerged. In the first two studies, the boys from different camps had the chance to develop a friendship before they were forced to compete. Instead of interpersonal hostility emerging between the two groups, there was a sense of sportsmanship. The experimenters eventually resorted to simulating a raid so that one group would have to blame the other.

The shared, common, inclusive sense of 'us' that emerged during the earlier two studies seems to have inoculated the groups from competing destructively with one another. This phase was missed out during the Robbers Cave study, which was marked by much greater intergroup animosity. We are less likely to treat others as a competitors or combatants, once we meet the humanness in others and have a sense of belonging to a larger context.

True leaders, therefore, set a wider context and facilitate people meeting as fellow human beings and not just as 'roles' or as competing 'human resources'. The Robbers Cave study informs us that we are not doomed to aggression and hostility, despite appearances to the contrary. When leaders create a 'field' of shared endeavour, people come together to serve something larger than themselves.

How to create a sense of belonging

Here are some things to try when conflict between two teams arises. The overall aim is to reduce 'negative interdependence' (where one group wins, the other loses) and increase 'positive interdependence' (where it's a win-win).

1. **Enable people to connect.** At the start of the session, have a 'check-in' (see page 91). Invite each person to respond to the following:

   ■ What's one thing that's energises you about working with the other team?

   ■ What's one thing that's drains you about working with them?

   Reflect together on the common themes that emerge. Help people to see each other as fellow human beings with similar struggles and motivations.

2. **Calculate the cost.** Form small mixed sub-groups that are each made up of people from the two different teams. Ask each sub-team to explore the following questions:

- What are the unintended consequences of us not collaborating (e.g. duplication of work, unaddressed customer complaints, missed opportunities to share ideas)?

- What are the three most concerning undesirable outcomes?

- What is the cost to the organisation of these three outcomes? If possible, put the cost in monetary or tangible terms (e.g. loss of opportunity or reputation).

Each sub-group shares the estimated costs and the thinking behind them. As a whole group, reflect together on what you're learning about the cost of not collaborating. Explore where there are any 'quick wins' to greater collaboration, e.g. the teams agree to have a weekly catch up to share their current priorities.

3. **Identify a shared project.** Ask each sub-group to identify a shared project requiring collaboration from both teams. For example, co-production of a strategy or a new operational plan. Have a whole group dialogue to agree the project that feels most engaging and then explore what steps to take to deliver this project as part of the organisation's purpose.

SEE THE WHOLE

When leaders attend to dysfunctional dynamics in their organisation, they can powerfully orientate an organisation to its true purpose.

Returning to the 'fishtank' metaphor, when leaders place their attention on the whole of the 'fishtank' (and not just the 'fish' or individual people), they understand that the health of any one part of the ecosystem depends on the health of the whole. By attending to whatever might be polluting the atmosphere, 'fishtank owners' (or leaders) identify and remove toxins, such as festering resentments or unhealthy competition. They inject life-giving oxygen into stale waters, whether this is an honest conversation, a new incentive for collaboration or a team away day that builds trust. Cleaning the fishtank is not easy but it is a more sustainable solution than focusing only on 'sprucing up the fish'.

If 'stuckness' is left unaddressed, an organisation will never live its most potent purpose, no matter how inspiring it is on paper. Plopping a compelling purpose statement into a stagnant fishtank will not work; the fishtank must be cleaned so that there is a good flow of finance, resources and rewards in the system and a sense of vitality in people.

From a systemic perspective, organisational health is predicated on a number of principles being synchronised, which I'll come to shortly. If these principles are ignored or misaligned, an organisation's energy stops flowing and it loses competitive advantage. While these 'symptoms' are visible, the root causes are often invisible to the untrained eye.

What's great is that our understanding of these hidden dynamics has deepened in recent years. The growing practice of 'systemic constellations' has brought into focus an architecture of underlying principles. When these are seen and, more crucially felt, this quickly reveals the underlying 'invisible dynamics' in a system, freeing up stuck energy and releasing fresh insights.

The originator of this thought framework, Bert Hellinger, a German psychotherapist, discovered these systemic principles over many years by observing and studying many different systems, including families and organisations. Since his pioneering work in Europe and beyond, hundreds of thousands of people across the world have experienced 'systemic constellations' as Hellinger's approach has become known. There are also thousands of practitioners worldwide who apply and adapt Hellinger's insights to an array of personal, organisational, environmental and political issues with great effect and success.

A HEALTHY ORGANISATION

Leaders who develop an understanding of these invisible, underlying forces have a lens to scan quickly a team or organisation in order to identify where crucial systemic issues might be located. Leaders can then identify the 'acupressure points' for creating healthy change in a system. Solutions and resources that were previously hidden start to come into view, and purpose can become a real wellspring of energy, joy and fulfilment.

A healthy organisation has several systemic dimensions. Leading practitioner John Whittington expresses this succinctly:

> *In a healthy system, everyone who has contributed is acknowledged and the history of the system is spoken about, including all the difficulties. Everything has a place. Roles are created in conscious connection with the purpose of the whole system. There is a balance between what each individual and team gives and what they receive. Everyone feels safe and able to relax into their own authority, and apply it, willingly, for the good of the system.*[7]

When we tune in, we know when a system is out of alignment; but we often don't know why nor how to realign it. Understanding these systemic principles, which permeate the whole field of an organisation, is a powerful way to reveal the deeper territory of how to create movement in line with a compelling organisational purpose.

Each of us can learn to attune to these systemic principles, in part, by tuning into ourselves more deeply. They are not abstract; they are forces that we can feel. The work of Hellinger and other organisational practitioners has shown that there are universal principles that underpin all human relationship systems – families, organisations, teams and governing bodies. They create invisible energetic fields that shape organisational life.

When people experience these systemic principles in their bodies (not just understand them in their heads), they have an intuitive sense that they are 'right'. At systemic constellations programmes, I've witnessed many times the visceral sense with which people experience these principles when they feel their effects. In organisations, we often learn to suppress our emotional experiences and bodily sensations as a way of being 'civilised'. In this different way of working, we play close attention to our 'embodied intelligence' (our feelings, sensations and intuitions) and what this tells us about the state of the 'fishtank'.

MULTIPLE WAYS OF KNOWING

To connect on purpose, we need to include multiple ways of knowing rather than relying only on our rationality. Psychologists have, for a long time, recognised how important it is to cultivate four dimensions of 'knowing' to become a 'whole' person. The four ways of knowing, in relation to purpose, are:

- thinking – knowing with our intellect whether something is for us or not
- feeling – knowing with our inner atmosphere whether something feels 'right' or not
- sensing – knowing with our bodies whether something is true for us or not
- intuiting – knowing, without knowing why, whether something is ours to do or not.

The challenge is that we are primed, by our schooling and society, to use our intellect as our dominant, and sometimes only, way of knowing. In organisations, thinking is privileged, analysis is trusted and rationality is rewarded. The other three ways of knowing – feeling, sensing and intuiting – are a greatly underutilised resource. They are, however, key to working systemically and bringing purpose to life.

PLUGGING INTO THE 'KNOWING FIELD'

At the heart of systemic constellations is creating a 'map' of a system. A system could be a whole organisation, a team or a department. Elements to place on the map might include people such as customers, suppliers and other stakeholders as well as abstract elements such as purpose, profit and strategy.

A 'desktop' approach, which was described in the previous chapter, involves mapping the key elements of a system using objects, props or sticky notes with arrows. In the more traditional way of constellating, a 'living map' of a system is created where, once the key elements of a system have been identified, people stand in to represent these parts, considering two key dimensions (as we did with the desktop approach in Chapter 6):

- How close or distant are the elements to each other?
- What direction are they going/facing?

Once they are placed on the map, 'representatives' take their time to settle in and notice what they observe in their bodies. They might tune into changes in temperature and any impulse to move. They might observe that something or someone is capturing their attention or that they have a strong desire to leave the room. People start to tune into what they know 'phenomenologically' – using their sensing, feeling and intuiting – as they stand (literally) in the energetic field of the system.

What quickly becomes apparent is that representatives have access to insights and rich information about a system that they previously knew nothing about. Plugging into the 'knowing field' (a term coined by Albrecht Mahr, a German physician, psychoanalyst and early adapter of the method) is the distinctive essence of the systemic constellations approach. One stakeholder might turn towards an organisation's purpose and feel drawn to it; another might turn away. The representative for purpose might be in alignment with the 'rep' for strategy or face different directions. Representatives might speak or stay silent as the whole field comes alive in unexpected ways.

THE 'FORCE FIELD' OF PURPOSE

What's exciting is how this mapping approach reveals powerful insights about the purpose of an organisation. Having facilitated and observed many constellations, I've witnessed that purpose is an incredible 'force' that connects a system. Just as placing a magnet under a field of iron filings pulls them into a pattern of coherence, a clear and compelling purpose attracts people's energy. The following image reflects how purpose creates a 'force field' across a whole organisation and its stakeholders. The image shows the 'force field' of purpose: true and potent purpose is the 'magnetising' force that attracts stakeholders to pull in the same direction and deliver a sustainable and successful organisation.

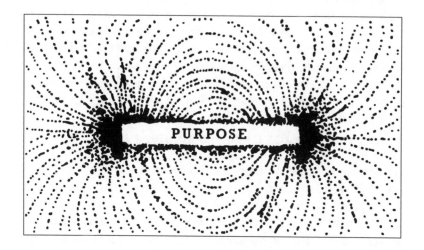

There is, however, a critical caveat. *The purpose needs to be a true purpose in order to have the power to connect a system.* Think back to the Organisational Purpose Diamond (covered in Chapter 6): it is the true, most potent purpose of an organisation that generates a strong 'magnetic field'. The espoused purpose, actual purpose and founding purpose do not have this 'charge' unless they are resonant with the most compelling purpose of an organisation.

When a substitute takes the place of purpose, such as growth for growth's sake or the pursuit of a goal, the 'field' does not line up in the same way. When Volkswagen focused on being the biggest carmaker in the world, rather than on a true purpose, it became unstuck. The 'fake purpose' led some of VW's stakeholders, such as future 'green' customers, to be repelled instead.

When a true organisational purpose is forgotten or replaced it becomes problematic for the whole system. In a constellation, it can show up in various ways: representatives for staff members stare out of the window, wander around unable to find their place or have an impulse to leave. Leadership team members are unable to settle and spin round and round instead. When the true purpose is subverted by meeting targets or making money, it depletes the free flow of energy in a system with real conse-quences for the health of the organisation and its people.

In less than an hour a constellation can reveal a terrific amount of data – data that matters and that makes a real difference to decision making. It can take a team of consultants using more analytical approaches several months to generate insights, which often do not reveal what's hidden beneath the surface. Despite several PhDs being carried out, no one can really explain how the phenomenon of 'representation' works. It might be 'mirror neurons', the result of 'morphogenetic fields' that biologist Rupert Sheldrake describes or some other quantum phenomenon that currently eludes the scientific mind. No one knows how it works but it does and the message is clear: the primary function of leadership is to set the right purpose for their organisation and to align the systemic influences at play.

THE FOUR SYSTEMIC PRINCIPLES

In systemic constellations, problematic repeating patterns are a system's way of showing that something wants to be seen, learned or completed. An ongoing conflict at senior levels could be because a hard truth needs to be acknowledged. A lack of leadership could point to a founder being forgotten or excluded, their place in the system lost. A lacklustre organisation might be the result of an organisation's co-founder having left acrimoniously and the system trying to re-member them to bring them back into belonging.

Dysfunctional behaviours are understood as an unconscious attempt to realign the systemic principles. When there is a lack of flow – of leadership, energy or resources – it is a symptom that deeply held unconscious dynamics and loyalties are at work and need attending to.

These imbalances make themselves known in unusual but strangely familiar ways. The 'ejector seat' phenomenon is an example: a repeating pattern of people having difficulty occupying a role, regardless of how talented they are. Whatever we try to exclude – a founder who left unacknowledged, a team member who was fired or a customer who was cheated – will always hold a powerful energy that will distract until we re-include it.

The thought framework of systemic constellations includes four systemic principles that need to come into alignment, in addition to an organisation having a true purpose. Using this framework helps leaders to diagnose where there are issues in the fishtank to address. The four systemic principles are:

1. **Acknowledgement.** Facing up to reality creates alignment in an organisation. Acknowledgement without judgement frees people from old stories, releases fresh energy into the system and strengthens

At the second session, we mapped the team and found a 'constellation' where each person felt in their right place with one another and the purpose of the CIC. Through some authentic and, at times, testy dialogue, we clarified the purpose of the executive team: 'To run the company effectively by providing strong and compassionate leadership.' The SLT also arrived at a critical question: How can we become a more empowering, listening and outstanding team that really serves all our stakeholders? We explored ways to do this.

At the third team coaching session, the team members felt safe enough to give one another robust feedback. They acknowledged what they genuinely appreciated about one another and what they had found challenging. During this open and honest exchange, the atmosphere really shifted. I was heartened to receive the following email from the CEO with his observations shortly afterwards.

* * *

Dear Sarah,

Thank you for last week's session. Reflections are excellent, despite there having been some trepidation about next steps and dealing with the fallout from the past. Without exception they all feel much more heard, enabled, engaged, valued and supported than when we started and overall I think we are a more capable team. You must be doing something right!

The impact has been really noticeable. We managed to get proper buy in to the paper creation for the board so it feels we have submitted something we can all stand behind. Our board meeting now has an opening 'check in' followed by a short update presentation and a dialogue section with guiding topics for members. We have a clear list of decisions that need to be made, but we won't frame the agenda around this to keep a free flow of energy.

It's been great to work with you. How would you feel about running a joint session with the rest of the board – the chairman and the non-execs – in a few months' time?

Best wishes,
Adam

* * *

SUMMARY

- An organisational system is a complex web of continuously changing relationships among internal and external stakeholders. It behaves in ways different from the sum of its parts.

- A repeating pattern such as a poorly performing team, a turf war between leaders or fighting between departments requires a systemic approach in order to resolve it in a sustainable way.

- The more that leaders develop their understanding of systemic principles, the more they will be able to influence their organisation around a truly compelling 'why'. When leaders see their whole 'fishtank' (or system) and not just the individual 'fish' (people), their interventions will be far more effective.

- Creating a sense of belonging among team members is a powerful way to cut through conflict. Reducing 'negative interdependence' (where one group wins, the other loses) and increasing 'positive interdependence' (where it's a win-win) brings opposing camps together.

- There are five underpinning systemic principles that shape systems. When leaders attune to these forces, they know how to 'clean the fishtank' and create a flow of positive energy. The underpinning principles are:

  1. Purpose: a clear and authentic purpose unifies and energises stakeholders.

  2. Acknowledgment: creating change starts with acknowledging that what is, is.

  3. Time: what comes first has a natural precedence over what comes later.

  4. Place: everyone has a right to a unique and respected place in the system.

  5. Exchange: a dynamic reciprocity of giving and receiving creates a healthy system.

- A compelling purpose acts like a 'magnet', bringing alignment to a system that has become fragmented. When leaders orientate their teams, projects and services to the real reason for an organisation's existence, this unlocks the energy to achieve excellence and strengthens the system as a whole.

- Unresolved issues create burdens systemically. Effective interventions restore harmony to the underlying systemic principles. Acknowledging length of service helps team members to find their 'right place' in relation to one another and the organisational purpose.

NOTES

1. Dr Whitaker (2015) 'A Critical Condition', *New Statesman*, 5 March.
2. Hurth, V., Ebert, C. and Prabhu, J. (2018) Organisational Purpose: The construct and its antecedents and consequences, Cambridge Judge Business School, Working Paper No. 02/2018.
3. Hurth, V. (2017) Organizations as open systems that need purpose and integrated thinking, *Board Leadership,* March–April.
4. Saïd Business School and Heidrick & Struggles (2017) The CEO Report: Embracing the paradoxes of leadership and the power of doubt. See https://www.sbs.ox.ac.uk/sites/default/files/2018-09/The-CEO-Report-Final.pdf.
5. University of Cambridge Institute for Sustainability Leadership (2017) *Global Definitions of Leadership and Theories of Leadership Development: Literature Review,* 27 June. See https://www.cisl.cam.ac.uk/resources/publication-pdfs/Global-Definitions-Leadership-Theories-Leadership-Development.pdf.
6. Oshry, B. (1995) *Seeing Systems: Unlocking the Mysteries of Organisational Life*, Berrett-Koehler.
7. Whittington, J. (2012) *Systemic Coaching and Constellations: An Introduction to the Principles, Practices and Application,* Kogan Page.
8. Heffernan, M. (2015) *Beyond Measure: The Big Impact of Small Changes,* Simon & Schuster.
9. See https://www.theguardian.com/women-in-leadership/2013/oct/14/blind-auditions-orchestras-gender-bias.

PART III

THE THREE BRIDGES OF PURPOSE

CHAPTER 8

LIGHT UP THE WHOLE ECOSYSTEM

Organisations do better when everyone is rowing in the same direction. A well-integrated, shared purpose casts that direction.

EY Beacon Institute

Pioneering leaders take their organisation on the journey of becoming purpose-driven. They clarify the meaningful reason for their organisation's existence and move away from being focused solely on profit for shareholders towards creating value by serving a whole ecosystem of beneficiaries. By embodying each of the four capacities of purpose-led leadership – leadership presence, authentic dialogue, stakeholder engagement and connecting on purpose – leaders transform their organisation towards its wider purpose so it becomes an agent of positive change in the world.

* * *

'The purpose of the bank is to make money!'

A conversation had opened up among a cohort of 40 participants at a leadership programme of Standard Chartered Bank. I was one of several coaches on the programme, hosted by Saïd Business School at the University of Oxford. Some participants had waited years to be invited and saw their attendance as a badge of honour for all their hard work. They'd flown in from Africa, Asia and the USA to meet their colleagues and expectations ran high.

It was the perfect 'pressure cooker' environment. Fintech developments was creating pressure to innovate. Bill Winters, the CEO, wanted to create a 'culture of challenge' after a period of restructuring, which had created significant upheaval and the inevitable exits of people. Many leaders had been required to step up into broader roles with more responsibility, while dealing with a sense of loss and 'survivor guilt'.

During one of the whole group forums, where people were trying to make sense of their and others' roles in the new world, a question about the bank's purpose had arisen, provoking some strong assertions.

'We need to be profitable, of course, but if that's our only purpose, it won't inspire our customers.'

'It's the people around here – colleagues and customers – with rags to riches stories that motivate me, not working to maximise profit.'

'Well I didn't do all this work over all these years just to have someone come along and move the goalposts!'

As the heated exchange continued, I found myself reflecting it was no surprise that the group were struggling to have a deeper dialogue about the bank's reason to exist. For some leaders becoming more purpose-driven is threatening, as they prefer the apparent certainty of business-as-usual. For others, it is a real opportunity that will enable an organisation to stay competitive while being a force for good in the world.

The question of how to light up the whole ecosystem of stakeholders – employees, customers, suppliers, communities and shareholders – is not unique to this bank. Coming to a shared understanding about the evolving purpose of an organisation in a world of hyper change is a new frontier that many leaders will have to grapple with.

* * *

Reinventing an organisation through redefining its purpose is high on the business agenda. There are many signs that our organisations, including our banks and financial institutions, need to be transformed. Although some organisations do have happy, engaged and productive employees, many don't. There is a growing recognition that overall levels of employee engagement are shockingly low as distrust of business deepens and a climate of fear among employees takes hold.[1]

Beyond individual organisations, there are many indications that our whole economy is not delivering. Martin Wolf, writing in the *Financial Times,* describes how 'rentier capitalism' – where privileged individuals and companies extract a disproportionate amount of 'rent' from everyone else – has created economic outcomes that benefit the few and leave society as a whole worse off. A global environment of feeble productivity growth, growing inequality and slowing innovation has led to a call for capitalism itself to be reset.[2]

'Business must make a profit but should serve a purpose too' was the *FT* headline on 18 September 2019. The newspaper defined the 'new agenda' in three ways: (1) to stand up for wealth creation and free enterprise as drivers of development; (2) to promote better business by holding companies to account; (3) to empower each other to lead the way in business, society and the wider world. They acknowledged that in our fragmented world, where many see difficulty, they see opportunity. In response, this chapter covers the following:

- The changing context of business as a new consciousness about capitalism, the purpose of corporations, the environment and climate change takes hold.

- Why delivering a compelling purpose is key to business success in the disruptive world in which we live.

- How leaders can embody the four core capacities of purpose-led leadership to transform their organisation, its performance and become a force for good in the world.

THE NEW CONSCIOUSNESS SHAPING BUSINESS

The *FT*'s call to action followed an announcement a month earlier by the Business Roundtable (BRT), an influential US business group that represents the CEOs of 181 of the USA's largest companies, chaired by Jamie Dimon, CEO of JPMorgan Chase. On 19 August 2019 the Roundtable amended its two-decade old statement that 'corporations exist principally to serve their shareholders'. They said, 'While each of our individual companies serves its own corporate purpose, we share a fundamental commitment to all of our stakeholders'.[3]

This move to drop the 'shareholder first' creed that has driven capitalism for the last four decades is a standout moment. Their 300-word statement, in which shareholders didn't appear until word 250, made commitments to create value for customers, invest in the training of employees, foster a culture of diversity and inclusion, deal fairly and ethically with suppliers, support the communities in which they work and protect the environment.

While many welcomed this move, including social interest groups and environmental, social and governance (ESG) investors, there was also a strong backlash. Economists and investors claimed that companies would be thrown into legal confusion. The Council of Institutional Investors, a US lobby group, 'respectfully disagreed' with the BRT's statement, saying that 'accountability to everyone means accountability to no one'.

At the heart of this debate is the question: 'What are companies for?' Gillian Tett, writing in the *FT* a few days after the Business Roundtable announcement, suggested that we ponder the root of the word 'company'. Whereas this often conjures up images of balance sheets and profit margins, the word originally comes from the twelfth-century French, *compagnie,* meaning a 'society, friendship, intimacy; body of soldiers', which comes from the Latin *companio*: 'one who eats bread with you'.[4]

While breaking bread together is a far cry from much of corporate life, strengthening social bonds is central to the various new forms of capitalism being propounded. Bill Gates in a speech at the World Economic Forum, Davos, in 2008 spoke of 'creative capitalism'. Wholefoods co-founder John Mackey has proposed 'conscious capitalism' and Salesforce CEO Marc Benioff has written a book on 'compassionate capitalism'. The common thread is to take care of people and the planet rather than maximise profit as an end in itself.

Strengthening social bonds is key to the growing 'B Corps' movement. Over the past decade, almost 3,000 organisations have become B Corporations, including Patagonia and Danone Fresh Dairies UK. Their ethical, social and environmental practices are assessed and certified by independent monitors to meet the rigorous standards laid down by B Lab, a not-for-profit group in Pennsylvania, who make the results public. B Corps are required to legally commit to act in the interests of all stakeholders, not just shareholders. In the UK there are over 200 B Corps enterprises, which are required to include a purpose in their articles of association and provide measures to prove it is being fulfilled.

What is striking is that increasing numbers of companies are proactively choosing to go through this process of stringent measurement, including of their sustainability credentials. Although some are cynical about 'virtue signalling' or 'purpose washing', business leaders are meeting an urgent need. Given the changing global consciousness, particularly in relation to climate change, the decision to follow a purpose-driven approach not only makes good long-term business sense but means that business leaders *are* starting to fill the leadership vacuum that our gridlocked politics has left behind.[5]

There is, amid all the challenge, a huge opportunity. At highly successful Brompton Cycles, they arrived at their bold purpose by becoming clear about what they cared about and how they could serve the world. As Will Butler-Adams, MD of Brompton Cycles, says in *The Power of Purpose*, developing global consciousness was key. Once they were exporting at a certain level and became more aware of what was happening on a global scale, their purpose – to change the way that people live in cities – became clear.[6]

WHY DELIVERING A COMPELLING PURPOSE IS KEY TO BUSINESS SUCCESS

In addition to the business case that supports purpose-driven business, one other reason trumps all the others. As scientists warn of the likelihood of catastrophic climate change, leaders have a vital role to play. Companies such as Patagonia, Unilever and Iceland, which are taking a stand for sustainability, are trail blazing the way ahead. Their attitude that purpose is not about profit but how to create benefit to people and minimise harm to the planet, and in the process produce a profit, is a vital and urgent orientation.

Climate action has become the defining challenge of our times. With the rising number of floods, heat waves and forest fires, climate change is no longer a distant threat, but, for the first time in history, something that we all experience in our everyday lives. Gone are the days when we might have dismissed environmental degradation as a risk only to people in far-away places that we cared little about; the alarming and uncertain impact of our changing weather system now confronts us all.

There is an increasingly diverse array of voices calling for business to change. Dr Jem Bendell, professor of sustainability leadership and founding director of the Institute for Leadership and Sustainability at the University of Cumbria, acknowledges that this is a tough call. In his paper, Deep Adaptation, Dr Bendell outlines his belief that due to large-scale crop failure and food shortages, societal collapse will happen in developed countries within ten years.[7] In a recent podcast series, *Leading in a Climate Changed World* hosted by Olivier Mythodrama Leadership Lab and Robin Alfred of Findhorn Consultancy Service, Dr Bendell spoke about the pressing need for us to prefigure how we relate to one another – with greater presence, curiosity, compassion and care – before societal collapse sets in.[8]

Public interest in climate action and corporate responsibility is at an all-time high, particularly among the young. In a poll by Fortune/New Paradigm, 80% of 25–34-year olds said that they wanted to work for 'engaged companies'. Companies are increasingly aware that in order to attract the best young talent going forwards, they need to be plugged into what younger generations want and their call for taking a stand on public issues such as climate change, gun ownership and religious liberties.[9]

Having a purpose that engages the next generation is key. In their book *Thinking the Unthinkable,* Nik Gowing and Chris Langdon summarise hundreds of interviews with corporate leaders and highlight the role clarity of purpose plays in dealing with the pace of change. They state that disruption – 'the new normal' – requires leaders to think, and plan for, 'unthinkables'. A clear organisational purpose is pivotal: it provides the 'North Star' for decision making, strategy setting and people pulling power in an uncertain world.[10]

Despite the growing success of purpose-driven business, many leaders are, however, still unaware that a compelling purpose is critical to the success of the organisation and unleashing the energy of the workforce. As a result, they may lack the capacities to both define their purpose *and* the 'know-how' to bring it to life.

The rest of this chapter illustrates how vanguard leaders are getting to grips with purpose. Using the four capacities of purpose-led leadership, they are articulating and delivering a compelling organisational purpose for their ecosystem of stakeholders. And, in so doing, they are laying down the tracks for other leaders to follow.

How to find inspiration for becoming purpose-driven

Think of an organisation or brand that lights you up. What is it about them that resonates?

What are the signs that tell you this organisation lives its purpose? (Customers love their products, it takes a stand on an important social issue, it supports a meaningful cause, etc.)

What can you learn from this that would help your organisation to go on a journey of becoming more purpose-driven?

EXPANDING LEADERSHIP PRESENCE

The journey of purpose-led leadership starts with our own wholeheartedness. In his book *Do Purpose: Why Brands With a Purpose Do Better and Matter More* (2014), David Hieatt shares how building a powerful brand begins with a leader's passion for creating positive change in the world. Having worked for Saatchi and Saatchi and built one of the most influential sports brands of the last decade, Hieatt is a good guide to this territory.[11]

Hieatt argues that purpose-driven brands excite us because there is something they want to contribute to. Zipcar changed car ownership.

Patagonia changed how clothes get made. Apple changed the game with technology. These companies stir us because we, as customers or employees, want to be part of the change too.

As humans, we are wired to want to connect with something bigger than ourselves. Think back to the moment you heard about 9/11 or the Berlin Wall coming down: where were you? We can often remember being 'rooted to the spot' in such moments because they connect us with a much larger story of what is unfolding on this shared planet of ours.

Purpose-driven brands stand for something bigger; more meaningful than profit alone. The magic of the most successful brands in the world is the promise of change. This promise *is* the brand. The best brands don't appeal so much to logic or reason, they touch our hearts. Successful founders stay true to their impulse of knowing what they want to change and what they care about. As Hieatt pithily puts it: 'Love scales'.

Jack Ma, founder and CEO of Chinese e-commerce giant Alibaba, argues that what sets true leaders apart is not what we typically think it is. Addressing the Bloomberg Global Business Forum in New York in September 2017, Ma shared his belief that no matter how smart machines become, the solutions to our biggest collective challenges such as social inequality, climate change and global epidemics, will come from humans:

> *A machine does not have a heart, does not have soul, and does not have a belief. Human beings have the souls, have the belief, have the values; we are creative, we are showing that we can control the machines.*

While organisations need leaders with a well-developed IQ and MQ (or management quotient so that they get stuff done) what is most critical is their LQ or 'love quotient'.[12] While 'love' is rarely used in the leadership lexicon, this is ultimately what we're talking about with the shift from command-and-control to purpose-led leadership (see page 60).

Pioneering business leaders are forging ahead with new ways to describe leading with purpose and presence. Tony Hsieh, CEO for over 17 years of the hugely successful online retailer Zappos, is one of these trail blazers. In an interview published in the *McKinsey Quarterly* (2017, No. 4), Hsieh argues that mobilising collaboration both within the organisation and beyond its boundaries is at the heart of Zappos' success.[13]

Hsieh describes how each of the 1,500 employees occupies a valuable niche in the ecosystem: 'To harness collective intelligence, we think of every single employee as a human sensor.' In effect, each one is deploying presence.

Using the metaphor of an aeroplane, Hsieh describes how all the different 'sensors' are needed. While some sensors such as the altimeter might be more critical, attention must be paid to all. If the low-voltage warning light comes on, it is not to be ignored. If an intern raises a flag about the organisation exploring Instagram, this 'sensing' is not to be dismissed by older or more senior people. The whole system at Zappos is set up to process the signals that different 'sensors' or people raise so that the organisation stays resilient and innovative in a constantly changing environment.

To enable self-organisation, Zappos encourages employees to move around and find the 'sweet-spot' where their purpose intersects with what adds value to the organisation. Individuals are seen as full of creative potential, intelligence and resources – in short, 'whole' people. Their ability to sense, particularly tension between their own purpose and the organisational purpose, unlocks performance.

To connect their own purpose with the organisational purpose ('To Live and Deliver Wow'), team members are free to join and leave as many of the 500 'circles' in the company as they wish. Purpose statements, for circles or individuals, evolve over time. As Hsieh reflects: 'It's not just a systems-change, it's also a personal journey for each individual employee.' And it begins with each person bringing their leadership presence to bear.

HAVING AN AUTHENTIC DIALOGUE ABOUT PURPOSE

Recent research has found that having an organisational purpose can be insufficient to drive higher levels of financial performance unless certain factors are present. Better conversation has a crucial part to play. A study carried out by Claudine Gartenberg at NYU Stern School of Business, Andrea Prat of Columbia University, and George Serafeim of Harvard Business School drew on the responses of around 500,000 employees from 429 companies in the USA. The data stretched over a six-year period, across five different levels of employee – from senior executives to frontline staff – and across a broad range of industries.[14]

Overall, they found that for their measure of purpose to relate to financial performance two factors are needed. Firstly, only organisations with *high clarity of purpose* systematically show superior financial results. Secondly, *the perceptions of middle managers* rather than senior managers or frontline staff were found to drive the relationship between financial performance and purpose. The very people for whom clarity of purpose is most important are also, however, the ones that senior management are most at risk of failing to communicate effectively with. Vibrant and visible leadership that brings purpose clarity and engages the 'frozen middle' in the conversation is essential to bring purpose to life.

Returning to Standard Chartered Bank, the conversation about purpose spanned many months. The leadership programme – *Leading Across Boundaries* – provided a unique opportunity for leaders from different parts of the organisation to talk with colleagues that they might otherwise never have met. I learnt some powerful lessons about how dialogue helps leaders to re-purpose their organisation.

Firstly, leaders need to have a 'safe space' in which to talk and be fully present. During the course of our 30-, 60- and 90-day follow-on small group coaching calls, a more generative conversation about purpose became possible. Participants shared concerns they said they wouldn't have aired with their own team. They spoke out about them with colleagues from other parts of the bank as we had created a 'container' in which to talk.

Groups often need to move through the four conversational fields in order to have a meaningful conversation (see page 95). Reflecting on this, I asked the bankers: What does it take to move the conversation about purpose beyond polarisation? They observed:

- Curiosity. A sincere desire to understand what I don't know.
- Realising that I haven't got a clue about how the other person really feels.
- A pause. Just stopping for a moment and taking a breath.
- A moment of kindness, compassion and care.
- A question instead of yet another opinion. A sense of wanting to understand more.
- Letting my body relax. Noticing where I'm holding some tension and letting it go.

Secondly, it was a spirit of inquiry – not knowing, wanting to understand more – that unlocked a deeper dialogue. People moved out of entrenched positions and into a much more expansive space. When we let go of rigid thought patterns, such as 'I'm right, you're wrong', it opens the way for new thinking to emerge.

Finally, purpose conversations require not a 'Let's fix this' mentality but a 'Let's have a conversation and see what emerges' mindset. Dialogue has a flow in which deeper insights effortlessly arise. We don't need to force anything to happen or try to get anywhere. When a 'generative image'[15] – a turn of phrase, metaphor or actual image – surfaces and captures people's imaginations, it is electrifying to feel.

Back at the bank, 'Being human' started to emerge as a generative image – a 'dot on the wall' for the change journey that the bank needed to go on. Some leaders were receptive, others more cynical but people stayed in the conversation. In the coaching groups I worked with, searching questions were asked: what does the Bank stand for? If the Bank ceased to exist tomorrow, who would care, and why?

From these conversations where leaders discussed 'being human', the Bank defined its purpose: 'Driving commerce and prosperity through our unique diversity'. This purpose statement reflects what differentiates the Bank: the diverse people that intimately understand the local clients and markets in which they work.

Senior leaders then engaged their people to answer the question: 'If we are to bring our purpose to life in a human way, how do we do this?' They crowdsourced and analysed the responses of 70,000 people with the help of smart machine learning and defined the behaviours they most valued. 'Never settle' connected with the 'driving' element of their purpose. 'Do the right thing' brought 'commerce and prosperity' to life. 'Better together' is how the Bank harnessed 'unique diversity'.

Several leaders I worked with reflected that, had it not been for a safe space in which to do some sense making, they might have exited. When leaders are able to voice their vulnerabilities, it can make the difference between a decision to stay or go. By engaging people in an authentic dialogue about the reason the Bank existed, the Bank not only clarified its purpose but retained some of its top talent at a time of turbulence and change.

ENGAGE NOT ENRAGE YOUR STAKEHOLDERS

Listening to the voice of customers, as well as employees, is critical in order to cope with new disruptions. In their book, *Thinking the Unthinkables,* Nik Gowing and Chris Langdon share the story of how Safaricom, Kenya's telecommunications giant, turned around an 'unthinkable moment' by taking stakeholder engagement to a new level and re-examining their organisational purpose.

Since it began in 1997, Safaricom has been widely lauded for being an innovative market leader. Having pioneered a money transfer system enabling anyone with a mobile phone, even if they had no landline, electricity or bank account, to conduct business. The number of users rose from 2 million in 2008 to over 27 million in 2018.

In 2016, the unthinkable happened. Angry, young customers accused Bob Collymore, its CEO, on social media of being a 'thief'. These 'digital ninjas' took issue with what they perceived as overcharging for new data bundles. They complained in their thousands of 'being screwed' financially and threatened revenge for what they saw as exploitation.

Safaricom executives realised that their brand could be trashed within weeks, maybe even days. What shocked them most was that they had become so out of touch with the next generation. In a country where half the population is under 26, these digital natives had the power to cause huge reputational damage and an exodus of subscribers.

After re-checking Safaricom's pricing policy, Collymore realised they had a point. The tariffs were more complicated than they needed to be and the company had taken money for things customers weren't using. Within days, the company had to change not only its tariffs but its mindset and behaviour toward their vociferous and suspicious customers.

By listening to their critics, senior leaders at Safaricom realised that they had failed to understand that this generation had very different needs from their own. For millennials, the mobile phone is a lifeline to a livelihood and a better future. They saw Safaricom not as a profit generator for investors and shareholders but as an enabler of their own creative purpose of having an impact in the world. Safaricom's revolution of money transfer had created an expectation that the company was more than a corporate 'cash cow'.

To respond to the crisis, Safaricom quickly established a youth network, BLAZE. Created by young people for young people, it 'supports unconventional journeys to success' by providing summits, boot camps and a TV show. All executives at Safaricom are reverse mentored and spend two hours a month with a digital native. As a result, instead of a mass subscriber defection, both revenues and profits went up (by 14.1% and 8.8%, respectively) for year ending March 2018.

What strikes me most about this story is how Safaricom turned around an existential threat by listening to its customers, a major stakeholder. This avoids a potential pitfall of purpose-driven business, highlighted by *The Economist,* that while collective capitalism 'sounds nice', it is not clear how CEOs should know what 'society' wants from their companies. They argue that as ordinary people do not have a voice, CEOs, politicians and campaigning groups will 'set goals for society that range far beyond the interests of their company'.[16] The Safaricom story shows us that ordinary people using a company's products *do* have a voice and, when a CEO has the humility to listen, a company can not only survive but thrive when the unexpected strikes.

CONNECT ON PURPOSE

Disruptions, which have become the new normal, require leaders to lead with a clear purpose and a moral compass. When purpose boils down simply to a meagre goal about profit or growth, rather than a company producing goods and services that benefit customers and consumers, it has real consequences. In education and health services, as people lose sight of the organisation's purpose and strive to hit performance targets, people become stressed. Burnout and high staff turnover characterise both sectors.

A system that is not addressing its true purpose will turn in on itself. Many parts of the NHS are stressed and sick when its true purpose is to heal. The education system has been eclipsed by an obsession with targets and league tables. Teachers are in the grip of a 'culture of fear, over-regulation and lack of trust' and one fifth plan to leave within two years.[17] Given the pressures they're under, leaders often can't see their purpose and/or they have lost sight of their beneficiaries. They see their targets and regulators but have forgotten the patients, the children and their best future possibilities.

An organisation gets into trouble when goal setting replaces a true purpose. Sales targets, market share and growth metrics are seductive because they are measurable but they are not a real 'why'. In the HBR article, 'Goals Gone Wild', the authors argue that while goal setting can bring many benefits such as increased motivation, it has many unseen downsides such as focusing attention on the short-term, inhibiting learning and people behaving unethically due to the fear of not meeting a goal.[18]

Organisations are too often over managed and under led. Senior people focus on performance against targets (management's job) while neglecting the purpose of the organisation (the leaders' true role). For an organisation to make a positive contribution in the world, leaders need to stop treating goal setting as a pseudo-purpose and attune their organisation to a compelling purpose instead.

Whereas every organisation on the planet knows *what* they do (the products they sell and the services they offer) and some organisations know *how* they do what they do (what sets them apart from their competition), very few organisations know *why* they do what they do. And yet, as Simon Sinek reminds us in his best-selling book, *Start with Why,* 'People don't buy what you do, they buy why you do it.'[19] The following figure of Sinek's (which has become a classic illustration of purpose) illustrates that an organisation's 'why' is at the core of what matters most.

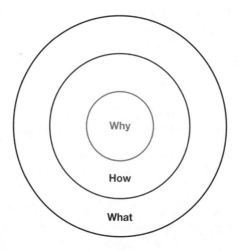

Start with Why
Based on Sinek S. (2011) *Start with Why: How Great Leaders Inspire Everyone To Take Action*, Portfolio.

An organisation's 'why' is the very reason it exists. In their seminal paper, Building Your Company's Vision, James C. Collins and Jerry I. Porras describe it as the 'guiding star on the horizon'. Whereas organisational goals have a clear finishing line, an organisation's purpose is never completed. It is not a statement about the company's products, services or market segments; it is articulation of what the organisation endlessly pursues. For example:

- Walt Disney's purpose is not to make cartoons, but to make people happy.

- McKinsey & Company's purpose is not to do management consulting, but to help corporations and governments be more successful.

- Fannie Mae's purpose is not to repackage mortgages, but to strengthen the social fabric by continually democratising home ownership.[20]

A compelling organisation purpose is uncovered rather than constructed. Crystallising a purpose is neither an intellectual exercise nor an exercise in wordsmithery. Leaders often find it difficult to articulate the true purpose of their organisation, as they cannot analyse their way into the future. Instead of a powerful purpose that guides action, many organisations end up with a mishmash of goals and aspirations instead.

Uncovering an organisation's 'why' calls on leaders to look inside themselves and discover what is meaningful. They also need to look outside themselves and see what is happening in the world that moves them to want to create change. They need to listen to their hearts.

Finally, leaders need to engage those within the organisation and explore what engages and energises them. A true purpose, rather than an espoused purpose that will never really be lived, can then come into view (see page 119 for the difference between these different 'levels' of purpose).

To articulate a vibrant purpose, below is a process to follow.

How to distil a compelling organisational purpose

When leaders tap into their own motivation about why they work for an organisation, fragments of the purpose emerge, which can be combined into a statement later on.

1. **Form a core group.** Imagine you've been asked to recreate the very best version of your organisation on another planet. You only have seats on the rocket for seven to twelve people. Choose individuals who have an instinctive understanding of your organisation's DNA, making sure you include some middle managers.

2. **Hold an authentic dialogue.** Invite people to respond to questions that tap into what they care about and the reason that the organisation exists:

    ■ What do we, as an organisation, stand for?

    ■ What change do we really want to make in the world?

    ■ What's the critical problem that we can uniquely address?

    ■ Who do we most care about and what do they most need from us?

    ■ What difference would it make to them if our organisation ceased to exist?

    ■ What are we so passionate about that we'll go the extra mile for it?

3. **Reflect on the 'field' together.** Look back on the conversation you've just had. Notice where the 'hot spots' were. What fired people up? When were people at their most enthusiastic? Look at what, if anything, lowered people's energy. There could be some powerful indications of what *not* to include.

4. **Capture the essence.** Based on these observations, invite people to write down 'fragments' of the purpose. Give each person several sheets of paper and ask them to capture a single fragment on each. They could be single words or short phrases. Bypass people's desire to wordsmith by getting them to focus only on the essence.

5. **Let it percolate.** Agree when you will reconvene. When you do come back together, review all the fragments. Take your time to combine them into a statement that lights people up. Remember that there might be a multitude

of ways to express the purpose. Near enough is good enough. You can always hone the statement again at a later date.

What matters is to develop a shared understanding of the organisation's purpose with a real 'feeling' dimension to it. The statement can then, when it finally appears, be taken more widely to explore how it resounds with stakeholders.

LIGHTING UP THE WHOLE SYSTEM

'We want a zinger!' Colin Mills, founder and chairman of The CFO Centre Group Ltd, said to me. In our conversation about evolving their organisational purpose, he laid out exactly how he wanted the new purpose to feel.

The CFO Centre had been created 18 years ago to help its founders and clients find freedom from conventional corporate life. It places part-time CFOs into businesses that do not require full-time professionals, enabling these CFOs to have a 'portfolio lifestyle' with more time to do the things they love while doing rewarding work. The founding energy of the business, while clear, hadn't been crystallised into a clear purpose statement for the organisation to align around; the challenge was now to do this.

A year after we'd done our work together, I caught up with Sara Daw, CEO at The CFO Centre. I learnt three valuable lessons about how a purpose lights up an ecosystem of stakeholders.

Firstly, people have to feel inspired by the organisational purpose. For team members to connect with it emotionally, the purpose needs to tap into our innate desire to make a difference, joyfully. For it to make customers zing, it needs to provide a sense of excitement and trust, which helps to build brand loyalty. A true purpose embodies a boldness that feels invigorating.

Corporate psychologist Gurnek Bains in his book *Meaning Inc.* lays out different sources of meaning that organisations can draw on to identify a purpose, for example:

- Walmart, Google and IKEA embody 'universalisation' where the purpose is to work for the good of all by democratising access to goods and services.
- Ecotricity, Uber and Ovo Energy capture the purpose of 'fresh challenge' by up-ending the complacency of incumbents.
- Tesla, Samsung and ARM Holdings embody 'innovation' and going where no company had gone before.[21]

We used this typology (which contains a fuller set of categories) as a 'starter for ten' to explore what felt compelling. Seeing that their 'why' was linked with innovation was clarifying for The CFO Centre. The future of work and 'the modern CFO' arose as topics in many conversations, reflecting their DNA as an innovator. Their combination of offering a disruptive business model and a sense of belonging for CFOs as the 'gig economy' takes hold helped to bring their purpose into sharper focus.

Secondly, an organisational purpose comes to life when unfinished business is dealt with. One senior leader had left The CFO Centre under difficult circumstances. When Ed Rowland and I created a live 'map' of the system (using the methodology of systemic constellations, see page 136) it became clear that there was some unsettled energy. While attending to these issues can be delicate, as difficult feelings are often involved, the risks of doing nothing are much greater; for example, resentments about unfair exchange, lack of acknowledgment or extra burdens of work remain. 'Cleaning the fishtank' (see page 135) releases a clear flow of positive energy so that everyone can be in their right place and deliver the purpose.

Finally, a compelling organisational purpose draws people together to achieve the organisation's best future potential. Colin and Sara had already collected significant data on why individuals join the business as part of the research for their recently published book, *Executive Freedom.*[22] They engaged the niche consultancy The House, founded by Steve Fuller and Graham Massey, to continue to consult with team members around the articulation of the purpose, framing these conversations as 'strengthening our brand' – something that individuals could easily relate to. After several months of consultation with their teams around the world, they crystallised a new purpose statement: 'We help you live the life you choose.'

'People love it!' Sara said to me. 'We've had brilliant feedback. The stories people have shared about why the purpose matters to them have been phenomenal.'

I felt excited by her enthusiasm.

'We wanted to unhook people from thinking that nothing will really change. We sat down with everyone in the business and started a dialogue. Asking them, "How do you understand our brand?" has brought our power together.'

Sara observed that the new purpose statement had helped The CFO Centre to live its brand more fully.

'Defining our purpose has helped us to see our brand more clearly. Our brand, our culture is our competitive advantage – no one can copy that!'

Sara also shared that the purpose definition had helped The CFO Centre to differentiate itself at a time when lots of competition was popping up. With developments in technology, placing freelancers into businesses was becoming 'Uber-ised'.

'But they tend to be very transactional,' Sara observed. 'We're not a technology business; we're a people business. Defining our purpose on this human basis has kept us ahead of the curve so that we can really serve our clients and help them to navigate the future.'

SUMMARY

- Disruption has become the new normal. A changing consciousness about capitalism, the purpose of corporations and the environment is creating pressure on companies to become a force for good in the world and not only financial wealth generators.

- Progressive companies are proactively orienting around a compelling purpose that creates positive change in society as well as financial success. The growing B Corps movement reflects the growing trend of 'engaged companies'.

- Embodying a compelling organisational purpose and engaging stakeholders with the purpose is the real function of leadership. When money making, goal setting and target meeting replace a true purpose, it damages an organisation.

- Uncovering a true organisational purpose is not an analytical exercise – it is a full-body experience. An organisation's 'why' needs to feel invigorating, bring clarity to decision making and draw stakeholders together so that they contribute to long-term well-being of people both inside and outside the organisation.

- By developing the four core capacities of purpose-led leadership, leaders inspire their organisation to become an agent of transformation and value creation for all its stakeholders.

NOTES

1. Keegan, S. (2015) *The Psychology of Fear in Organizations*, Kogan Page, Kindle Edition.
2. Wolf, M. (2019) Why rigged capitalism is damaging liberal democracy, *Financial Times*, 18 September.

3. (2019) Business Roundtable Redefines the Purpose of a Corporation to Promote 'An Economy That Serves All Americans', updated statement, 19 August. Available at: www.businessroundtable.org.

4. Tett, G. (2019) Does capitalism need saving from itself? *Financial Times,* 6 September.

5. Murray, A. (2019) Business finds itself left out of the party, *Financial Times*, 19 August.

6. O'Brien, J. and Cave, A. (2016) *The Power of Purpose*, FT Pearson.

7. Bendell, J. (2018) *Deep Adaptation: A Map for Navigating Climate Tragedy*, IFLAS Occasional Paper 2, University of Cumbria, 27 July.

8. *Leadership in a Climate Changed World* podcast series. See https://podcasts.apple.com/gb/podcast/leading-in-a-climate-changed-world/id1463196797.

9. Murray, A. (2019) America's CEOs seek a new purpose for the corporation, *Fortune*, 19 August. See https://fortune.com/longform/business-roundtable-ceos-corporations-purpose.

10. Gowing, N. and Langdon, C. (2018) *Thinking the Unthinkable: A New Imperative for Leadership in the Digital Age,* John Catt Educational Ltd.

11. Hieatt, D. (2014) *Do Purpose: Why Brands with a Purpose Do Better and Matter More*, Chronicle Books.

12. Ma, J. (2017) Building the Economy of the Future, 20 September. See https://www.youtube.com/watch?v=BhCCAbDSsNc, Bloomberg, YouTube LLC.

13. De Smet, A. and Gagnon, C. (2017) Safe enough to try: An interview with Zappos CEO Tony Hsieh, *The Quarterly*, No. 4, McKinsey & Company.

14. Gartenberg, C., Prat, A. and Serafeim, G. (2016) Corporate purpose and financial performance, *Organization Science* 30(1), January–February 2019: 1–18, Harvard Business School.

15. Bushe, G.R. and Marshak, R.J. (2016) The dialogic mindset: leading emergent change in a complex world, *Organization Development Journal* on Developing Culturally Adaptive Leaders for Turbulent Times.

16. *The Economist* (2019) What are companies for?, 22 August. See https://www.economist.com/leaders/2019/08/22/what-companies-are-for.

17. See https://www.theguardian.com/education/2019/apr/16/fifth-of-teachers-plan-to-leave-profession-within-two-years.

18. Ordóñez, L.D., Schweitzer, M.E., Galinsky, A.D. and Bazerman, M.H. (2009) *Goals Gone Wild: The Systematic Side Effects of Over-Prescribing Goal Setting*, Working Paper 09-083, Harvard Business School.
19. Sinek, S. (2011) *Start with Why: How Great Leaders Inspire Everyone to Take Action,* Portfolio.
20. Collins, J.C. and Porras, J.I. (1996) Building your company's vision, *Harvard Business Review.*
21. Bains, G. (2007) *Meaning Inc: The Blueprint for Business Success in the 21st Century,* Profile Books.
22. Mills, C. and Daw, S. (2019) *Executive Freedom: How to Escape the C-Suite, Create Income Security, and Take Back Control by Building a Part-Time Portfolio Career*, BrightFlame Books.

CHAPTER 9

TUNE A TOP TEAM

*When you're surrounded by people who share a passionate
commitment around a common purpose, anything is possible.*[1]

Howard Schultz

For an organisation to be successful, everyone in it has to work really well together and this calls for the power of teamwork. Pivotal to team effectiveness is the articulation and embedding of a shared team purpose. A clear 'why' enables team members to resolve conflicts and find their common ground amid the diversity that is necessary for excellent delivery. An inspiring purpose that infuses the whole team 'tunes' team members with one another and connects them with their stakeholders and wider environment. The four capacities of purpose-led leadership enable a team to go on this journey.

Let's take a look at the challenge facing one leadership team to navigate this territory.

* * *

'It's not a tell.'

It was the opening line of the meeting. The chief technology officer (CTO) of a UK Government Agency had called his senior leadership team (SLT) together to explore their purpose. They'd set aside a whole day with the objective of articulating a clear purpose statement for the SLT, drawing on everyone's input.

'It could be a tell,' he continued, 'I've done it that way before – two hours and several sticky notes later, you've come up with something. It's expedient but it's not effective. I want our team purpose to be lived not laminated.'

This leader, I thought, gets it. He understands how purpose needs to be co-created not mandated. While I felt excited, I wasn't sure that the team was. I'd caught the look on a couple of their faces when they'd walked into the room and seen the circle of chairs. I'd heard a couple of these IT experts mutter that it had better not be group therapy. As they sat down, I'd done my best to reassure them that there wouldn't be any group hugs either.

'We've achieved an incredible amount in the last 18 months,' the CTO said. 'Our organisation has a clear purpose and now we need to play our part. I have this vision of us becoming a beacon of an IT department for the whole of Westminster but what matters is what we *all* agree on our team purpose.'

There were a couple of nods but also some blank stares.

'I've been here 28 years and I've seen a lot of days like this,' said the one woman in the team, kindly but provocatively. 'Things come and go – mostly go. It's not just about finding our purpose, it's about living it otherwise today will make no difference whatsoever.'

'I'm spinning lots of plates at the moment,' said another. 'I could easily not be here. If we don't get the output we say we want – a purpose state-ment for the SLT that we all agree with – today will have been a complete waste of time.'

I looked across at my co-facilitator, who was another member of the IT directorate. He was the mover and shaker who'd made this meeting hap-pen. To my relief, he looked relaxed, which helped to settle my nerves. I had a strong sense that we had our work cut out.

* * *

A purpose that is totally adopted, believed in and then brought to life is critical for a team's success. Katzenbach and Smith define a team as fol-lows: 'A team is a small number of people with complimentary skills who are committed to a common purpose and set of performance goals and an approach for which they hold themselves mutually accountable.'[2] Note the level of engagement achieved here.

With a believed-in common purpose, team members have collective responsibility for an output. Without a shared purpose, a team is not a team but a group of individuals. A team might be a fixed entity that endures for years or a project team that exists for a few months; what matters is that there's a collective 'why'.

Teamwork can be a difficult 'nut to crack'. When a team lacks a shared purpose, many issues arise. Personality clashes, strained relationships or individuals working in 'silos' are common, as well as members accusing one another of working their own agenda and feeling frustrated that others are not 'on board'.

Research shows that when a team aligns around a compelling purpose, many of these challenges are overcome.[3] With a purpose agreed, a strategy becomes possible. With a strategy in place, a team has a clear direction. With a shared direction, team members resolve their differences by having a sense of belonging and 'we're in this together'. The actions that leaders need to start and stop doing become clear and people become energised.

Identifying a team purpose that engages everyone is, therefore, a high leverage intervention that improves team delivery. The articulation and embedding of such a purpose calls for all four leadership capacities covered in Part II, as we shall see shortly.

This chapter includes the following:

- What an effective team purpose is.
- Why a team purpose matters.
- How to bring a team purpose to life using the *four purposeful leadership capacities.*

WHAT AN EFFECTIVE TEAM PURPOSE IS

A team purpose is distinct from a goal, objective or vision. It's the deeper reason that a team exists. One senior leadership team I worked with decided that their purpose was to be a 'rogue unit' by bringing clarity to other parts of the business 'one conversation at a time'. Their vision was an organisation where everyone felt able to contribute and thrive. Their objective was to bring people together to share 'little pockets of success'. Their goal was to break down silos between different departments. It was the team *purpose* that described what the team exists to do.

A compelling team purpose has several distinct features.

Firstly, a team purpose has to be authentic. To inspire people to bring their best energies, a team purpose needs to be real. Jargon or fine words alone won't cut it – it will simply create cynicism. It has to reflect the real challenges and opportunities the team faces.

Secondly, a team purpose has to be shared. Articulating a purpose is not about the team leader crafting a purpose statement behind closed doors – a fundamentally different approach is needed since team members need to be emotionally engaged; a potent team purpose needs to be *felt.*

Thirdly, a team purpose must be lived. Purpose cannot just appear on the office wall or as a screensaver. It must be at the heart of everything that a team does. For purpose to be woven throughout a team, it must be expressed in day-to-day activities and in interactions with customers, suppliers and other stakeholders.

Finally, the team purpose needs to be the 'true' purpose of the team not a pseudo purpose. We saw in Chapter 7 that the true purpose of an organisation is often distinct from the founding purpose, the espoused purpose and the actual, lived purpose. If an organisation has a truly inspiring purpose, people's energies will be drawn to it as a magnet is drawn to steel. Other purposes – such as making money – do not hold the same power to engage people's energy and deliver outstanding results.

For a team to perform at the top of its game, it has to have a 'true' purpose. As for an organisation, there are different 'levels' of purpose, outlined in the figure below. At the centre are the beneficiaries that the team serves. These stakeholders could be customers, senior leaders, investors – whoever is involved in the ongoing success of the enterprise.

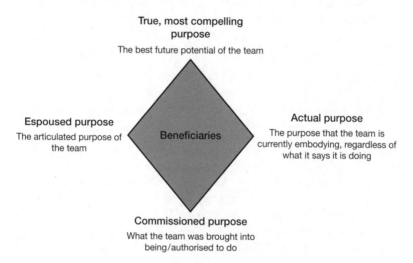

Team Purpose Diamond: the levels of purpose

Organisational Purpose Diamond by Edward Rowland and Sarah Rozenthuler (www. wholepartnership.com) is licensed under the Creative Commons Attribution-ShareAlike 4.0 International License.

The four levels of purpose are:

- **Commissioned purpose** – This is what the team has been officially created to do, usually by senior management or the board.
- **Espoused purpose** – This is what the team says that it's about, whether this is formally written down or not.
- **Actual lived purpose** – This is the purpose that the team is actually fulfilling, regardless of what it says it's doing.
- **True, most compelling purpose** – This is a team's best future possibilities and aligns with the purpose of the organisation.

A true purpose is the 'glue' that holds a team together. For a team's 'why' to become this connective tissue, it involves evolving a team's commissioned purpose into its true, most compelling purpose. The gap between the espoused and the lived purpose can create the momentum for change necessary for a team to go on this journey.

How to uncover a potent team purpose

This exercise is best done with your team. Using the Team Purpose Diamond, reflect on these questions:

1. Who is your team there to serve? What difference do you make or intend to make to your beneficiaries?

2. What was your team created to do? How relevant is your commissioned purpose today?

3. What does your team say it's about? Does this align with what it is actually about?

4. When team members are most engaged and energised, what are they doing? What does this reveal about your team's true, most potent, purpose?

Now take a sheet of paper and write the emerging true team purpose at the top of the page. Divide the rest of the page into three columns headed 'Start', 'Stop' and 'Continue'. Using the purpose as a reference point, fill in the three columns with activities that are on your horizon. If the purpose enables each team member to see clearly what to do and not do, it's a positive sign. If the purpose does not lead to clarity of thinking, review it.

LETTING A TEAM PURPOSE EMERGE

Leadership presence allows the true purpose of a team to become more precise as people share what they know at a deeper level. When team members become present together, they can sense into their 'why'. Just as our peripheral vision rather than our centre of vision is more suited for detecting movement when we want to uncover our purpose, it helps to look with 'soft' rather than 'hard' eyes.

Presence is a capacity that teams as well as individuals can develop. When people are really 'in the room' with one another, the quality of the thinking is much richer. When people are in tune with their inner state and with each other, they operate in an expanded space of possibilities. Thoughts, feelings and intuitions move in a current of creative expression.

'Entrainment' refers to one entity, with one rhythm, causing another entity, with a different rhythm, to come into sync with it. The classic example is a room full of pendulum clocks with random rhythms gradually coming to swing in time. Women living under the same roof often find that, over time, they ovulate and bleed together. Even without any conscious intention of doing this, their cycles effortlessly synchronise. Research into 'chronobiology' has revealed that this synchronisation is not a learned behaviour but inherent.

This powerful 'field effect' applies in meetings. Our vibrations are inseparable from one another. The leader of a group often sets the tone for a whole meeting by their opening comment. If it's critical, defensiveness around the table soon creeps in. If it's scepticism, hesitation descends like a cloud over the meeting. If it's encouraging, a buoyant atmosphere spreads around the room.

Tuning into a team purpose happens most easily when people bring their hearts and minds to a conversation. When team members are each aware of what is engaging and energising among themselves, they can uncover their team purpose. A team's 'why' emerges out of the combination of what brings different team members alive. On sheets of A3 brightly coloured card, I ask them to create an alternative business card that includes:

- I feel most alive when ...
- The impact I most love to have is ...
- What I'd most like to contribute to the team is ...
- What I'd most like to receive from the team is ...

When team members share their insights, points of contribution, support and interconnectivity start to emerge. By reflecting together on how they can help each other to serve their stakeholders better, the team purpose comes effortlessly into view. This reflective dialogue leads to a mutual understanding about the team purpose. It is this shared understanding that keeps the purpose alive more than any big words on a page.

EXPLORING DISAGREEMENTS THROUGH DIALOGUE

For a team to attune to a purpose that is in the best interest of the whole, it is important to explore differences through authentic dialogue rather than sweep them under the carpet. By airing disagreements, the wisdom of the whole team can come through so that a well-crafted, co-created purpose emerges.

At the SLT meeting we created space – literally – to surface where there were tensions in the different perspectives people held. At the start of the meeting, people had paired up to discuss their initial responses to the questions:

- What is the real purpose of this team?
- What wants to flow through us into the rest of the organisation and beyond?
- What is the added value we bring?
- If we disappeared today, how would the world be different tomorrow?

Keeping the focus clearly on the bigger 'why' allowed for a different level of dialogue. Individuals captured the essence of their partner's response and fed back to the group. Out of this whole group dialogue, we distilled a set of four possible team purpose statements. These statements painted a picture of the team and its best future possibilities.

We put these four draft purpose statements on four separate large cards and placed them on the floor. Each person stood where they intuitively felt drawn. If a particular statement resonated with them, they stood close to it. If a statement didn't attract them, they stood at a distance and/or looked away. From this floor map, several things soon became clear:

- It highlighted where there was agreement. The team member who was stood directly behind the CTO said that he felt comfortable because they had chosen the same purpose statement and were facing the same direction.
- It amplified the differences. Those who saw the purpose as being more about providing governance were facing away from others who saw it more in terms of building capability. This led to a dialogue about what really mattered to the team.
- Some of the language that people had used came into sharper focus. One team member said that he felt drawn to one purpose statement because it had the words 'achieve' and 'deliver'. Others shared the words that had most inspired them.

It was striking that by being on our feet, the dialogue had become very lively. The usual rules of conversation – such as who spoke the most, who agreed with whom, who would object – had been helpfully disrupted. The embodied visual helped to provoke an engaging and respectful conversation – 'We do that; we don't do that!'

It also quickly became clear which of the four purpose statements was most energising for the team. It also felt significant that the CTO was facing outwards, looking out of the window.

'Our team purpose needs to connect with the external environment,' he said, looking thoughtful.

'And with the teams we lead,' another SLT member said.

It was a sharp reminder that to uncover a true team purpose, the focus needs to be not just on the team itself but also on the larger context in which the team works. A systemic approach is critical. To encourage the SLT to look at this bigger picture, I asked:

'Who would scrutinise your team purpose most closely?'

'The COO – she'd have a lot to say!'

'Our staff!'

'The divisional directors.'

'The CEO'.

'Finance would have an opinion.'

'So would the Non-Executives.'

It was clear that the SLT needed to see the purpose through the eyes of their key stakeholders as well. While the morning's dialogue had been insightful, the SLT had not yet discovered a purpose that lit them up. To help the SLT to uncover its purpose further, it was clear that we needed to come at it from a different angle and not just in a 'heady' way.

CRYSTALLISING PURPOSE THROUGH A STAKEHOLDER CONSTELLATION

To bring purpose to life in a team, it is essential to include the systemic context as part of the discovery process. Teams, departments and organisations do not exist independently – they occupy a niche in an ecosystem. When a team attunes to its purpose through engaging stakeholders and their wider perspective, the true purpose comes more clearly into focus.

I used the image earlier (in Chapter 6) of a child's hanging mobile to reflect the way in which stakeholders exist in delicate balance to one another. This dynamic applies to a team and its stakeholders as much as to an organisation. You might like to take a moment before reading further to reflect on the individuals and groups that surround your team. If you were to complete the following diagram by putting your team as one part of the 'mobile', which other individuals or groups do you co-exist with? You could write these in the remaining circles.

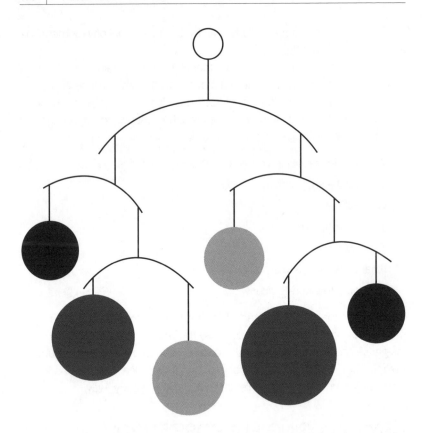

To explore purpose in its larger context with the SLT, I drew on the pioneering methodology of 'systemic constellations' (that I introduced in Chapter 7). This awareness-based approach is particularly insightful when we need to consider the perspective of multiple stakeholders, in order to release a greater flow of energy in a system. Practitioners in organisations are increasingly using this embodied mapping technology to reveal break-through insights that dialogue alone or more rational methodologies are unable to reach.

When a team connects with its real purpose, the excitement is clear to see. A true purpose draws people together and keeps them engaged. Just as a magnet pulls a random spread of iron filings into a coherent field, a shared purpose 'tunes' a team to be more harmonious. People no longer face different directions; their energies are all lined up.

Returning to the SLT, we created a stakeholder map to crystallise the team purpose further. I placed the emerging team purpose statement on a flipchart and invited each member of the SLT to volunteer to represent one of the key stakeholders.

I then asked the 'representatives' to put their own thoughts to one side and step into being the stakeholder or 'clump' of stakeholders that they'd chosen to represent. I invited them to place themselves at a distance from the flipchart to reflect the degree to which the purpose met their needs. The closer in, the more they felt they were well served by the SLT's 'why'; the further away, the less well served they felt.

It soon became apparent that we had an incomplete purpose statement. While a couple of the stakeholder reps were close to the flipchart, the others were spread right across the length of the room. The external stakeholders were almost out of the door at the opposite end of the room; the staff, CEO and COO were spread across the middle.

We explored the embodied map together by hearing what each person noticed about where they were stood. Some shared sensations ('I feel a knot in my stomach'), while others shared feelings ('I feel flat') or observations about how close or far apart they were from the purpose or each other. As we gathered the input, the intakes of breath, and bursts of laughter indicated that the data was resonating with the SLT. I asked:

'What's the one thing that would make you take a step closer to the SLT purpose?'

The responses came quickly and easily. We scribbled down these insights that were flowing in our midst. These included:

- 'The people are missing! It's all about the people and they're not included!' (The COO.)
- 'You need to add in "efficiently" or value for money as it's not our money we're spending but the country's.' (Finance.)
- 'Where's the timeliness?! We need things to be delivered on time.' (The divisional directors.)
- 'There's nothing about engaging us – we need to be included!' (Staff.)

The energy behind these observations felt very different from the cynicism at the start of the meeting. As our dialogue continued, a potent articulation suddenly – and unmistakably – arrived, to the relief of everyone present. The team now had a purpose statement to share more widely in order to hone it further. Engaging actual stakeholders in the purpose articulation process ensures that a team's 'why' really serves their beneficiaries.

ALIGNING TEAM MEMBERS WITH THE TEAM PURPOSE

To release fresh energy into a team, it helps for each team member to find their 'place' in relation to the team's 'why'. The exercise below helps team members to connect on purpose by finding their 'place' in relation to it.

How to help the team find their 'right place'

You'll need a large room with some empty floor space for this exercise.

Give each person a paper plate. Ask them to write their first name on the plate and to draw an arrow (→) on the plate so that it can face a certain direction.

Include a plate for the team's purpose, also with an arrow on it.

Current reality

Ask the team leader to place the plate for the team purpose intuitively on the floor. Notice in which direction the arrow points. Experiment with a few positions until the plate feels in its 'right' place.

Ask each person in the team to place their plate, paying attention to:

- **distance** – the stronger the relationship, the closer the paper plates
- **direction** – the more alignment there is, the more they go in the same direction.

Invite team members to stand on their own plate. Notice how the energetic 'field' feels when everyone is in their place.

Next invite people to walk around the room and to stand on plates other than their own. Notice how it feels to be stood in the different places.

As a whole group, pay attention to any 'hotspots' of alignment/misalignment or closeness/distance, whether between individuals or in relation to the team's purpose. Explore what this might mean.

Desired future

Invite each person to make an 'optimising move' that strengthens the whole map. This might involve moving their plate closer to or further away from someone else's or changing the direction that the arrow points so that there is more alignment with the purpose. Allow time for the whole map to 'settle' again (remember the image of the child's hanging mobile – when one part moves, the other parts move too).

> **Reflective dialogue**
>
> Give people the opportunity to reflect together:
>
> ■ What did the mapping reveal about the hidden potential of the team?
>
> ■ What allowed or prevented the 'optimising move'?
>
> ■ What might be needed to make that move easier?
>
> Ask people to share what they will do differently (if anything) as a result of this exercise to create more alignment with the team's purpose.

A further dimension to explore is how the team purpose connects with the organisation's purpose. Creating this 'line of sight' helps to promote 'cathedral thinking'. As the writer Antoine de Saint Exupéry said, 'A rock pile ceases to be a rock pile the moment a single man contemplates it, bearing within him the image of a cathedral.'[4]

It is purpose that enables us to look up from only seeing the bricks and mortar in front of us to take in the soaring ceiling and cavernous structure of the whole building. I shared the story earlier of how energising it was for the EMEA HR team at Discovery Inc. to see the connection between their purpose and the organisation's 'why' (see page xix).

ENABLE GROWTH THROUGH FEEDBACK

A further benefit of a team purpose made clear is that it enables continuous improvement. Sharing feedback ensures that the team now stays on track with delivering its purpose. Feedback can be shared as part of a formal appraisal session or given more informally. What matters is that the feedback is authentic and impactful.

Giving feedback has become a hot topic in recent times. An article in *The Guardian* entitled 'Why feedback is never worthwhile' resonates with the feeling of dread that many of us have when we hear the words, 'Can I give you some feedback?'[5] In a recent *HBR* article, the authors highlight how 'radical candour' has become the name of the game at organisations, such as Netflix, where employees are encouraged to give one another the unvarnished truth frequently, candidly and critically. The authors question the assumption that feedback is always useful and highlight ways to do it better, including paying close attention the language we use.[6]

From the perspective of becoming more purpose-driven, if people have acted in a way that detracts from the team living its 'why', it does need to be addressed *in an effective way*. If a leader has excluded others from a meeting without good reason or unfairly overlooked members of their team for a bonus, it is important to acknowledge this. Resentments fester if left unaddressed.

Feedback is not about making the other person feel incompetent or inadequate. The purpose of feedback is to support the other person to expand their thinking, enable their growth and contribute to a high-performing team. We need to own our perceptions as clearly and as honestly as we can rather than assume the stance of an expert who 'knows' how the other person needs to change.

While the focus of the conversation below is on 'developmental' feedback, the same principles apply for 'motivational feedback'. If you have a team member who is excellent at stakeholder engagement or sharing success stories that bring the organisation's purpose to life – tell them. People will excel only when we take the time to share what we see that really works and encourage them to do more of this.

Have a feedback conversation

Prepare by picking your moment to give feedback. If someone has given a poor presentation to a customer, it might be best to let the dust settle and share your thoughts a day or so later (if someone has done brilliantly, let them know straight away!).

Next, think carefully about the language you'll use. Aim for language that is respectful, simple and concise. Any element of judgement – whether in the words spoken or the tone used – will shut down the other person. Take a look at the statements in the column 'What we typically say' and identify any that you might use. Take a look at the alternatives under 'Give this a go instead' and see what might work for you, adapting any that you need to.

Use specific and observable data wherever possible. Rather than speaking in general terms, state precisely the behaviour or attitude that you want to highlight so that the receiver understands what they need to do (or not do) for future success.

What we typically say	Give this a go instead
Can I give you some feedback?	Can we talk about how x went? I'd like to share my response
You should ...	This is what I would do in a similar situation

What we typically say	Give this a go instead
You need to get better at ...	Here are a couple of suggestions about what you could do differently next time
You shouldn't have ...	When you did or said x, I felt y or the impact on me was ...
You need to be less arrogant ...	I started to feel agitated at the point when ...
You need to be more inclusive	When I heard that x hadn't been invited to the meeting, I felt concerned
You've been completely unfair	When I saw that x hadn't been given a bonus, I assumed that you thought they'd been under-performing

Explore how the messages you've given have landed with the other person by asking them how the conversation has left them *feeling*. You might ask what they are taking away and if they have any requests of you. Close by saying that the door to further dialogue is open.

When a team realises it faces behaviours that are 'off purpose', they can course correct and, by focusing on the positive behaviours that are working well, team members can do more of these to strengthen the team's delivery in line with their purpose.

SUMMARY

- A clear and strong shared purpose is central to being a high-performing team. It describes why the team exists in a way that inspires each team member.

- A team purpose needs to be authentic, shared and lived. An inspiring team purpose creates common ground and enables team members to 'tune' into one another rather than get stuck in conflict.

- There are four 'levels' of team purpose. The 'true' purpose of a team reflects its best future possibilities. This is often distinct from its 'commissioned' purpose, espoused purpose and actual purpose. Evolving the commissioned purpose into a true purpose takes a team on a transformative journey to more powerful delivery.

- To uncover a team purpose, the four capacities of purpose-led leadership are needed:
  - When people are present, they bring both their hearts and minds to explore what matters most.
  - Authentic dialogue surfaces differences and takes the conversation to a different level where team members talk about their collective identity.
  - Stakeholder engagement ensures that a team purpose really meets the needs of those whom the team serves.
  - A true team purpose emerges as each team member feels the connection with their own purpose.
- A potent team purpose connects with the purpose of the organisation. Team members each have a sense of belonging and of being in their 'right place'.
- When team members give each other constructive feedback, team performance is strengthened.

NOTES

1. Gallo, C. (2013) What Starbucks CEO Howard Schultz taught me about communication and success, *Fortune*, 9 December.
2. Katzenbach, J.R. and Smith, D.K. (2009) *The Discipline of Teams,* Harvard Business Review Classics.
3. Katzenbach, J.R. and Smith, D.K. (2009) op cit.
4. Antoine de Saint Exupéry (1942) *Pilote de Guerre,* Editions de la Maison Française.
5. See https://www.theguardian.com/lifeandstyle/2019/mar/22/ why-feedback-is-never-worthwhile-oliver-burkeman.
6. See https://hbr.org/2019/03/the-feedback-fallacy.

CHAPTER 10

ENLIVEN YOUR PEOPLE

Companies need the contributing vitality of all the individuals who work for them in order to stay alive in the sea of changeability in which they find themselves.

David Whyte[1]

Tue leaders uplift their people by restoring their zest for work. They have meaningful conversations where people feel seen and safe to express their full selves. They enable people to see the positive impact of their work on others, bringing a sense of aliveness. They are doing what they feel called to do and their vitality energises others. Developing leadership presence, authentic dialogue, stakeholder engagement and connecting on purpose creates a win–win–win, enabling individuals, teams and organisations to flourish. All of this begins with a leader feeling the 'warm glow' of their own purpose inside.

Let's take a look at one leader wanting to reconnect with his mojo.

* * *

'Is this it?'

I was at a 'chemistry meeting' with a prospective client in the travel industry. We were sitting in the hushed atmosphere of the British Library in London. As he lent back and tucked his arms behind his head, I thought: Here's a man who seems to have it all. I'd noticed the screensaver on his tablet – the beautiful wife and smiling children stood in front of the large family home with a luxury car parked outside.

'Is there more to life than this?'

It sounded like the line of a song, but I knew from the way his eyes searched mine that he was being serious. We'd met to discuss how some coaching might support him in taking the next step in his leadership. A conversation goes, however, where a conversation goes ...

'Am I the only person in the world who just can't stick with his job, go home, collect a pay cheque and see that as the way life is?'

'It sounds like you think there's something missing?'

'I had this profound moment recently,' Gary said. 'I realised I'd be 40 years old in four years' time. I want to be able to look back and feel that I made a difference.'

There was a pause while that sank in.

'I want to feel that I really lived.'

* * *

Finding work that brings deep satisfaction is one of life's great challenges. It can take time, persistence and courage to discover it, as well as patience to deal with the inevitable setbacks. The search, however, is truly worth it. When our daily work is connected with our purpose, it feels invigorating. As we willingly serve our beneficiaries, we feel connected with something larger than ourselves and have a felt sense of 'rightness' about what we're doing.

Discovering our purpose is not, however, a straightforward process. Unless we've been very fortunate, most families, schools and organisations don't show us the way to our North Star. We're often guided, sometimes goaded, to become what others wanted us to be. Some of us fall into the trap of parroting our parents by copying their career or going into the family business because it feels familiar even though it's draining. Others unwittingly try to live their parent's unlived dreams but betray themselves in the process.

I wanted to be an architect for most of my teenage years and was even given a place at university to study architecture. It took me many years to realise that I'd unconsciously taken on the burden of my dad's unfulfilled ambition – he was a civil engineer with artistic talents that were underused in his professional life. The sense of relief I felt when eventually I let go of a 'dream' that wasn't mine will always stay with me.

That visceral feeling of release still spurs me on – 30 years later – to do the work I do. Having stepped away from a career that would have been deadening onto a path that is enlivening, I want to share what I've learnt about coming fully alive at work. So much research tells us that employees' sense of purpose is directly related to their health, resilience and longevity; leaders have a unique responsibility to create an environment where well-being – their own and their people's – thrives.

This chapter, which focuses on how an individual discovers and follows their purpose, operates at two levels. Firstly, a leader needs to be in touch with what is theirs to do. We cannot energise another without being energised ourselves. We cannot engage a team unless we are engaged ourselves. Leadership begins with attending to our own flow of energy; our vitality positively 'infects' others more than anything we do.

Secondly, this chapter explores how a leader takes others with them across the bridge from feeling flat, exhausted or drained to feeling fulfilled at work. Spoiler alert: the story of Gary ends with his decision to leave the organisation rather than stay. Had I had access to his boss during the coaching, I would have shared what I've written here. I've seen more times than I care to remember talented people leave organisations because their leaders didn't engage and energise them. While leaving might be the right decision, a leader can connect their people with zestful work, which encourages them to stay.

This chapter covers the following:

■ What brings people alive at work.

■ Why enlivening your people matters.

■ How to energise yourself and your people using the four capacities.

WHAT BRINGS PEOPLE ALIVE AT WORK

Recent research, including in neuroscience, informs us what leaders can do to change the widespread lack of engagement at work. In *Alive at Work,* Dan Cable, a professor of organisational behaviour at London Business School, argues that disengagement is not a motivational but a biological problem. Our bodies are not built for routine and repetition, but rather exploration, experimentation and learning. Our intrinsic urge to be curious, creative and courageous comes from our 'seeking system'. When we learn something novel, develop a skill or have a conversation that brings new meaning, we are rewarded with a jolt of dopamine, the feel-good neurotransmitter that encourages us to explore more.[2]

Cable traces the deactivation of our seeking system back to the Industrial Revolution when work started to become bureaucratic and controlled. With the advent of assembly lines through to management by objectives, our 'fear system' has become more active, reflected in the feelings of anxiety and apprehension that still characterise many workplaces today.

There is a substantial body of research that indicates within many organisations there is a strong climate of fear. Employees are afraid of speaking out, losing their jobs and being demoted. While we have moved on from the physical dangers in the workplaces of the Industrial Revolution, in many organisations, these have been substituted with psychological ones. As a result, we keep our heads down and become anxious about the future.[3]

Activating the seeking system is the key to unlocking people's energy so that work feels engaging. This does not mean that we will always feel happy – there might be times when we feel inconvenienced and uncomfortable – what matters is that we find our work meaningful and stretching.

The surest sign that we are on our purpose path is that we feel engaged and energised. As our time and talents flow towards something meaningful, it brings joy rather than fleeting happiness. There might be difficult conversations to be had, sacrifices to be made and relationships to be disentangled but on we go, powered by a sense of purpose.

WHY ENLIVENING YOUR PEOPLE MATTERS

There are three key reasons that it is beneficial for leaders to help their people attune to purpose.

Firstly, purpose-oriented workers are more fulfilled by their work. The Workforce Purpose Index 2016 found that currently 37% of LinkedIn members across the globe (40% in the USA) identify themselves as 'purpose-oriented' – more motivated by doing work that matters rather than by status or money. Purpose-oriented workers are 50% more likely to be in leadership positions and 50% more likely to be ambassadors for their organisation.[4]

Secondly, it is beneficial for our well-being. Psychological research shows that people who have a sense of purpose in their work have better life outcomes than those who don't. A study carried out by researchers in the Department of Psychology at the University of South Florida found that academics who found their work meaningful and rewarding had higher levels of work engagement, well-being and job satisfaction than those for whom there was no sense of calling. This pattern of results has been well replicated over various studies spanning the last 20 years.

Where this study comes into its own is by including a group who experienced a calling but for whom this remained unanswered. These academics reported significantly poorer physical and psychological health than the other two groups. As the authors conclude, 'Having a calling is only of benefit if it is met, but can be a detriment when it is not compared with having no calling at all.'

In other words, ignoring a calling hurts us.[5]

Finally, research shows that employees want fulfilling work as part of their psychological contract. Leaders play a critical 'sense making' role, particularly in periods of change and uncertainty, by helping people to understand what new developments mean for them so that their work is in line with the organisation's purpose. When leaders lose a focus on this, engagement levels in the teams around them decrease.

Research by Korn Ferry Hay Group has found that in high change environments, leaders often overlook the need to develop the people they lead. They might be too busy, too stressed or too unclear about what the future holds. Leaders who are aware of this pervasive blind spot have a much better chance of addressing it and keeping their people on board by connecting them with their 'why'.[6]

THE DESIRE FOR FULFILLING WORK

In a hard-hitting article called 'Why You Hate Work', the authors highlight how many of us lack purposeful work.[7] They surveyed nearly 20,000 employees across a range of companies and industries and found that employees are significantly more satisfied and productive when four core needs are met:

- **Physical** – having regular opportunities to recharge, such as taking a break every 90 minutes.

- **Mental** – being able to apply focused energy and decision-making power to the task in hand.

- **Emotional** – feeling valued, appreciated and cared for, particularly by one's line manager.

- **Spiritual** – feeling connected to a higher purpose at work and doing what we do best and enjoy most.

While all four needs being met fuels productivity, loyalty and performance, one of them had a bigger impact than the others. Employees whose spiritual needs were fulfilled were *three times more likely* to stay with their organisation than those whose work lacked meaning.

There is, however, a rub. Whereas the authors made suggestions about how to meet more physical, mental and emotional needs, they did not cover how to strengthen the spiritual dimension at work. In our fast-paced, achievement-oriented, materialistic culture, we lack guidance about how to sense our deeper calling. Drawing on the first capacity of cultivating leadership presence, some 'how-to's are precisely where we go next.

HOW TO UNCOVER YOUR OWN PURPOSE

Our 'why' is something we receive more than conceive. As Steve Jobs famously said in his address to Stanford Commencement Address: 'Don't be trapped by dogma, which is living with the results of other people's thinking. Don't let the noise of others' opinions drown out your own inner voice. And, most important, have the courage to follow your heart and intuition. They somehow already know what you truly want to become.'[8]

To live our purpose, our journey moves through four different types of purpose, which are described in the figure below.

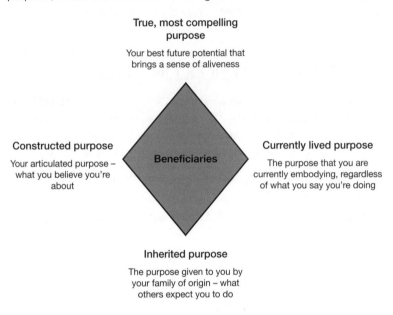

True, most compelling purpose

Your best future potential that brings a sense of aliveness

Constructed purpose

Your articulated purpose – what you believe you're about

Beneficiaries

Currently lived purpose

The purpose that you are currently embodying, regardless of what you say you're doing

Inherited purpose

The purpose given to you by your family of origin – what others expect you to do

Personal Purpose Diamond

Organisational Purpose Diamond by Edward Rowland and Sarah Rozenthuler (www.wholepartnership.com) is licensed under the Creative Commons Attribution-ShareAlike 4.0 International License.

The four different types of purpose evolve through the following sequence.

■ Our **inherited purpose** we receive from our family of origin. This includes positive experiences that drew out our essence as well as unhelpful expectations of our parents, siblings and other family members. Raising our awareness of how these 'overlays' from the past have shaped us frees us to step into our 'true work'.

■ Our **constructed purpose** is the narrative we create about our work that we intellectually believe. This purpose resides more in our head than in our heart, even though we might think and speak about it as if it were true. We often make the story sound good, which does not reflect the dissatisfaction we feel inside.

■ Our **currently lived purpose** is what we're actually doing, regardless of what we say to ourselves or to others. Sometimes we 'take on' the purpose of the organisation we work for in our desire to do something worthy or because of pressure to conform. This is our current reality that we've made our own, even if it doesn't feel authentic.

- Our **true, most compelling purpose** is what we feel life is calling us to do and be. When we live into our true purpose, we feel an inner glow. We have a deep knowing that we are where we belong and expressing who we really are. We are pulled from the past and present into the future and our best possibilities.

Our true purpose is not something that we develop out of a sense of obligation to others. When Parker Palmer, a US author and founder of the Center for Courage and Renewal, reflected on his own experience of feeling spilt between being good at his work as an aspiring 'ad man' lured by 'the fast car and other large toys' and living his true purpose, he had the chilling sensation that: 'The life I am living is not the same as the life that wants to live in me.'[9]

Many of us know the discomfort of the gap between our constructed purpose and currently lived purpose. Finding a way through this inner battle to live our true, most compelling purpose is critical.

One leader I coached, Annie, reflected on her four different purposes to move forwards. From her family of origin, she had inherited both a strong desire to make a difference in the world and a sense of heaviness about doing something worthwhile. Annie shared that while she could tell a good story about making a difference to children's lives, she'd 'taken on' the noble-sounding purpose of the government department where she worked and had started to feel hollow inside. She reflected:

'Really, I'm just a policy wonk! I keep busy having meetings and writing papers but I'm not sure whether it really makes a difference at all.'

While the gap between our *constructed purpose* and our *currently lived* purpose might feel disturbing, it can be a huge catalyst for change. As we become aware of the feeling that something is 'off' about the life that we're engaged in, this dissonance is a wake-up call. We start to have a sense of another life calling to us and we feel drawn to move into it since it is there that we pursue our *true, most compelling purpose*.

Having felt this mismatch, Annie navigated her way to become a CEO of a not-for-profit focused on children's welfare. In her new role, Annie was able to apply her natural ability to think strategically and engage her stakeholders authentically. While feeling heavy hearted had been her 'red flag' telling her that she was off track, feeling buoyant was the 'green flag' that told her she was on her purpose path.

Evolve your purpose

This exercise draws on the Personal Purpose Diamond.

Part 1 – your inherited purpose

Explore the messages that you were given by the 'big' people in your life when you were small. Explore what your parents and significant others wanted *for* you and *from* you.

- Who or what did my parents want me to be? Or, if they said or did nothing about this, how did that impact me?
- How might I be living out the unfulfilled dreams of my parents or ancestors? Am I in any way trying to accomplish what they wanted or failed at?

Explore the positive influence that your early life had on you. Your parents, siblings or long-standing friends might also have insights for you in relation to these questions:

- What did I really enjoy doing when I was younger? Where was I really effective?
- What did other kids love about what I did?
- When did I express myself most fully?

Part 2 – your constructed and currently lived purpose

Bring to mind any feelings you have of feeling trapped or stuck. Allow these feelings to surface without pushing them away. Remind yourself how discomfort can be a positive catalyst for change.

- Where do I experience a lack of congruence between my interests, values and aims and those of my organisation and/or profession?
- What's at risk if I were to make a change in my work situation? What's at risk if I don't?

Part 3 – your true, most compelling purpose

Remember that when our head and our heart are in tune, we make our best decisions.

- What is the most meaningful thing I could do with my life?
- What do I feel drawn to? Where do I feel a sense of ease? With whom?
- Where do I have that 'it feels right' feeling? In what way is the future calling me?

Finally, reflect on your responses. Notice any surprises. Be open to the possibility that the path that is really yours to walk sometimes finds you!

FOLLOW YOUR 'THREAD'

Each of us has unique potential. According to James Hillman, a US psychologist and author, just as an acorn unfolds into an oak, so we hold the blueprint for our individual possibilities inside ourselves. The big adventure in life is to find and then be true to our 'acorn' and allow the seed inside us to fully actualise. As Hillman writes:

> *There is more to human life than our theories of it allow. Sooner or later something seems to call us onto a particular path. You may remember this 'something' as a signal moment in childhood when an urge out of nowhere, a fascination, a peculiar turn to events struck like an annunciation: This is what I must do, this is what I've got to have. This is who I am.*[10]

We are given glimpses of our true purpose through 'signal moments' that happen throughout our life. Together, these signal moments weave a 'thread' that leads us to work that aligns with our purpose. Through my coaching of senior executives, I have observed that there are three kinds of signal moment which are captured in the following figure.

| Transmission moments | Crucible moments | Synchro moments |

Firstly, transmission moments are the times when we have a strong sense of who we are. We might experience this as a feeling of 'This is me! This is who I really am!' This feeling might come in a flash during a specific activity or a longer period, such as a stretch assignment. It might happen when we're simply doing something we're good at and enjoy.

Paul Merton, one of the most successful British comedians of recent times, began his fascination with humour at an early age when he saw the clowns in the circus and heard the crowd roar with laughter. In an interview, he recounts the thrill, years later, of his first ever stand-up gig at the Comedy Store in London. The crowd loved his routine and Merton walked the seven miles home, from Soho to Streatham, *'on pure ecstasy the whole way.'*[11] When our feet find the path that is ours to walk, it lights us up.

Secondly, 'crucible moments' are life-defining experiences that test us to the limits. They might be a single event or a pattern of experiences. They often involve pain or loss, difficulty or despair. Leadership thinkers Nick Craig, Bill George and Scott Nook, who coined the term, suggest that is the tough stuff and the hard times that give us our mettle – and meaning – as leaders.[12] These moments hold our attention. We keep revisiting them, as they help us to come to grips with who we really are. If we push them away, they 'have us' and result in us doing work that is too small for us. If we 'process' them – talk or write about them – these experiences burn off the dross of our personality to reveal more of our essence.

The high-profile UK investor and philanthropist Guy Hands has talked openly about how his difficult childhood has shaped him. Severely dyslexic and having moved to the UK from Zimbabwe at the age of three, Hands was an easy target for bullies at school. In an interview for the BBC, he shared how the bullying got worse and worse until 'One day I snapped, and I'm not proud of it, but I basically brought down a desk on another kid.'

Hands reflects that his difficult childhood gave him the drive to make something of his life. With his uncanny ability to spot good investments and build a culturally diverse team, he is the founder of the investment house Terra Firma, which has reported assets of £4.7bn.[13] Bearing no grudges against the kids that bullied him, he demonstrates a determination to make the most of the crucible moments that shaped him.

Finally, 'synchro moments' are meaningful coincidences that occur, which give us a sense that we're on our right path. The great Swiss psychologist Carl Jung coined the term 'synchroncity' to refer to unexpected and energising events that feel as though they're not spurious. These moments might be quite ordinary: a conversation, a magazine article or a radio show that you found particularly interesting. These incidents might seem like mundane occurrences, but they are not to be underestimated because they reinforce the undercurrents inside us.

Noticing what jumps out at us from the tapestry of our lives can be a valuable clue to the 'thread' of our purpose. As James Hollis, a Jungian psychoanalyst and author says:

When something is of us, it is for us, it sets off the tuning fork inside us. It resounds because it has always been there, archetypally. The resonance within us cannot be willed; it happens. No amount of willing will make it happen. But resonance is the surest guide to finding our own right path.[14]

The tuning fork resonating inside us brings clarity about our purpose. Years ago, I was sitting in the cinema watching the credits roll at the end of a film and the words 'dialogue coach' jumped out at me. On my LinkedIn profile, this turn of phrase has now become part of who I am, not on film sets but in the corporate world. The following figure illustrates some of the ways that resonance feels when we sense the 'tuning fork' going off our lives.

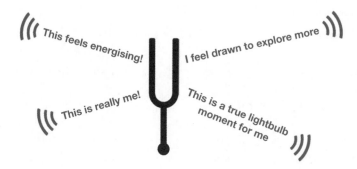

As our commitment to living our purpose deepens, it sets off a flow of activity around us. If we're sensitive to it, the right thing seems to happen at the right time and in the right place. People open doors to opportunities without us having to make a hard knock. Rather than using our force to make things happen, we 'magnetise' people, events and things to us, in a way that never would have happened by our own 'efforting'.

Attuning to our purpose calls for a new perspective. We let go of a 'planned future' so that our 'emerging future' can flow in. We open ourselves up to a felt sense of 'rightness' about our next 'true move' – the next step we will take to cross the bridge to living our purpose.

Follow your thread

Look backwards to go forwards and discover the 'thread' of your purpose.

Transmission moments

- When have you had an experience of 'This is really me!'?
- In which moments of your life have you felt particularly alive?
- When have you felt 'called' to help a purposeful cause?

Crucible moments

- Which moments or episodes of adversity have shaped you?
- How have these experiences strengthened you as a leader?
- What difficulties have you experienced that might enable you to help others who are struggling with a similar challenge?

Syncho moments

- What unexpected events or encounters have felt particularly energising?
- What meaningful coincidences come to mind?
- What 'generative images' have jolted you? A word, phrase, picture or symbol?

Weaving it together

Finally, reflect on your responses. See what patterns have played out. If there is a thread running through your life, what might it be? Describe it insightfully. How might you really take hold of this 'thread' and follow where it leads? What might be your next 'true move'?

SPEND TIME WITH YOUR PEOPLE

Turning our attention now to how a leader can engage and energise those around them, the 'Hawthorn effect' – a classic finding in organisational psychology – comes to mind. This term was coined after a series of experiments in the 1920s–30s at a factory outside Chicago to explore how to improve workers' performance. They increased lighting levels, changed the pattern of breaks, put workers in a separate room and, with each change, productivity increased. The productivity gain seemed to occur as a result of the effect on workers of the interest being shown in them, regardless of the specific intervention.

Making time for a meaningful conversation is a powerful way to give your people attention. We all need to be seen, valued and appreciated at work – without this we can fall into feelings of isolation and resentment.

Recent research has shown that professional coaching is a 'helpful vehicle' to support people in making positive career choices.[15] Talking with a boss, friend, trusted colleague or wise mentor can also be valuable. Another person is usually better to take a 'meta position' and see a situation with neutrality. As a result, a conversation can expand thinking, crystallise a decision or spur action. People become both calmer and more motivated.

A further benefit of conversation is that other people can sometimes see aspects of who we are that are pivotal to our purpose. We sometimes have abilities that are so effortless or passions that are so heartfelt that we take them for granted. The 'Johari window' – named after the two psychologists Joseph Luft and Harrington Ingham who developed the tool – is one way to understand this. The window has four 'panes' that are laid out in the diagram below.

Johari window
Based on Luft, J., Ingham, H. (1955) 'The Johari window, a graphic model of interpersonal awareness'. *Proceedings of the Western Training Laboratory in Group Development* (Los Angeles: UCLA)

Based on this layout, there are four 'selves':

- The Open Self which is known to self and others.
- The Hidden Self which is known to self but not to others.
- The Blind Self that is not known to self, but is known to others.
- The Unknown Self that is not known to both self and others.

Another person can reveal a valuable dimension of our Blind Self. I will always remember years ago my boss walking into the canteen and finding me talking animatedly with some colleagues. He commented on how I seemed to be able to effortlessly engage others. His observation crystallised something I'd known about myself but hadn't known that I'd known. The title of my previous book, *How to Have Meaningful Conversations,* still makes me smile when I recall his comment.[16]

To see how the Johari window might bring you and the people you lead insight, explore the following exercise. Our purpose reflects our unique, authentic self so seeing our Selves more clearly helps us to express more of our creativity, joy and talents.

How to see your Selves more clearly

Take some time to reflect on these three questions. Consider talking them through with a trusted friend or colleague who knows you well.

1. What am I pretending not to know about myself? What passions or strengths do I have that I don't acknowledge? What does this reveal about my Hidden Self?

2. What have others observed about my abilities? What encouraging comments stay with me? What aspects of my Blind Self have others brought to my attention?

3. Who's a leader who's very different from me that I admire? What qualities do they embody that I might also have? What might this tell me about my Unknown Self?

Reflect on what your answers tell you. Go for a walk in nature or somewhere relaxing. Allow any further insights to come to you, without striving for anything specific to happen.

Now take some time to reflect on someone who falls under your leadership who might benefit from your perspective.

- What do you observe about their abilities or 'superpowers'?
- When have you seen them express their heart's desire, essence or passion?
- What positive aspects of their Blind Self might you bring to their attention?

Pick your moment to share your insights with them.

By talking with your team members, you can explore whether what they are doing every day reflects their purpose and values. You can explore how aligned they are with the organisation's purpose. Helpful questions to ask include:

- What's most meaningful for you in your daily activities?
- How can I help you to accomplish more of your purpose in your work?
- What resources do you need?
- What obstacles might I be able to remove for you?

An open, honest and supportive conversation can help people to 'connect their soul with their role,' as author Nicholas Pearce[17] puts it, and overcome their resistance and fears. When you help someone to animate their everyday work with their own personal purpose, it is a true act of leadership.

CONNECT YOUR PEOPLE WITH YOUR ORGANISATION'S BENEFICIARIES

Purpose is about ensuring the long-term well-being of your beneficiaries. Research has shown that 'generativity' – doing something for the benefit of future generations – is the most common source of meaning.[18] Purpose does not land in our laps; it arises out of living an active and committed life where we want to make the world a better place.

Rather than follow the conventional US business school approach of 'learn, earn and return' to become a purpose-rich person (that many philanthropists have followed), purposeful work is best infused across the course of a whole career.[19] Putting purpose into 'deep freeze' by saying that we'll get to purpose 'later' is misguided. Reflecting on who we feel moved to serve and coming into contact with them is energising. Our beneficiaries might be other people, animals or nature; what matters is that we work wholeheartedly.

Connecting people with their stakeholders creates 'local meaning' according to Freek Vermeulen, a colleague of Dan Cable's at London Business School. Rather than leaders providing employees with a set of grand words – the typical way that organisational purpose is communicated – it is more effective to help people to observe and, more crucially, feel the direct impact of their work on their beneficiaries. Whereas lofty purpose statements can lead to cynicism, even a short conversation with a recipient who expresses genuine appreciation makes work meaningful. It transmits the message that we don't have to save a rainforest or do spinal surgery – day-to-day acts make a difference.[20]

Research carried out by Adam Grant on college fundraisers in call centres monitored the number of calls and the revenue generated by three groups of workers over a one-month period. The group who before making a call were taken into a separate room by a manager and read out a one-page letter from a student beneficiary about how their scholarship had made a difference, performed no better than the control group. The performance of the third group, who spent a few minutes in actual conversation with the beneficiary, shot up: they raised 171% more money. Purpose is not an abstract concept; it needs to be felt.[21]

Reflecting on Adam Grant's research, Dan Cable makes a pertinent observation for leaders. Generating a sense of an organisation's purpose through direct contact with beneficiaries needs to be authentic. If it is seen as a device for manipulating employees' feelings, it will backfire. Others have warned against the risks of 'corporate carrots' being used to trick people into aligning with an organisation's purpose.[22] A leader needs to ensure that contact with beneficiaries is sincere; only real emotional connection taps into the power of purpose.

CONNECT ON PURPOSE

As a leader it is important to create a supportive environment where people can grow. Purpose activates our 'seeking system', encouraging us to experiment, but we need to feel safe to explore. Research on highly productive teams at Google over a five-year period, Project Aristotle, found that 'psychological safety' – team members feeling safe to take risks and be vulnerable in front of one another – was 'far and away the most important of the five dynamics that set successful teams apart'.

Amy Edmondson, a professor of leadership at Harvard Business School, who coined the term 'psychological safety', highlights how it enables teams to have difficult conversations.[23] Instead of people feeling that they're walking on eggshells or tiptoeing around the truth, they are willing to admit to making mistakes, ask for help or propose an off-the-wall idea. People trust one another not to ridicule, reject or punish someone for speaking up; they share ideas and do something new to bring purpose to life instead.

When a leader is able to deepen the understanding between team members of what brings them alive, they will be much better at getting the best from one another. Each person is unique – what engages one individual might be very different from what energises another.

When I coach a leadership team, I encourage each team member to tune into their own sense of purpose using a fun activity, inspired by Dan Cable's work. I ask people to come up with an alternative job title that reflects their talents, strengths and unique contribution to the team. When the CFO introduces herself as the 'queen of the bank', the CEO as 'chief cheerleader' and the chairman as 'company conscience rep', the atmosphere becomes playful. People quickly and easily get a sense of who they really are and who others are. This connectivity helps to build psychological safety and to open up an authentic dialogue where people feel that they can be themselves without wearing the corporate mask.

According to Dan Cable, this exercise improves team dynamics because people increase their understanding of each other's roles and responsibilities. This greater role clarity aids decision making because it reduces ambiguity – a team gets on with the task that it is there to do, with more zest and confidence. It releases joy, creativity and energy. It clicks people into thinking in a different way. Who am I really? What am I about? What is the unique contribution I bring? When people engage with questions in this way, purpose on a personal level really starts to come alive.

* * *

The coaching with Gary spanned many months. He took his time to digest the dissatisfaction he felt and waited for his next 'true move' to become clear. Ongoing conversations with his wife were important so that he balanced providing for his family with taking care of his own need to do something more meaningful. Gary gradually came to see that he needed to leave his salaried job to run his own business instead.

While I was pleased for Gary that he had his mojo back, his decision to leave reminded me of how much talent organisations lose when leaders fail to engage and energise their people. As Richard Branson famously said in 2014, 'Train people well enough so they can leave, treat them well enough, so they don't want to.' This statement from the founder of the Virgin empire could be the mantra of every leader who wants to lead with purpose.

A couple of years after we'd completed the coaching, Gary and I caught up on a video call. I noticed that he looked much more relaxed than when we'd met at his office. Gary said that he loved being able to have breakfast most days with his girls, given that he worked from home and was master of his own diary.

As our conversation drew to a close, Gary shared that he was off to China the next day to meet with a possible new business partner.

'I feel so excited!' he said. 'I no longer feel I'm just a cog in a wheel. I'm creating something positive and leaving a legacy. I actually think this is it!'

* * *

SUMMARY

- Finding and following our heart's desire feels both exciting and scary. Discovering our purpose is important for our physical and psychological health.
- The four capacities of purpose-led leadership enable us to walk our purpose path:
  - Our presence allows us to acknowledge where we are and listen for more expansive possibilities.

- Authentic dialogue supports us to be true to ourselves, courageous with our actions and open to new dimensions of who we are.

- Having clarity about who we feel moved to serve makes our work meaningful.

- Connecting on purpose calls on us to explore four different types of purpose using our whole selves.

- Our journey to discovering more energising work involves letting go of our *inherited purpose*. When we notice a dissonance between our *constructed purpose* and *currently lived purpose*, this can be a catalyst for change. It can spur us to live into our *true most compelling purpose* rather than get stuck living a counterfeit version.

- Noticing 'signal moments' – including the times when we've felt 'this is really me!' – is key to uncovering our purpose. 'Crucible moments' and synchronicities weave together a 'thread' of our unique purpose.

- As we step into our true work with clarity and commitment, we experience a flow of meaningful events that take us more deeply into living our purpose.

- Support the people around you to gain a deeper understanding of their personal purpose, to find 'local meaning' and feel an emotional connection with the organisation's purpose.

NOTES

1. Whyte, D. (2002) op cit.
2. Cable, D. (2018) *Alive at Work*, Harvard Business Review Press.
3. Keegan, S. (2015) *The Psychology of Fear in Organizations*, Kogan Page, Kindle edition.
4. See https://cdn.imperative.com/media/public/Global_Purpose_Index_2016.pdf.
5. Gazica, M.W. and Paul E. Spector, P.E. (2015) *Journal of Vocational Behavior*, Elsevier.
6. Bywater, J. and Lewis, J. (2019) Leadership: What competencies does it take to remain engaged as a leader in a VUCA world? *Assessment and Development Matters,* The British Psychological Society.
7. Schwartz, T. and Porath, C. (2014) Why You Hate Work, *New York Times.* See https://www.nytimes.com/2014/06/01/opinion/sunday/why-you-hate-work.html.

8. Stanford University (2008) *Steve Jobs' 2005 Stanford Commencement Address.* See https://www.youtube.com/watch?v=UF8uR6Z6KLc YouTube Inc.

9. Palmer, P. (1999) *Let Your Life Speak: Listening for the Voice of Vocation*, Jossey Bass.

10. Hillman, J. (1997) *The Soul's Code: In Search of Character and Calling*, Ballantyne Books.

11. Graham, J. (2016) Paul Merton: 'I wanted my dad to be a hero, but he was very distant', *The Big Issue*, 14–20 March.

12. Craig, N., George, B. and Snook, S. (2015) *The Discover your True North Fieldbook A Personal Guide to Finding Your Authentic Leadership,* Wiley.

13. See https://www.bbc.co.uk/news/business-48266511.

14. Hollis, J. (2000) *Creating a Life: Finding Your Individual Path,* Inner City Books.

15. Viorela Pop, G. and van Nieuwerburgh, C. (2019) Listening to your heart or head? – An interpretative phenomenological analysis of how people experienced making good career decisions, *International Coaching Psychology Review,* 14(2), Autumn 2019.

16. Rozenthuler, S. (2007) *How to Have Meaningful Conversations*, Watkins, 2nd edn, 2019.

17. Pearce, N. (2019) *The Purpose Path: A Guide to Pursuing Your Authentic Life's Work,* St Martin's Essentials.

18. Schnell, T. (2011) Individual differences in meaning-making: Considering the variety of sources of meaning, their density and diversity, *Personality and Individual Differences,* 51, 667–73.

19. *The Purpose Economy,* op cit.

20. Vermeulen, F. (2019) Companies don't always need a purpose beyond profit, *Harvard Business Review,* 8 May.

21. Grant, A.M. (2008) The significance of task significance: job performance effects, relational mechanisms and boundary conditions, *Journal of Applied Psychology,* 93, 108–24.

22. Kenni, T. (2019) No purpose, no problem published on LinkedIn, 11 October. See https://www.linkedin.com/pulse/purpose-problem-theodore-kinni/?trackingId=5%2Bv0N546TEBeZHPukz1hCQ%3D%3D.

23. Edmondson, A.C. (2012) *Teaming: How Organisations Learn, Innovate and Compete in the Knowledge Economy,* Jossey-Bass, San Francisco.

EPILOGUE: A NEW DAWN

by Dr Victoria Hurth

We are moving into the sixth biggest extinction of life on planet earth, the last being when the dinosaurs were alive,[1] with an estimated 10,000 species going extinct each year.[2] While we have gained 7% tree cover since 1982 due mostly to climate change,[3] we have cut down almost half of trees that existed before humans and are now losing them at a rate of 15 billion a year.[4] Each year 24 billion tonnes of fertile top soil is lost – about 3.4 tonnes per person[5] and even mainstream politicians are suggesting countries such as the UK are only 30–40 years away from loss of soil fertility.[6] In the EU alone this is estimated to cost the economy US$490 billion.[7] Twenty-one of the world's largest 37 long-term groundwater stores are in distress with long-standing water tables being run down faster than they are replenished.[8] And then there is climate change, mental health, inequality, biogeochemical cycle disruption, ocean acidification … At the same time much progress has been made on certain indicators, for example as popularised by Hans Rosling (Gapminder.org). However, set against the above systemic failures, these often cherry-picked statistics of 'progress' are unhelpful distractions from the fundamental way our system of production and consumption has ravaged our asset base. Charities consistently argue that reaching climate change tipping points could undermine all development efforts of the past decades. If economics is the way in which scarce resources are allocated to provide well-being, in the long term, for all members of society, then on that measure our dominant economic experiments to date have failed us – be it the destructive Soviet communist system or the still dominant 'profit-maximisation' shareholder capitalism.

The 2007/8 financial crisis marked a turning point in the world's belief in the profit-maximisation shareholder capitalism ideology. Since then it has taken a while for the cogs of the paradigm shift to turn and the world to organise around a new vision of capitalism and business leadership that is fit for the future. Purpose-driven capitalism is the answer that has emerged from that process.

After years spent circling the problem with corporate philanthropy, CSR, cause-based marketing or even 'creating shared value',[9] we have finally zeroed in on the heart of the issue and source of the solution: that we cannot assume that market forces will deliver long-term well-being for everyone by businesses focusing on profit-maximisation for shareholders, as if this is an accurate proxy for success. Purpose recognises that business needs to be unshackled so it can directly focus on delivering well-being, not just for shareholders, and not just this year, but for generations to come. It is no accident that 'long-term well-being for all' is, as well as being arguably the original point of the economy, in essence the definition of sustainability.[10] With this as the most likely meta-purpose that company purposes 'ought' to be anchored against, purpose, the economy and sustainability all share the same goal.

This represents a huge shift for business that cannot be underestimated. Drawing from the primary and secondary research I have undertaken with my colleagues in the University of Cambridge, I would emphasise the following four features of purpose.

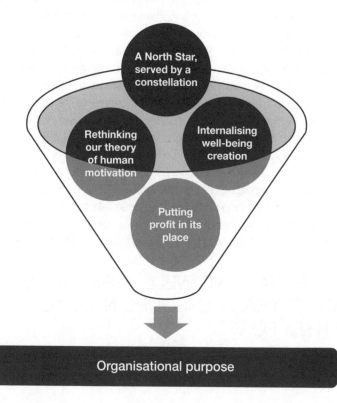

Each of these features has been chosen as vital to the concept, in that they need to be noticed individually by those wishing to lead for purpose and optimise its potential for performance – and yet all four need to be attended to at once. Together they illuminate the challenging and exciting shift in organisations that Sarah's capacities talk to directly:

1. PUTTING PROFIT IN ITS PLACE – AS A VITAL INPUT AND MARKER OF SUCCESS BUT NOT THE POINT OF BUSINESS

Purpose at its heart represents a new dawn as the sun begins to set on the economic experiment that placed profit-maximisation as the core objective of organisations. Since the 1960s the 'financialisation' of companies has taken hold, meaning success has been narrowed to monetary indicators.[11] Executives, like all humans, are prone to 'perceptual filtering' to help simplify decision making by ignoring what is less important.[12] Hence, if you orientate a business to elevate a single intermediary variable (monetary revenues) as the prize from which all other important outcomes will result, then, over time, the complex natural and human foundations that drive those profits are bound to be filtered out and eroded – as they have been. That means that in service to profits, we have undermined the very basis of our well-being. While some have gained massively and we have delivered many impressive poverty gains, the more impressive and sustainable outcomes for society that we might have achieved have gone unaddressed as we have been distracted from the real goal and, as some argue, real innovation has been dulled.[13]

It goes without saying that having enough profit to survive is critical to the ongoing success of any organisation; but more than that, if you are sure what you are doing is providing meaningful value, then trying to optimise profit and growth within the bounds of purpose often falls out of this. As a senior executive noted in our recent interviews: they wanted to optimise growth because they knew theirs was the most sustainable product on the market.

2. INTERNALISING WELL-BEING CREATION RATHER THAN OUTSOURCING IT TO MARKET FORCES

For some, purpose is just a dictionary concept – it is about why a business operates; however, this could be about anything. Using this approach, the mafia is a very purpose-driven business. However, purpose is far from agnostic about why a company should be in business. The concept is fundamentally tied to the *other* human-based meaning of purpose – that a fundamental basis of our well-being is to live a life in service of others, i.e. to have a meaningful purpose.[14,15] An organisation is a human organism and, taken to the organisational level, purpose is about orientating the whole business around directly delivering well-being outcomes for a specified group(s).

Perhaps necessarily, purpose is a world apart from the thinking that has dominated. Conventional thinking assumes profits or sales are a proxy for how well an organisation has converted scarce resources into well-being. This is because the best way to increase societal well-being is assumed to be a freely operating market where companies keep at arm's length from people's well-being decisions to avoid distorting the invisible hand of the market. The reasoning goes that people, as long as they are always self-serving and rational (which they are not) and not influenced by hopes, fears and values etc. (which they are), and have all the information they need about choices on offer (which they don't), will theoretically choose what is best for optimising their well-being (utility/welfare) within the constraints of how much money they have and what things cost. It is with this logic that businesses have been freed, and even morally encouraged, to focus on profit maximisation, within the law, while government's role is focused on setting those laws and policing them. So, a profit-maximising business will look at a market and first ask:

- What are people buying, or likely to buy, that we have the skills to produce at a profit?
- Where are my competitors leaving money on the table by not designing a product in *x* way, for *x* group and where we have the capacity to capitalise on this?
- How can we grow the categories we are in so we grow the business?

However, purpose-driven business instead first asks questions like:

- What does well-being in the long term look like for *x* group(s) of people?
- What skills do we have that could deliver their long-term well-being in a way that isn't being met properly in the market, and at enough profit?
- How does this translate into vision, mission, strategy and targets we can deliver and be accountable for?

- How can we grow our business relative to others because they aren't doing a good job at delivering well-being for the group we care about?

- How can we help lead people to value new innovations that do a better job at delivering their well-being than the ones they have become used to?

3. RETHINKING OUR THEORY OF HUMAN MOTIVATION – UNLEASHING THE HUMAN DRIVE TO SERVE THE WELL-BEING OF OTHERS

Purpose it not just about technically focusing on long-term well-being rather than profits. With the rejection of the profit-maximisation ideology comes the freedom to act with more accurate idea of what drives behaviour – of ourselves, employees, customers … all human stakeholders. As Sarah has outlined on page 36, the view that we are rational, self-interested decision makers has been undermined by decades of psychology research – and leadership theories as outlined below. These psychological insights show that in the workplace and beyond, we are driven by acceptance, altruism respect and shared values,[16,17,18] the need for a coherent identity[19] and a sense of belonging.[20] Human drivers such as this were taken for granted in the years before the financialisation of business.[21] While this list of motivators is powerful, it is the insight that, as humans, we are driven deeply by purpose – the need to live a meaningful life in service to the well-being of others – that is core here.

Purpose, naturally, still requires paying people fairly to meet the 'hygiene' threshold[22] and motivating people towards attending to profitability in a technical sense. At the same time, by focusing on motivations other than money, profits are likely to flow. As Sarah outlines in Chapter 2, although the evidence is still emerging, there is a raft of evidence that purpose drives profits. For example, Unilever's pioneer sustainable living brands, which focused on purpose, in 2016 grew 50% faster than the rest of the business and accounted for 60% of the company growth.[23]

We already know something about the mechanisms that connect purpose to success. For example, that if a company is engaging with purpose *in order* to be more profitable, the likelihood of success may be diminished, as Frankl notes: 'Success, like happiness, cannot be pursued; it must ensue, and it only does so as the unintended side-effect of one's personal dedication to a cause greater than oneself or as the by-product of one's surrender to a person other than oneself.' However, embedded in this is a change in how 'success' is defined, so either way pursuing purpose *for* profits is not reconcilable, rather profits are most accurately positioned as a vital resource and one marker of success.

Furthermore, there are documented performance benefits of connecting personal motivations to professional contexts. For example, studies on inter-related concepts of working for a cause[24] with passion[25] or through meaningful work.[26] Additionally, there is emerging field data that indicates a range of established desirable culture attributes that are likely to be enhanced through interventions to increase purpose in the organisation – something myself and Cambridge colleagues have been supporting Contexis Index CIC with.[27]

4. A NORTH STAR, SERVED BY A CONSTELLATION

One of the main features of purpose, which can tend to be overlooked, is that it provides the most powerful version of a Big Hairy Audacious Goal.[28] Purpose is about clarifying an organisation's identity and its unique reason for existing. Therefore, it is about being really clear who your primary service group(s) are and how your company will uniquely address their long-term well-being. Despite how some have interpreted it, even Ed Freeman (the father of stakeholder theory) would agree purpose is not about all companies saying their purpose is to serve all stakeholders, but instead stakeholder orientation is 'a means by which business organisations could achieve their purpose'.[29] Therefore it is different from stakeholder theory. That doesn't mean stakeholder theory isn't relevant. Because purpose is a long-term, systems-based concept, with it comes a recognition that it is vital to serve all stakeholders so they are able to help achieving the purpose in the long term. As a human concept, purpose also builds permission to recognise this is the right and rewarding thing to do. Furthermore, if an organisation's purpose is created against a global shared purpose of long-term well-being for all, then pursuing well-being goals for your service group at the expense of someone else's becomes illogical – because ultimately they are interdependent: can it be purposeful to address poverty in Cameroon with your campaigns but source goods for your shops made from slave labour in China? Why preserve forests in Brazil via your garden furniture but destroy forests in Indonesia with the soaps you sell?

In this way, if implemented well, purpose should be the North Star that anyone, no matter where they sit within the stakeholder constellation, can see and act in relation to – including to connect energy across organisations and sectors. It is for this reason that purpose is often connected with shifts to more organic organisational structures that can adapt flexibly to the environment.[30]

Acting as a North Star that reflects the very essence of a company's identity, purpose helps orientate people and unite their energy. This is likely to have further effects of helping provide a way for people to identify more deeply with their organisation, which we know is connected with greater levels of customer satisfaction.[31] The sense of belonging that comes with such a sense of collective membership[32] is important to human well-being, something Sarah clearly notes. But in order to contribute effectively to a shared human purpose, leaders need to take care to use this power to connect energy throughout the wider system. It is all too easy to revert to a blinkered approach that unites through creating 'in-groups' and 'out-groups'. Purpose done well should help more easily find common ground both within and beyond organisational boundaries.

PURPOSE AS OUR LONG-TERM HOPE, NOT A PASSING FAD

We have a small window to transform our mode of consumption and production. Purpose is the only method I can see that harnesses the best of capitalism with all its freedoms and efficiency. It is therefore not lightly that I say that purpose is here to stay. It is not a fad. It represents the best hope we have as humanity for addressing the dire situation we are in. As the realities of our unsustainability unfold further, purpose will increasingly be the staff we lean on. However, we cannot leave to chance when and how purpose-driven capitalism comes about – we have to be part of realising this, supporting companies on their journey and holding them to account for dramatic change rather than fine words.

The idea of purposeful business is not new – in fact the very earliest management gurus such as Barnard[33] were clear about the vital role of a humanly emotive purpose for business success. Others such as Bartlett and Ghoshal,[34] Hollensbe and colleagues[35] and Gartenberg and colleagues[36] have progressed our understanding of the role of purpose in business.

As many, such as Professor David Grayson, have pointed out,[37] for many businesses the idea that they exist to serve society was once commonplace (e.g. Unilever, Centrica, Cadbury). However, the profit-maximisation model of business crowded out anything but a mechanised, values-bereft view of business.

We have now had about a decade of a revived, and now mainstreamed, space for purpose. Most major consultants have a purpose offering and some of the great symbols of profit-maximisation capitalism such as Larry Fink and the US Business Roundtable have stated they now need to work primarily for social outcomes, not shareholder profit. Finally, we are at the point that we can start to get really serious about how we quickly transform the culture, structures, process, policies and functions that shape decision making in an organisation at all levels. As Sarah aptly points out, in essence this is a leadership challenge, and yet the leadership we have is not fit for purpose.

GIVING LIFE TO PURPOSE THROUGH LEADERSHIP

Leadership is a notoriously slippery topic, with it being widely said that there are as many theories of leadership as people who have written about it. The definition by Bolden and colleagues[38] is useful as it makes clear that management and leadership are in effect not far apart, but that leadership focused on the repeatable *relational* act of mobilising people towards a shared goal: leadership is 'a process of social influence to guide, structure and/or facilitate behaviours, activities and/or relationships towards the achievement of shared aims'. Embedded in this definition is the sense that leadership is about being clear about a destination, understanding the starting point or context that you are leading from, and a sense of the process to move from one place to the other.

However, when it comes to purpose-led leadership, while there is a huge amount to draw from, at the same time there is not very much. This is perhaps because, as one of a few academic papers directly on the topic notes: 'It is our experience that purpose is so fundamentally tied up with leadership that it is almost invariably subsumed and taken for granted by leadership scholars.' For this reason, some have argued that 'leadership as purpose' needs to be something that is uniquely understood and practised if we are to develop it.[39] This means understanding purpose as the invisible, ultimate, force that leads the organisation. The role of 'leaders' then becomes less about guiding others and instead about nurturing a leadership context that allows purpose to take this role and to connect stakeholder energy around it.

This is great in theory, and we now have access to a range of books that help us understand the kinds of areas leaders need to pay attention to. However, these rarely help leaders on the ground trying to develop themselves to be able to embrace what is needed. This is where Sarah's work comes in. Her integrated set of four capacities brings to life the practices each one of us needs to build to be the leaders, and followers, required to enable purpose to live in an organisation. In doing this she provides people with tools to transform the head, heart and hands of purpose-led-leadership. She draws on decades of work that have developed our understanding of leadership and particularly those that take us well beyond the narrow, mechanistic and individualistic view of leadership that fitted the profit-maximisation philosophy of business so well.

Traditional leadership theories (which are often interconnected), all have something that may be of use, depending on the stage a company is on in their purpose journey and their specific context – as such their potential contribution cannot be ignored. 'Great man' theory and the associated charismatic leadership theories[40] – while highly critiqued, can be useful as a follower theory based on the realities of hero worshipping;[41] trait-theories – which emphasise in particular that individuals' traits, including charisma, can be more helpful than others;[42] behavioural/style theories – which emphasise the importance of how leaders act rather than their traits[43] and that assumptions about the behaviour of followers is critical to how people lead; and contingency or situational theories – which bring to the fore the fact that leadership cannot be extracted from the context in which it is carried out.[44] They all have important insights for leading for purpose. However, much of the dominant theory building and analysis has been developed to serve profit-maximising businesses. It is not surprising then that many are critiqued for being overly based on individuals, males and in general on a transactional view of human interaction.

In this context, a number of progressive ways of looking at leadership have emerged over the decades that start firmly from a different view of human behaviour and the role of leadership. In essence, this represents a move to a constructivist/systems-based view. As humans we are understood to be purposeful, ethical beings whose behaviour is continually shifting based on meanings we draw from interactions with people, systems and process. It is these theories that Sarah's capacities connect with and develop most directly. Of these theories, perhaps the most notable are MacGregor's Theory Y,[45] which specifically sought to break with a limiting view of human behaviour, and Burn's original 'transformational leadership'.

This was situated in direct contrast to the traditional transactional leadership theories (note: this pre-dates the more instrumental and popular interpretation of transformational leadership that followed).[46]

As well as drawing from a more evidence-based way of thinking about human behaviour, these leadership theories, of which there are many, specifically open up a distinct place for leadership to connect individual human purpose to a shared organisational purpose, and beyond to a shared purpose for humanity. As Kempster[47] and Yukl[48] point out: Burn's transformational leadership, for example, is based on a quest for higher morality between leaders and followers where they focus on 'not only what is good for themselves, but also what will benefit larger collectivities such as their organisation, community, and nation' and Greenleaf's servant leadership included: 'standing for what is good and right even when it is not in the financial interest of the organization … '.

These theories pre-date some of the more recent wave of theories such as authentic leadership[49] and identity-based leadership, which, while not specifically about purpose, are highly relevant to it.[50] Some of the newer thinking elaborates the idea that 'leadership is purpose': 'Leadership is more than a person; it is a sense of purpose, a force that gives people a common direction'.[51] Others emphasise how leaders can develop new perspectives and practices that are aligned to purpose. Sarah draws on these most prominently and explicitly makes reference to Torbert's Action Logics (Chapter 3) and Otto Scharmer's widely acclaimed Theory U (Chapter 4), which plots the importance of letting go of prior assumptions, listening deeply to ourselves and what the system is saying through us, and bringing the future to realisation.

The transformed view of human behaviour that all these more advanced theories rest on, situates leaders as being embedded within leadership contexts with roles (which are distributed throughout the organisation)[52] as meaning-makers, emotional artists, facilitators and story-tellers, more than all-knowing, all powerful icons with amazing oratory skills and deft arguments.

While these theories offer us vital ways of thinking about the leadership needed to deliver purpose, they rarely offer hands-on advice for developing the capacities required to bring this leadership to life. Sarah has made an important contribution to this gap with her four capacities. Together, these will help readers to understand and build their own contribution to purpose, listen deeply to what the system is asking for, help move others to purposeful action and bring the energies in the system together to deliver purpose.

CONCLUSIONS

Purpose offers the promise of solving many intractable issues for business. By removing the intermediary barriers that obscure the path to well-being impact, organisations can effectively do the job society has authorised them for. Rather than being anti-business or anti-profit, purpose hence again gives business the right to energetically focus directly on well-being, profitably – thereby assuring its real value creation, viability and social licence in the longer term (sustainably). Profits are vital to business but they are not the point of business. At the same time the focus on well-being maximisation (rather than profit maximisation) allows us to reclaim' profits' from being a dirty word.

More than that, purpose is as much about bringing the best of humanity back into business as it is about anything else. Hence it gives permission for businesses to engage emotionally with staff and stakeholders as humans; to harness and develop the best of what it is to be human. It is for this reason that the word 'meaningful' is so important in our description of organisation purpose: 'An organisation's meaningful and enduring reason to exist that aligns with long-term financial performance, provides a clear context for daily decision making, and unifies and motivates relevant stakeholders.'[53]

Purpose also gives a clear identity-based goal that everyone can, and wants, to rally towards without being micro-managed against prescribed actions. Finally, because it is about a long-term systems approach, it provides the imperative for a business to distribute value to a range of stakeholders (not just shareholders) so that they can in turn support the company's purpose into the future.

A range of leadership theories has provided the foundation for a new way of thinking about leadership that is more aligned with humans as ethical, purposeful beings. Sarah takes these and distils the capacities that leaders need and how, in real terms they can develop them. Her four leadership capacities, taken together, are designed to help develop a deep and ongoing understanding of oneself, the organisation, stakeholders and the wider system. Sarah has done us a huge service by synthesising the four capacities of purpose-led leadership so that leaders can move forward not just conceptually, but practically.

NOTES

1. Barnosky, A.D., Matzke N., Tomiya S. *et al*. (2011) Has the Earth's sixth mass extinction already arrived?, *Nature*, 471, 51–7.
2. WWF (2019) How many species are we losing? See http://wwf. panda.org/our_work/biodiversity/biodiversity/.

3. Song, X.P., Hansen, M.C., Stehman, S.V., Potapov, P.V., Tyukavina, A., Vermote, E.F. and Townshend, J.R. (2018) Global land change from 1982 to 2016, *Nature*, 560(7720), 639.

4. Crowther, T.W., Glick, H.B., Covey, K.R., Bettigole, C., Maynard, D.S., Thomas, S.M. and Tuanmu, M.N. (2015) Mapping tree density at a global scale, *Nature*, 525(7568), 201.

5. UNCCD (2014) Land degradation neutrality resilience at local, national and regional levels, Bonn, Germany: United Nations Convention to Combat Desertification.

6. https://www.theguardian.com/environment/2017/oct/24/uk-30-40-years-away-eradication-soil-fertility-warns-michael-gove.

7. Panagos, P., Borrelli, P., Poesen, J., Ballabio, C., Lugato, E., Meusburger, K. and Alewell, C. (2015) The new assessment of soil loss by water erosion in Europe, *Environmental Science & Policy*, 54, 438–47.

8. NASA (2015) see https://www.nasa.gov/jpl/grace/study-third-of-big-groundwater-basins-in-distress.

9. Porter, M.E. and Kramer, M.R. (2011) Shared value: How to reinvent capitalism—and unleash a wave of innovation and growth, *Harvard Business Review*, 89(1/2), 62–77.

10. Hurth, V. and Whittlesea, E. (2017) Characterising paradigms of marketing for sustainable marketing management, *Social Business*, 7(3-4): 359–90.

11. Lazonick, W. (2010) Innovative business models and varieties of capitalism: Financialization of the US corporation, *Business History Review*, 84(4), 675–702.

12. Starbuck, W.H. and Milliken, F.J. (1988) Executives' perceptual filters: What they notice and how they make sense. In: D. Hambrick (ed.) *The Executive Effect: Concepts and Methods for Studying Top Managers*, Greenwich. CT: JAI Press, Greenwich, CT, pp. 35–65.

13. Ibid.

14. Frankl, V.E. (2003) *The Will to Meaning*, Zeig Tucker & Theisen.

15. Schnell, T. (2009) The sources of meaning and meaning in life questionnaire (SoMe): Relations to demographics and well-being, *Journal of Positive Psychology*, 4(6), 483–99.

16. Ghoshal, S. (2005) Bad management theories are destroying good management practices, *Academy of Management Learning and Education* 4(1): 75–91.

17. Tyler, T.R. (2006) Social Justice Research, S. f. S. o. Justice, Cambridge, MA.

18. Stout, L.A. (2003) On the proper motives of corporate directors (or, why you don't want to invite homo economicus to join your board), *Delaware Journal of Corporate Law*, 28, 1.
19. Mick, D.G. and Buhl, C. (1992) A meaning-based model of advertising experiences, *The Journal of Consumer Research*, 19(3), 317–38.
20. Baumeister, R.F. and Leary, M.R. (1995) The need to belong: desire for interpersonal attachments as a fundamental human motivation, *Psychological Bulletin*, 117(3), 497.
21. Smith, A. (1790/2010) *The Theory of Moral Sentiments*, Penguin, London.
22. Pink, D.H. (2011) *Drive: The Surprising Truth About What Motivates Us*, Penguin, London.
23. See https://www.unilever.com/news/Press-releases/2017/unilevers-sustainable-living-brands-continue-to-drive-higher-rates-of-growth.html.
24. Hirschi, A. (2012) Callings and work engagement: Moderated mediation model of work meaningfulness, occupational identity, and occupational self-efficacy, *Journal of Counseling Psychology*, 59(3), 479–85.
25. Vallerand, R.J., Houlfort, N. and Fores, J. (2003) Passion at Work: emerging perspectives on values in organizations. In Gilliland, S.W., Steiner, D.D. and Skarlicki, D.P. (eds) *Emerging Perspectives on Values in Organizations*, Information Age Publishing, Greenwich, CT, pp. 175–204.
26. Lips-Wiersma, M. and Wright, S. (2012) Measuring the meaning of meaningful work. Development and Validation of the Comprehensive Meaningful Work Scale (CMWS), *Group & Organization Management*, 37(5): 655–85.
27. See https://www.contexis.com/how-we-do-it-measuring-purpose/.
28. Collins, J.C. and Porras, J.I. (1991) Organizational vision and visionary organizations, *California Management Review*, 34(1), 30–52.
29. Freeman, R.E. and Ginena, K. (2015) Rethinking the purpose of the corporation: Challenges from stakeholder theory, *Notizie di Politeia*, 31(117), 9–18.
30. Laloux, F. (2014) *Reinventing Organizations: A guide to creating organizations inspired by the next stage in human consciousness*, Nelson Parker, UK.
31. Homburg, C., Wieseke, J. and Hoyer, W.D. (2009) Social identity and the service-profit chain, *Journal of Marketing*, 73(2), 38–54.

32. Ashforth, B.E. and Mael, F.A. (1996) Organizational identity and strategy as a context for the individual, *Advances in Strategic Management*, 13, 19–64.

33. Barnard, C.I. (1938) *The Functions of the Executive*, Harvard University Press.

34. Bartlett, C.A. and Ghoshal. S. (1994) Changing the role of top management: beyond strategy to purpose, *Harvard Business Review*, 72(6), 79–88.

35. Hollensbe, E., Wookey, C., Hickey, L., George, G. and Nichols, C.V. (2014) Organizations with purpose, *Academy of Management Journal*, 57(5), 1227–34.

36. Gartenberg, C., Prat, A. and Serafeim, G. (2019) Corporate purpose and financial performance, *Organization Science*, 30(1), 1–18.

37. Grayson, D., Coutler, C. and Lee, M. (2018) *All In: The Future of Business Leadership*, Routledge, UK.

38. Bolden, R., Hawkins, B., Gosling, J. and Taylor, S. (2011) *Exploring Leadership: Individual, organizational, and societal perspectives*, OUP, Oxford.

39. Kempster, S., Jackson, B. and Conroy, M. (2011) Leadership as purpose: Exploring the role of purpose in leadership practice, *Leadership*, 7(3), 317–34.

40. House, R.J. and Howell, J.M. (1992) Personality and charismatic leadership, *The Leadership Quarterly*, 3(2), 81–108.

41. Spector, B.A. (2016) Carlyle, Freud, and the great man theory more fully considered, *Leadership*, 12(2), 250–60.

42. Colbert, A.E., Judge, T.A., Choi, D. and Wang, G. (2012) Assessing the trait theory of leadership using self and observer ratings of personality: The mediating role of contributions to group success, *The Leadership Quarterly*, 23(4), 670–85.

43. Blake, R.R., Mouton, J.S. and Bidwell, A.C. (1962) *Managerial Grid*, Advanced Management-Office Executive.

44. Blanchard, K.H., Zigarmi, D. and Nelson, R.B. (1993) Situational Leadership® after 25 years: A retrospective, *Journal of Leadership Studies*, 1(1), 21–36.

45. Douglas, M. (1960). *The Human Side of Enterprise*, McGraw Hill.

46. Kempster, S., Jackson, B. and Conroy, M. (2011) Leadership as purpose: Exploring the role of purpose in leadership practice, *Leadership*, 7(3), 317–34.

47. Ibid.

48. Yukl, G. (2006) *Leadership in Organizations*, 6th edn, Prentice-Hall Upper Saddle River, NJ.

49. George, B. (2003) *Authentic Leadership: Rediscovering the Secrets to Creating Lasting Value*, John Wiley & Sons.

50. Haslam, S.A., Steffens, N.K., Peters, K., Boyce, R.A., Mallett, C.J. and Fransen, K. (2017) A social identity approach to leadership development, *Journal of Personnel Psychology,* 16, 113–24.

51. Drath, W.H. (1998) Approaching the future of leadership development. In McCauley, C.D., Moxley, R.S. and Van Velsor, E. (eds), The Center for Creative Leadership handbook of leadership development (pp. 403–32), Jossey-Bass, San Francisco.

52. Ibid.

53. Ebert, C., Hurth, V. and Prabhu, J. (2018) *The What, the Why and the How of Purpose: A Guide for Leaders*, Chartered Management Institute and Blueprint for Better Business White Paper.

AFTERWORD

When we lead with purpose, we express our natural desire to participate wholeheartedly in this beautiful and troubled world of ours. When we don't do this, the wider system loses our contribution, our team loses its glue and we lose our vigour. We must build bridges to address these losses.

To help you to go on this journey, here are the core messages of being *Powered by Purpose* to keep close by:

- Attract and retain talented people by uncovering and living a compelling 'why'.
- Build a robust team by creating a sense of belonging and making work meaningful.
- Take care of your team members who will then take care of your customers and other stakeholders.
- Enhance performance by treating employees as fellow human beings (not 'human resources') who want to make a difference.
- Do some 'cathedral thinking' by taking time to reflect on what really matters.
- Create connectivity by making time for meaningful conversations and being real about how you're feeling.
- Stay energised by doing what is yours to do; it's not money, power or status that drive you at a deeper level, it's being in touch with what you feel called to do.

I wish you all the very best for crossing the bridge to a better future. Please do get in touch and let me know how you get on either via my website (www.bridgeworkconsulting.com) or via social media where we can share the learning using #poweredbypurposebook

I look forward to hearing from you.

sarah@bridgeworkconsulting.com

INDEX